The Tories

D1381947

00103995

The Tories

From Winston Churchill to David Cameron

Timothy Heppell

B L O O M S B U R Y

LONDON • NEW DELHI • NEW YORK • SYDNEY

Bloomsbury Academic

An imprint of Bloomsbury Publishing Plc

50 Bedford Square
London
WC1B 3DP
UK

1385 Broadway
New York
NY 10018
USA

www.bloomsbury.com

Bloomsbury is a registered trade mark of Bloomsbury Publishing Plc

First published 2014
Reprinted 2014 (twice)

British Library Cataloguing-in-Publication Data
A catalogue record for this book is available from the British Library.

ISBN: HB: 978-1-7809-3039-8
PB: 978-1-7809-3040-4
ePDF: 978-1-7809-3114-2
ePUB: 978-1-7809-3116-6

Library of Congress Cataloging-in-Publication Data
A catalog record for this book is available from the Library of Congress.

Heppell, Timothy.
The Tories: from Winston Churchill to David Cameron/ Timothy Heppell.
pages cm
ISBN 978-1-78093-039-8 (hardback) – ISBN 978-1-78093-040-4 (paperback) –
ISBN 978-1-78093-116-6 (epub) 1. Conservative Party (Great Britain)–History.
2. Political parties–Great Britain–History. 3. Conservatism–Great Britain–History.
4. Great Britain–Politics and government. I. Title.
324.2410409'045–dc23
2014001632

Typeset by Deanta Global Publishing Services, Chennai, India
Printed and bound in Great Britain

In Memory of David Ball 1945–2011

CONTENTS

ACKNOWLEDGEMENTS

I would like to acknowledge the importance of the support provided by my parents, Irene and Neil, and most notably that of my wife Gayle. I dedicate this book to her and to our sons, Matthew, aged nine, and Oliver, aged six. I would also like to express my gratitude to Mark Richardson and Caroline Wintersgill at Bloomsbury for their support with this book.

Introduction

The Conservative Party has traditionally viewed itself as the 'natural party of government'. This phrase has been used in most books written about the history of the party. It was argued that their electoral competitiveness had enabled them to govern, independently or in coalition, for such a large proportion of the twentieth century that it was the 'Conservative century' (Seldon and Snowdon 2001: 27). Their dominance of the second half of the century was particularly significant. They had two multi-term periods in power. The one-nation era of affluence between 1951 and 1964 and then Thatcherism provided four terms between 1979 and 1997. Of the eight victories between 1951 and 1992 three justified the term landslide, that is, the victories in 1959, 1983 and 1987. All the remaining provided them with the opportunity to complete full parliamentary terms. Of their four defeats between 1951 and 1992 three were marginal and only 1966 constituted a significant reversal. The losses of October 1964 and 1974 gave Labour majorities under five, and Labour only entered office in March 1974 as a minority government (Table 1).

The end of the Conservative century would coincide with a number of important books being written on the Conservatives by political historians (Ball 1998; Blake 1998; Charmley 1996; Davies 1996; Evans and Taylor 1996; Gilmour and Garnett 1998; Ramsden 1995, 1996, 1999). Within this historical tradition there have been a number of core assumptions that were seen to explain their electoral success. It is worth reconsidering these:

1 It was argued that their electoral success could be explained with reference to their 'appetite for power' and their willingness to subordinate doctrinal considerations in that pursuit.

2 Their desire for office, rather than an adherence to an ideological creed, meant that they relied heavily on demonstrating internal discipline and unity. In these narratives the notion of loyalty was so significant that it was described as their 'secret weapon'.

3 Tied to this was the assumption that the Conservatives were a party of tendencies rather than a party of factions (Rose 1964: 33–46). Factions amounted to stable, cohesive and organized groups furthering a broad range of policies. Such factions are said to be conscious of their group identity and they advance a programme for government.

Tendencies constituted fluctuating alignments between political elites on specific policy arenas; but these transient alignments are said to lack the cohesiveness and organization of factions. Rose argued that Labour was a party of factions, and the Conservatives were a party of tendencies.

Table 1: The electoral record of the Conservative Party 1945–2010

Election	Elected Conservatives	Percentage share of votes	Total vote received	Government and majority	
1945	213	39.8	9,577,667	Labour	146
1950	299	43.5	12,502,567	Labour	5
1951	321	48.0	13,717,538	Conservative	17
1955	345	49.7	13,311,936	Conservative	59
1959	365	49.4	13,749,830	Conservative	100
1964	304	43.4	12,001,396	Labour	4
1966	253	41.9	11,418,433	Labour	97
1970	330	46.4	13,145,123	Conservative	31
1974 F	297	37.9	11,872,180	Labour	Minority
1974 O	277	35.8	10,464,817	Labour	3
1979	339	43.9	13,697,923	Conservative	44
1983	397	42.4	13,012,315	Conservative	144
1987	376	42.3	13,763,066	Conservative	101
1992	336	41.9	14,092,891	Conservative	21
1997	165	30.7	9,602,957	Labour	179
2001	166	31.8	8,357,622	Labour	167
2005	197	32.4	8,772,473	Labour	66
2010	307	36.1	10,726,555	Conservative-led Coalition	

Source: Kavanagh and Cowley 2010: 350–1.

Before proceeding any further it might be worthwhile to reflect upon these assumptions from the perspective of the early 1990s, and to consider the reaction of academics to the Conservatives 1992 general election victory. Respected political scientists appeared to reaffirm the assumptions from within the political historical tradition. Consider these:

1 King argued that the Conservatives had reaffirmed their status as the natural party of government within a dominant party state. If the Conservatives could secure an electoral mandate when, first, opinion polls were predicting their imminent defeat; second, they were facing the electorate in the midst of an economic recession; and third, despite the fact that had been in office for over a decade already, then their continued electoral dominance seemed assured (King 1992: 224).

2 Norton also commented on the evolving configurations of party political competition, with one peripheral party, the Liberal Democrats; one minor party, Labour; and one dominant party, the Conservatives. Writing in 1998 he noted that in 1992 most political commentators had assumed that a fourth term of Conservative office would enable the party to orchestrate an economic recovery and thus the groundwork for a fifth successive electoral victory (Norton 1998: 75).

3 Dunleavy placed the continued electoral hegemony of the Conservatives in a comparative context. He noted that the Conservatives should be compared to the Japanese Social Democrats who had governed for generations, or with the Christian Democrats in Italy, who had been in government almost continuously since the war (Dunleavy 1993: 133).

4 Working on the assumption that the Conservatives would govern in perpetuity, there was an affiliated assumption that the intriguing dilemma was which brand of Conservatism would dominate. Cowley argued that the transformation of Britain into a dominant party state system had increased the importance of internal groupings and thus leadership selection within the Conservatives. Cowley implied that if general elections merely confirmed that the Conservatives are dominant, then political scientists needed to turn their attention to intra-party selection processes to determine which brand of Conservatism is dominant within the dominant party itself (Cowley 1996: 198).

Those political scientists who had implied, or had merely reported upon, an assumption of the Conservatives governing in perpetuity overemphasized the extent of Conservative hegemony. The supposed natural party of government were almost immediately forced onto the defensive politically. The Major administration imploded and destroyed their party of government credentials. They became viewed as incompetent; the Parliamentary Conservative Party (PCP) was divided; Conservative parliamentarians were seen to be sleazy and untrustworthy; and John Major was felt to be a weak and ineffective Prime Minister (Heppell 2006: 2–5).

The prolonged era of Conservative opposition between 1997 and 2010 challenges the merit of the assumptions that have underpinned the historical tradition. Significantly they do not provide us with an adequate explanation for Conservative electoral failure and specifically prolonged electoral failure (Hayton 2012a: 7). Their claims to unity and cohesion seem 'questionable' after the events of the last two decades (Seawright 2010: 2). The period between the fall of Margaret Thatcher and the emergence of David Cameron was characterized by a degree of ideological feuding that contravened the Conservatives self-proclaimed inclination towards discipline and unity, and their supposed preference for being in office rather than dogmatically adhering to set ideological positions.

This book questions the assumptions that have permeated the historical tradition of Conservative academic work. It assumes that the key issue to be examining when studying the Conservatives is their adaptive capability (or otherwise). Examining processes of adaptation enables us to understand adaptations which are accepted and/or are successful, and those which are disputed and/or unsuccessful. This is critical as

> adaptation is an intensely political, not technical process and is seldom smooth or unproblematic because adaptation challenges the extant definition of what Conservatism is. Parties exist in a system of rules producing stability (or inertia) which inhibit adaptation. Adaptations are more radical than the tactical shifts of electoral politics, they occur at a deeper level and in response to influences broader than the electoral cycle. Adaptation requires the party to reinterpret policies and style, modulating these with the perceived changes in the party's milieu, thereby redefining Conservatism. Successful adaptation delivers power. If not, further adaptation occurs. (Taylor 2005a: 133)

Therefore, this book provides students of British politics and general readers with a way of interpreting the historical development of the Conservatives in the post-war era which focuses on these processes of adaptation. The book will be influenced (but not overcome) by the statecraft model. This was advanced by the late Jim Bulpitt, to evaluate how the Conservatives have attempted to win office (the politics of support) and then govern competently (the politics of power) so as to then retain office (Bulpitt 1986a: 19–39). There are four dimensions to the cycle of statecraft analysis – successful party management, a winning electoral strategy, political argument hegemony, governing competence – which if all are successfully achieved should lead to another winning electoral strategy (i.e. re-election) (Bulpitt 1986a: 21–2).

The first dimension is successful party management. This recognizes the centrality of internal discipline, unity and loyalty to external perceptions of the party. It encapsulates how the leadership uses the powers of policy formulation and appointment to engender cohesion within the PCP and the wider party (Bulpitt 1986a: 21). The second dimension is the constructing of a winning electoral strategy. Such a strategy needs to energize Conservative party activists to ensure that they contribute to the mobilization of support. It also needs to penetrate into the traditional core Labour Party vote (Evans and Taylor 1996: 280).

The third dimension is political argument hegemony. This constitutes a component central to the self-confidence of a governing party and its acquisition and maintenance will better assist in the execution of internal party management. Political argument hegemony involves manufacturing a political scenario in which the arguments made by the leadership obtain predominance in terms of elite debate, that is, ensuring that the Conservatives are perceived to be the more plausible party for addressing specific public policy concerns. This process is entwined with the acquisition of a winning electoral strategy. It is a dual process in which Conservative administrations are attempting to organize their own core values into the political domain while forcing the core values of their political opponents out of the political domain, thus mobilizing bias in their favour (Stevens 2002: 119). Therefore, the successful execution of statecraft enables the Conservatives to secure the primacy of their policy prescriptions and it aims to define the political terrain over which political arguments occur (Hickson 2005: 181).

The fourth dimension is having acquired office does the electoral strategy and the political argument espoused enable the Conservatives to govern competently? The central determinant of perceptions of competence is the choice and appropriateness of policies both domestic and external. The successful execution of the governing competence dimension of statecraft requires that the Conservatives pursue policies that can be implemented successfully (Bulpitt 1986a: 22).

The statement model does, however, operate under a number of assumptions. It assumes that the Conservatives have traditionally possessed a willingness to seek electoral support from any and all sections of the electorate. By this we are implying that traditionally the Conservatives have sought to 'accommodate' the preferences of the electorate (Bale 2010: 7). Traditionally Conservative electoral strategy has reflected a recognition that the party could not afford to leave itself 'stranded outside' the crucial 'zone of acquiescence' in 'which the plurality of largely moderate voters would be prepared to reward you with office' (Norris and Lovenduski 2004: 99–100). Therefore, prior to the onset of Thatcherism, post-war Conservative leaders from Winston Churchill to Edward Heath had aimed to position the party towards the centre ground of British politics and the location of the median voter. By centre ground we mean the electoral centre rather than the ideological centre (Quinn 2008: 179).

The second assumption was that upon the acquisition of power, incumbent Conservative governments wished to insulate themselves from domestic and external pressures and that they would seek to manipulate social, economic and international pressures to maintain a degree of governing competence (Hickson 2005: 182). The goal of statecraft when occupying power was therefore centre autonomy. This suggests that once in government, Conservative governments would want to secure relative autonomy for the centre – that is, the Cabinet and the Civil Service – on matters of high politics, most notably economic management. Simultaneous to this pursuit, Conservative governments would aim to delegate issues viewed as 'low politics' to governmental agencies beyond the centre. However, it is the domain of high politics that is most pertinent to the execution of statecraft and, within this context, the formulation of a depoliticized mode of economic management is the pre-eminent concern (Evans and Taylor 1996: 224). Depoliticization involves a deliberate political strategy of attempting to place responsibility for decision-making 'at one remove' from government (Burnham 2001; Flinders and Buller 2006). This amounts to a form of statecraft which is 'designed primarily to service the continuation of power and the maintenance of political office by reducing the risks of failure', in which the governing party aims to 'distance themselves from accountability while enhancing their electoral prospects' (Kerr et al. 2011: 200). Buller and James take the notion of depoliticization as statecraft one step further by arguing thus:

> Faced with problems that are difficult to resolve and where decisions may lead to unpopularity, it will be rational in statecraft terms for leaders not to do anything themselves, but to devolve responsibility for these problems to other individuals, groups or organisations. If these individuals, groups or organisations then end up solving these difficult problems, party leaders can claim credit for the act of devolution. If things go wrong, the self-same leaders will have the option of distancing themselves from responsibility while letting others take the blame. (Buller and James 2012: 541)

The third assumption that we can make with regard to the statecraft model relates to the notion that it appears to be supported by the valence model of voting behaviour. The gradual decline of voting behaviour being orientated around stable class-based cleavages resulted in the growth of valence politics (Butler and Stokes 1969; Stokes 1992). This differentiates between issues on which the electorate will differ – that is, positional politics, from issues in which there is general agreement on the ends if not the means – that is, valence politics. Positional politics referred to how voters interpreted a range of political issues and then voted for a party whose positions were nearest to their own – that is, ends. Valence politics referred to how voters evaluated the general political competence of parties in relation to the means by which they would aim to secure their political goals. The importance of valence-based politics was evident in the seminal work *Political Choice in Britain*, which argued that valence politics and judgements on the relative competence of the two main political parties was the most important factor underlying electoral choice (Clarke et al. 2004: 9). Within this the central determinant of party identification based on competence was leadership evaluations. From this Buller and James conclude that the 'key statecraft task for political leaders is to cultivate such an image of competence, especially in the area of economic management' (Buller and James 2012: 541).

Buller notes that the statecraft interpretation 'has made an important contribution to our academic understanding of twentieth century political development' (Buller 1999: 691). This seems an entirely justifiable assertion as variants upon it have been applied to the study of territorial politics (Bulpitt 1983); race and British politics (Bulpitt 1986b); the contours of British foreign policy, with particular reference to the position of Britain within the European Union (Bulpitt 1988, 1992; Buller 2000). More recently, Buller and James have utilized statecraft as a means of assessing the Prime Ministerial leadership of Tony Blair (Buller and James 2012). However, although this book assumes that as a framework the statecraft theory is of value, it is important to avoid the accusation that critiques and competing perspectives of statecraft are being ignored. Discussions and debates on statecraft are offered by Stevens (2002: 119–50), Buller (1999: 691–712) and Buller (2000: 319–27).

Within the critiques has been the accusation that it shows a bias towards the agency of political elites and pays insufficient attention to structural constraints. For example, Stevens argues that Bulpitt offers an essentially 'high politics' view of history, as his model 'sees the role of political actors as overwhelmingly important in creating political outcomes', when their agency should be seen to operate within the context of the 'underlying institutional and ideological structures' (Stevens 2002: 123). Stevens suggests that structures, and the constraints that they may create, are crucial to the framework of governance and party leadership, and thus they form a critical aspect of the rules of the political game. Moreover, statecraft has been criticized for its limited sensitivity to the impact of international events upon domestic politics, and this limitation, alongside its predominant focus on political change over other explanations for change – be that economic or ideological – means that the statecraft model adopts a 'uni-dimensional' approach to politics (Kerr and Marsh 1999). However, the statecraft approach should not be seen as 'uni-dimensional' as it is the manipulation of these rules of the political game – the interaction between the agency of elites of the wider political structures – which forms the basis of statecraft strategies (Stevens 2002). As Hickson concludes:

> Statecraft should be viewed as an examination of how the Conservative Party has sought when in power to *insulate* itself from social, economic and international pressures and how it has sought to *manipulate* them in order to maintain some degree of governing competence. (Hickson 2005: 182)

The emphasis on manipulation is critical here. The Conservatives have always wanted to give the impression to the electorate that they can govern effectively and are broadly unified, but such judgements about them should be viewed in relative rather than absolute terms. When using statecraft we must not understate the importance of perceptions of the Conservatives relative to Labour in relation to the various dimensions of statecraft. As such, the activities and condition of opposition parties also need to be considered. A weak and badly divided opposition, for example, in the 1951–62 or 1979–87 period, was a contributing factor to successful Conservative statecraft.

In addition to noting its international dimensions and the importance of the opposition, Hickson makes two critical observations with regard to statecraft which are intrinsic to the way in which this book aims to utilize the model. First, Hickson argues that Bulpitt 'reduces the salience of ideology' within the Conservatives. Rather than subsume ideology within statecraft, it would be better to interpret statecraft as the way in which we can observe how the Conservatives have pursued, (successfully or otherwise), their ideological objectives at any one time (Hickson 2005: 183–4). Second, Hickson argues that we must not overstate continuity when examining the Conservative statecraft strategies. When assessing them over time it is possible to identify 'several' statecraft strategies which can be seen as being time specific, that is, given that economic, social, cultural and political climates evolve and change, so statecraft strategies will have to evolve to reflect the new and altered terrain (Hickson 2005: 182).

Therefore, this book is about the electoral strategies, governing approaches and ideological thought of the Conservatives from Churchill to Cameron. It will consider how the statecraft strategies adopted by the Conservatives have evolved since 1945 as mechanisms designed to ensure that they gain and retain access to power. Implicit will be the argument that adaptations to the narrative of Conservatism may be required to manufacture a viable form of statecraft. The book argues that post-war Conservatism can be seen in terms of five significant blocks of time in statecraft terms:

1 The first period (1945–64) involves a successful adaptation of Conservatism in the immediate post-war era as the Conservatives re-orientated themselves to the state and the one-nation narrative helped to provide a viable statecraft strategy to the mid-1960s.

2 The second period is the Heathite era between 1964 and 1975 which was characterized by a failure of statecraft. Although the objective of winning power back was achieved in 1970, the Heath administration was unable to maintain political argument hegemony or demonstrate governing competence. The Heath era ended with Conservatism in a state of flux.

3 During the third period (1975–92) Conservatism engaged in a process of adaptation in the form of Thatcherism which abandoned the state

and embraced the market. This provided an appropriate time-specific instrument of statecraft that propelled them to four successive general election victories between 1979 and 1992.

4   The fourth period is best described as the post-Thatcherite era. Embracing the end of the Major era and the 1992–97 administration, as well as the period of opposition between 1997 and 2005, this period embraces the three cataclysmic electoral defeats of 1997, 2001 and 2005. The post-Thatcherite era has been characterized by a failure of statecraft with clear evidence of a complete collapse in the four dimensions of statecraft, and more specifically once this mode of statecraft ceased to be of value to the Conservatives, there was an inability to transcend it. This contributed to a prolonged period of electoral rejection.

5   The fifth and contemporary mode of statecraft to be considered relates to the Cameronite modernization strategy; built around transcending Thatcherism and the construction of a liberal conservative outlook as a statecraft strategy (2005–). This retains the economic liberal mentality associated with Thatcherism (and Euroscepticism), but welds this to a liberally social outlook in moral matters, and reflects the altered terrain after a generation of New Labour governance. Liberal conservatism provides the basis of the Cameronite statecraft model and the central narrative to this approach has become the emerging notion of the Big Society.

The aim of this introduction has been to demonstrate how the identification of an operational form of statecraft is the eternal concern for the Conservatives, that is, what strategy will secure an electoral mandate (the politics of support), which will enable them to govern effectively (the politics of power). The remaining chronologically structured chapters provide scope through which to evaluate, first, the evolving statecraft strategies and to explain their viability when they have provided electoral hegemony and governing competence, and second, their non-viability when governing incompetence has contributed to electoral rejection. The following chapters are thereby structured in a way that allows the reader to follow the chronological development of the party in each of the time periods identified, leading to an analytical overview of their statecraft strategies.

1

New Conservatism and the ascendency of the one-nation tradition 1945–1964

The scale of the electoral defeat that the Conservatives suffered in 1945 was deeply shocking (Ramsden 1999: 312). There was a swing of 12 per cent to Labour as the Conservatives won only 213 seats on a vote share of 39.8 per cent and a turnout of 9.5 million. Labour secured 47.8 per cent of the vote and 11.9 million votes, and critically secured a parliamentary majority of 146. To put the scale of defeat into even sharper context it is worth noting that at the previous general election in 1935 the Conservatives had polled 11.8 million, which represented 53.7 per cent of the overall vote and provided them with 432 MPs (Gamble 1988: 62).

In the aftermath of defeat the Conservatives were said to be facing a hostile intellectual climate in which Labour was in the ascendency. Alongside the vacuum that this left at the heart of Conservatism – that is, what was the core narrative and how could this be translated into policy – the difficulties that were facing the party were deemed to be compounded by their own organizational weaknesses. The size of the Labour majority, alongside the ambitious programme of reform that the Attlee administration would aim to implement, would mean that the political landscape would be considerably altered by the end of the Parliament. There was much Conservative depression in 1945 not just at the 'violent turn of the electoral tide' but the fear that while their 'problems seemed acute, they would now get worse' (Ramsden 1999: 315). 'Chips' Channon recalled the sense of despondency within the PCP at an August 1945 meeting of the 1922 Committee. He noted that Winston Churchill 'seemed totally unprepared, indifferent and deaf, and failed to stir the crowded audience. . . . I came away fearing that the Tory party was dead' (Rhodes James 1967: 412).

Lord Woolton, who became the Party Chair once in opposition, identified the scale of the problem:

> We had our backs to the wall. We had been heavily defeated. We had very little money. The Party was depressed. The political press of the country was largely staffed, on its reporting sides, by members of the Labour Party, and everywhere there was a slant towards socialism and disbelief that in the new post war world this old Conservative Party could ever govern this country again. (Woolton 1959: 334)

Yet between 1945 and 1951 the Conservatives added an additional 3.2 million votes to their July 1945 vote share, which was sufficient to bring them back into office in the autumn of 1951. This constituted 'an extraordinary political revival' (Willetts 2005: 171). Not only did the Conservatives regain power from Labour within 6 years, but at the 1955 general election they increased their parliamentary majority from 17 to 59; and then at the 1959 general election they increased it again from 59 to 100. The 1959 general election victory was tied into the 'never had it so good era' associated with the high points of Conservatism – the era of Harold Macmillan and the age of affluence (Evans and Taylor 1996: 101). This chapter considers the period between the general election defeat of July 1945 through until their own removal from office in October 1964, thus embracing the process of renewal in opposition between 1945 and 1951, and their 13-year tenure in power between 1951 and 1964.

'New' Conservatism 1945–1951

The Conservatives lost the general election in 1945 due to a range of factors. It was a mistake to assume that the popularity of Churchill would be sufficient to propel them to victory (Lindsay and Harrington 1974: 142). As Mass Observation surveys from the time demonstrated, the electorate were 'quite capable of feeling intense gratitude to Churchill and at the same time not wanting him as post-war Prime Minister' (Ramsden 1999: 313). This misplaced emphasis on Churchill the individual was compounded by their failure to offer 'the constructive *domestic* policies for which the country looked' (Lindsay and Harrington 1974: 143).

However, these short-term tactical miscalculations associated with the campaigning period masked a deeper underlying problem. By 1945 Conservatism was 'discredited' by the associations from the 1930s with appeasement, unemployment and unpreparedness for war (Blake 1998: 254). Willetts observed the 'move away' from the Conservatives by noting three critical publications (Willetts 2005: 169). First, the Conservatives failed to grasp the extent to which they were condemned for the pre-war depression and high unemployment and appeasement. These negative associations were constantly emphasized and propagated through the activities of the Left Book Club, which was captured best by the 1940 book *Guilty Men*, which was co-authored by Michael Foot and others (Cato 1940). Second, not only did such publications question the governing competence of the Conservatives, they also emphasized how the Conservatives 'only represented the narrow self-interest of the affluent' (Willetts 2005: 169). This view was pushed forward in the pre-war book, *Tory MP*, again published by the Left Book Club, (Haxby 1939), which claimed that 'the reluctance to confront Hitler was directly related to the conspicuous commercial interests and property holdings across the Empire of many Tories' (Willetts 2005: 170). Finally, Willetts identifies the significance of the 1942 Beveridge Report which laid out an ambitious domestic policy agenda, which was 'massively popular and had been wholeheartedly endorsed by Labour' (Willetts 2005: 170). Although the Conservatives had accepted the principles of the Report, their acceptance was 'hesitant' and 'qualified' (Lindsay and Harrington 1974: 145). The cumulative effect of these three influences was that the Conservatives were 'faced with a critique of their record, an attack on them for sleaze, and a shift in the political agenda to which they had no clear response'. Consequently the Conservatives 'had lost the battle of ideas' and were intellectually on the 'defensive' (Willetts 2005: 170).

Could the Conservatives recover? The process of reconstruction in the post-war period was seen to combine three aspects. First, organizational reform that was geared towards creating a mass party orientated towards electoral mobilization. Second, moves towards candidate selection reform to make the party appear more socially representative. Finally, there was policy innovation. Put together, these processes have become portrayed as part of the 'modernising' narrative of 'New Conservatism' (Evans and Taylor 1996: 76). It is also worth noting that this 'drastic overhaul' of the party and the 'sweeping changes' that were to be initiated had more to do with the influence of Woolton and R. A. Butler, than to Churchill himself (Davies 1996: 26). Norton also notes the influence of Ralph Assheton, (predecessor to Woolton as Party Chair), and suggests that between them they 'not only resuscitated the Party but effectively galvanised it' (Norton 1996: 44).

In the aftermath of defeat Conservatives tended to take comfort in the idea that their rejection was a by-product of their own organizational weaknesses (Lindsay and Harrington 1974: 145). In this aspect of Conservative recovery, the Party Chair Woolton played a critical role in their eventual return to office. While Woolton would later state that Churchill had been 'vague' with him in terms of what was required, he demanded and got a 'completely free hand' in the overhaul and running of the party organization (Hoffman 1964: 81). His strategy to win back power was based on members and money. This involved a major recruitment drive and increasing the prioritization of fund-raising at the constituency level (Evans and Taylor 1996: 77). This would relieve pressure on Central Office to underwrite the activities of the constituency parties, although the target that Woolton set (an annual constituency target of £2,000–3,000) left 'some constituency officers gasping' (Hoffman 1964: 88). The recruitment drive was successful, especially in bringing in younger members from the middle classes and also women, and was tied into the establishment and growth of the Young Conservatives (Willetts 2005: 176). Membership had dipped below 1 million in the autumn of 1946, so party morale was clearly boosted as the membership target that Woolton set of 1 million members (made in April 1948) was hit by June of that year, and then increased to 2.5 million in 1950, and to over 3 million members by 1951, which was perhaps 10 times as many as in 1945 (Hoffman 1964: 83–90). The financial base of the party was improving as the membership was growing, which in turn enhanced the organizational efficiency and effectiveness of the party – for example, in 1928 there had been 180 people working for Conservative Central Office, but by 1947 that figure was 233 and increasing (Clark 1998: 328).

The issue of candidate selection was to be closely linked to the organizational reforms of the opposition era. Here the reforming mentality sought to address two concerns. First, there was the concern that constituencies were felt to be selecting their candidates on the basis 'of their capacity to meet their election expenses', which deterred constituencies from seeking subscriptions from the mass of electors (Willetts 2005: 177). As Woolton had noted, the 'organisation of the party was weakest in those places where a wealthy candidate had made it unnecessary for the members to trouble to collect small subscriptions' (Woolton 1959: 345). The second consequence of this was that this 'restricted candidates to a narrow social strata' and 'made it difficult' (not impossible) for less wealthy but 'talented Conservatives to secure nomination' (Evans and Taylor 1996: 77). Although the expected contribution seemed to be around £100 (and this was fixed as the maximum expected contribution in 1944), a young Quintin Hogg (later Lord Hailsham), after seeking nomination in 1943, found that the average tariff for a safe seat was around £500 per annum. He then condemned the 'virtual sale of safe seats' as 'a festering sore in the party' (Gilmour and Garnett 1998: 39).

To address these concerns, a committee was set up under the chairmanship of David Maxwell-Fyfe, with the objective of reviewing the financial arrangements of prospective parliamentary candidates. The Maxwell-Fyfe findings ensured that the candidates would no longer be asked about financial contributions as part of the selection committee. Rather once selected as the candidates they would be permitted to make a voluntary contribution to their constituency association, but that would be limited to £25 per annum for new candidates or £50 per annum for existing Conservative parliamentarians. Moreover, individual constituency associations would be made responsible for covering the election expenses of Conservative candidates, which would encourage constituencies towards broadening and deepening their fund-raising activities within the constituency (Evans and Taylor 1996: 77).

Candidate selection reform would be presented as a 'potent symbol' of 'New' Conservatism and was endorsed by the 1948 and 1949 Annual Conferences (Evans and Taylor 1996: 77). As Willetts notes, the party 'lost no opportunity' to promote the significance of having reformed their financial base and their means of candidate selection (Willetts 2005: 177). Opinions vary on its actual impact in addressing the second of the aforementioned concerns – the social composition of candidates selected. Iain Macleod would argue that the reforms had 'a profound effect on the *changed image* of the Tory party' (Ramsden 1995: 94). However, Hoffman notes that their actual impact on those candidates selected for 1950 was limited. Many of those who were nominated were selected before the new procedures came into place. Moreover, when analysing the class and occupation background of successful candidates over the next decade or so, there was little real evidence of changes to the type of candidate chosen for the safest of seats (Hoffman 1964: 96–7). However, although Clark acknowledges that the 'turnaround was dramatic', he states that

> setting these results against the worst possible trough for a benchmark does not necessarily present a balanced picture. In the 1930s, and before, the party – certainly by comparison with its competitors – had been extremely well organised and efficient– and to some extent the post 1945 modernisers were merely regaining the ground which had been temporarily conceded. (Clark 1998: 327)

However, 'strengthening party organisation was a necessary but not sufficient condition for electoral success' and such changes came in tandem with policy renewal (Norton 1996: 45). The Conservatives were initially constrained by Churchill's attitude to opposition politics. His instincts told him that the role of the opposition was to critique the Attlee government and no more (Theakston 2012: 9–12). He explained his approach to the 1922 Committee in 1947 by stating that it is 'dangerous to prescribe until you are called in' (Goodhart 1973: 143). He had also informed the 1946 Annual Conference that 'I do not believe in looking about for some panacea or cure-all on which we should stake our credit and our fortunes' and 'which we should try to sell in a hurry like a patent medicine to all and sundry' (Ramsden 1995: 142).

Addison argued that Churchill was more interested in 'politics than policy' (Addison 1992: 397). As a consequence the leading influence in terms of policy-making, and thereby intellectual renewal, was Butler. When the 1946 Annual Conference demanded that statements of policy intent were required, a reluctant Churchill delegated the responsibility to Butler, who was to spearhead the agenda as chair of the Industrial Policy Committee (Norton 1996: 45). Butler combined this role with being chairman of the Conservative Research Department (involving Macleod, Reginald Maudling but also Enoch Powell), and thus this combined role gave him 'considerable authority' and it was he who 'really put drive and coherence into the policy exercise' (Mayer 1992: 162–3). The composition of the Industrial Policy Committee was also significant – including Macmillan, Maxwell-Fyfe and also Oliver Stanley, Oliver Lyttelton and David Eccles. Most of these figures were associated with the one-nation wing of the party, who could assist Butler in 'ensuring that things moved in a progressive direction' (Ramsden 1980: 109).

That Butler needed to show this form of leadership was necessary given the attitude of Churchill. They feared that the party was 'still damagingly identified with the thirties', and as such their desire was for 'some new and different policies to convince the voters that the party had changed' (Gilmour and Garnett 1998: 32). Although Churchill instructed Butler to avoid 'detailed policy', and to ensure that the findings showcased underlying principles rather than specific promises (Ball 2001: 326), Butler viewed the exercise as one in which his remit was to ensure that the 'party was facing in the right direction before it made firm commitments' (Gilmour and Garnett 1998: 33). The output of the Committee, affirmed at the 1947 Annual Conference, was the famous *Industrial Charter*.

The document was designed to showcase how New Conservatism could offer an alternative to a laissez-faire approach associated with the liberalism of the nineteenth century, and the supposedly dominant state socialism as advanced by Labour. It was a carefully crafted document. Norton notes that it was a

> ... blend of Tory and neo-liberal strands within the Conservative Party, maintaining continuity with past policies whilst introducing innovative proposals clearly influenced by wartime experience. The neo-liberal strand was reflected in the assertion of the need for free industry from "unnecessary controls and restrictions," to abolish restrictive practices such as the closed shop, to return road haulage to private ownership and to finance tax reductions through cuts in public expenditure, thus encouraging investment and, consequently, output.

Norton argues that the traditional Tory element was 'to the fore' in the

> ... advocacy of a degree of voluntary co-operation between government and industry, the two working together to agree a "national budget"; in the acceptance of full employment and the status as bodies of the public sector of the Bank of England, the railways and the coal industry and in the proposal for a Workers' Charter establishing in essence good practice guidelines on issues such as job security and status. (Norton 1996: 45–6)

By recognizing the need for a greater role for the state in managing and regulating the economy it was interpreted as endorsing Keynesian solutions. The 'strong role in coordinating economic policy with the trade unions and industrialists' caused some disquiet on the right (Clark 1998: 326). They would describe the document as being 'pink' and 'semi-socialist', but nonetheless despite the reservations of Churchill himself it was accepted at the 1947 Annual Conference (Willetts 2005: 179). With the 1922 Committee and the front bench endorsing the proposals, the right wing was marginalized and 'consigned to a long uphill struggle' (Clark 1998: 326). The *Industrial Charter* was then followed up with a subsequent policy statement entitled *The Right Road for Britain* in 1949 which accepted the welfare state, full employment, and broadly reaffirmed the language of the *Industrial Charter* and the role of the state therein. However, the increased emphasis on advancing property ownership ensured that it was more acceptable to the whole of the party than the *Industrial Charter* (Evans and Taylor 1996: 90).

It was the *Industrial Charter*, however, which would generate a considerable amount of retrospective appraisal. Lindsay and Harrington described it as 'the most important post war policy document produced by the Conservative Party' (Lindsay and Harrington 1974: 151). Taylor regarded it as 'an early milestone' in the adaptation of the Conservatives to post-1945 politics, while Howard felt that not only did it mark that the party was 'coming to terms with the mixed-economy welfare state' but also that it had 'sealed it off from its pre-war past'. Howard later commented that in broader historical terms it constituted 'the most memorable concession a free market party ever made to the spirit of Keynesian economics' (Taylor 1994: 513; Howard 1987: 135, 156). As an exercise in policy renewal and political adaptation it appeared to recognize that by 1947 'the centralised war economy, the spread of Keynesian ideas and the paramount need to preserve full employment had altered the circumstances' – as such Conservative elites were seeking to be sensitive to the new terrain upon which party competition would evolve (Gilmour and Garnett 1998: 35).

Butler would later suggest that the significance of the *Industrial Charter* was its contribution to the Conservative attempt to 'wrest from the left much of the middle ground in the battle of ideas' (Butler 1971: 135). In this context, much of its value came from what Butler called 'impressionism' (Ramsden 1977: 422). Of the two and half million who bought a copy of the charter, Beer would comment: 'whether many of [them] read much of the Charter's lucid, but earnest prose is not vitally important . . . [but] . . . its *symbolism* was clear to party members and the public' (Beer 1969: 316). On the importance of its symbolic value, Butler would later acknowledge:

> Our first purpose is to counter the charge that we were the party of industrial go-as-you-please and devil-take-the hindmost, [and] that full employment and the Welfare State were not safe in our hands. (Butler 1971: 146)

This suggests that the Conservatives utilized the publication of the *Industrial Charter* as a means of addressing negative assumptions that they were associated with, and that would be central to Labour electioneering. At the same time Hogg would publish *The Case for Conservatism* within which he stated that the party opposed the 'ungodly and rapacious scramble for ill-gotten gains' that one associates with laissez-faire capitalism 'in which the rich appeared to get richer and the poor poorer' (Hogg 1947: 51–3). Such sentiments informed the justification that Butler advanced in his own memoirs:

> Our need was to convince a broad spectrum of the electorate, whose minds were scarred by inter-war memories and myths, that we had an alternative policy to socialism which was viable, efficient and humane, which would realise and reward enterprise and initiative but without abandoning social justice or reverting to mass unemployment. Until the progressive features of our thought had been fully exposed to public view, no one was going to kill Attlee in order to make Churchill king. (Butler 1971: 132)

Thus, the *Industrial Charter* symbolized the Conservatives attempt to articulate a 'middle way' alternative located in between laissez-faire capitalism and state socialism, which Macmillan had been arguing for in his 1938 book (Macmillan 1938). At the time of the endorsing of the *Industrial Charter*, Macmillan himself wrote that 'between the two ways there has always been a progressive element in the party; but it never dominated the party. Now it has seized control, not by force or palace revolution, but by the vigour of its intellectual argument' (Dorey 2011: 81). Although criticism from a minority on the right was evident, we can conclude that the value of the *Industrial Charter* lies in making the accusation that the Conservatives were laissez-faire an 'unconvincing' one (Gilmour and Garnett 1998: 34). Debates would rage about its actual long-term value in terms of translating policy ideas into practice once in power, but on this Macmillan deserves the final word. Macmillan concludes that the importance of the *Industrial Charter* was 'not so much in the detailed proposals as in their general tone and temper' (Macmillan 1969: 303).

'Never had it so good?' Dominance and the politics of prosperity 1951–1960

Despite these processes of organizational change and policy renewal the Conservatives failed to win back power at the first opportunity. The Conservatives increased their vote share from 39.8 per cent in 1945 to 43.5 and their 12,502,567 votes represented a significant improvement on the 9,577,667 secured 5 years earlier. The erosion of the massive parliamentary majority that Labour had held (from 146 to 5) was not simply a reflection of improving Conservative strategy. It also reflected the difficulties that Labour had experienced when governing in hugely constraining economic circumstances. Their objective of achieving a 'politically and economically viable combination of full employment, low inflation, modest wage settlements and welfare benefits' was undermined (Pugh 2010: 287). Their credibility was damaged by the devaluation of the pound in 1949, which fuelled inflation and had the dual effect of making it harder to secure wage restraint from trade unions and further eroded the popularity of the Attlee administration. Within 18 months Labour were forced to face the electorate again with not just their economic credibility under question. A heated internal debate within Labour was gathering pace regarding future policy development. From the socialist left came the call for further nationalization as a symbol of their continuing commitment to socialism. From the social democratic right came the argument that they should consolidate the accomplishments of the Attlee government, that is, the objective of a future Labour government was the effective administration of the new welfare state. The resignation of Nye Bevan, provoked by the imposition of health service charges levied on false teeth and spectacles, was a prelude to left-right feuding in opposition between Bevan and Hugh Gaitskell, of which the real victor was to be the Conservatives (Crowcroft 2008).

Eighteen months after narrowly failing to remove Labour from power, the Conservatives had another opportunity to propel Churchill back into Downing Street. They added a further 1.2 million voters (up to 13.7 million and 48 per cent of the vote) which increased their parliamentary representation to 321 and a majority of 17. However, with the Liberal vote collapsing from 2.6 million to 730,556, the Labour vote actually increased from 46.1 per cent and 13,266,592 in February 1950 to 48.8 per cent and 13,948,605. So the Conservatives may have secured a parliamentary majority but they were constrained by the fact that Labour had actually secured more votes.

Indeed, the incoming Churchill administration was strongly influenced by its inheritance. In the domestic sphere, policy post 1945 had embraced an extensive programme of nationalization which had placed one-fifth of the economy under public ownership, and the establishment of the National Health Service was the jewel in the crown of the new welfare state. Foreign policy had involved independence for India and Pakistan, which had acted as a prelude to the transition from Empire to Commonwealth, while the establishment of the North Atlantic Treaty Organisation secured the alliance with the Americans within the defence of Western Europe. Political historians would come to argue that the Attlee era would shape the contours of policy for a generation. They would embed what became defined as the post-war consensus, and its associated policy pillars – full employment thus justifying Keynesian demand techniques; a mixed economy thus legitimating public ownership of core industries; active government; trade union conciliation within industrial relations; a welfare state underpinned by the notion of universal national insurance; and foreign and defence policy guided by maintaining Britain as a nuclear power and membership of the Atlantic Alliance (Addison 1975; Kavanagh 1987a).

Before considering the evidence of policy 'continuity' between the Labour and Conservative administrations of 1945–51 and 1951–64 respectively, it is worth reflecting on the 'achievements' of the Conservatives. The legacy from the Attlee administration was constraining, with 'public spending running out of control' (Evans and Taylor 1996: 94). However, within 2 years it was becoming apparent that the economic circumstances were improving, and the Conservatives reaped the electoral dividend from the shift from the age of austerity to the age of affluence (although the Conservatives also benefitted from an upturn in the world economy in the 1950s) (Davies 1996: 288). Rationing was abolished and significant governmental focus was placed on housing. As Housing Minister, Macmillan pushed through a commitment to build 300,000 new homes. Significantly by 1964 the proportion of families owning their own homes stood at 47 per cent as opposed to 30 per cent in 1951 (Norton 1996: 47). In the same time period there was a 53 per cent increase in the average weekly wage for an adult male manual worker (from £8.30 to £17.51). The age of affluence was evident from the growth of consumer goods: increases were seen in terms of the production of vacuum cleaners (up by 33 per cent), washing machines (up by 40 per cent), television sets (up by 67 per cent) and passenger cars (up by 140 per cent). Unemployment averaged 1.8 per cent and never increased above 2.6 per cent, while economic growth was steady at a 'respectable' 2.8 per cent over the time period, sometimes hitting 4 per cent, while inflation was never more than 2–3 per cent (Evans and Taylor 1996: 108). It was an environment in which most of the economic indicators 'were favourable' until the latter stages of their time in office, and the cumulative effect was that 'the government was able to boast an increase in the standard of living during its time in office' (Norton 1996: 47). In this environment of supposed prosperity – or what became known as the age of affluence – the Government felt able to pursue measures that would aid electioneering. They sustained the commitment to full employment, while maintaining their commitments on spending on the National Health Service at the same time as finding scope to reduce taxation (Norton 1996: 47).

What has been most noted, however, by political historians is the policy continuity between the Attlee administrations and the successor Conservative administrations, which largely accepted their predecessors' commitments in terms of health, social security and education, and avoided attempts to reduce the size of the public sector (Seldon 1981: 80–8). The term 'Butskellism' encapsulated the assumed convergence between the policy objectives of the Attlee and Churchill administrations and their adherence to Keynesian demand management techniques and their commitment to full employment. However, it was an insinuation that did little to endorse either Butler or

Gaitskell to their respective parties, as 'Butler had long been regarded by the Conservative right, as being little better than a socialist, while the Bevanites tended to regard Gaitskell as rather worse than a Conservative' (Gilmour and Garnett 1998: 75). Butler would later admit that while he and Gaitskell 'spoke the language of Keynesianism we spoke it with different accents and a differing emphasis' (Butler 1971: 160).

The term reflected three key areas of perceived continuity: denationalization, full employment and the role of the trade unions. The new Conservative administration denationalized only two of the industries that Labour had moved into public ownership – iron and steel (1953) and road haulage (1954) (Turner 1996: 320). While Churchill continued to state his opposition to nationalization in principle, his administration broadly accepted their inheritance and then argued that they were trying to make a success of public ownership (Seldon 1981: 187). Such a perspective reflected the one-nation viewpoint that while they

> had not advocated public ownership per se, the existence of a mixed economy, albeit one in which 80 per cent of the economy remained in private hands, was one they could broadly accept, not least because it seemed commensurate with Macmillan's "middle way" vision of the state providing general or strategic coordination of the activities of a predominantly private sector economy. (Dorey 2011: 85)

In this scenario the one-nation solution was to 'establish the broad parameters' of 'national needs', while 'leaving the majority of firms relatively free' unless it was an industry 'deemed to be too strategically important to be left in private hands' (Dorey 2011: 85). Of the justification for pragmatically accepting a policy – nationalization – that they accepted was 'inefficient' (Kilmuir 1964: 163), Dorey concludes that this reflected how the Conservatives

> professed a non-ideological and flexible character, a philosophy which readily governs according to immediate circumstances rather than on the basis of theory or dogma, and which also seeks a consensual approach as far as possible, which in turn would buttress social stability and cohesion and ultimately foster national unity. These values meant that while one nation Conservatives were committed to private ownership of companies and industries in principle, and thus wholly in accordance with Conservative philosophy, they could, in particular contexts or on certain occasions, accede to nationalisation of a particular industry, albeit with little enthusiasm. (Dorey 2011: 85)

Such pragmatism clearly motivated their commitment to full employment. Here it is clear that Conservative elites, such as Macmillan and Butler, were moved by the social deprivation of the 1930s, which had for them 'made the provision of jobs paramount' (Davies 1996: 289). This concern was clearly evident in the 1953 Annual Conference speech by Butler, who responded to free market criticism of his approach by saying 'those who talked about creating pools of unemployment should be thrown into them and made to swim' (Davies 1996: 289). In addition to the moral objections to high unemployment, the Conservative administrations of the 1950s were also driven by economic and political (or electoral) calculations. Committing to full employment was deemed to be a political (electoral) necessity. The popularity of the commitment to full employment reflected the prevailing orthodoxies of the time-specific climate of expectations. It was the central quandary of the time. The commitment to the welfare state was dependent upon high employment levels to provide the necessary tax yields and National Insurance revenues that could finance cradle-to-grave social security, free education and the National Health Service. An administration that permitted unemployment to increase would be reducing such revenues while increasing pressure on social security payments. Such assumptions would be more openly challenged by the 1980s, but at this juncture such positioning was a 'rational calculation of electoral advantage' (Turner 1996: 321).

However, the commitment to full employment was closely aligned to the greatest difficulty for the Conservatives: the trade unions (Davies 1996: 285). Churchill was particularly sensitive to the danger that they represented through their class approach to politics and their leaders' commitment to socialism. More broadly, Conservative elites while deeply sceptical of trade unions felt that they could not antagonize them and simply write off millions of trade union votes by alienating them unnecessarily. On the transition to power, conciliation with the trade unions was the priority. As such, rather than appoint Maxwell-Fyfe to the Ministry of Labour, who had been 'frightening the unions' with speeches on reform, Churchill appointed the more emollient Walter Monckton with a clear brief to avoid antagonizing them (Seldon 1981: 68–70). Monckton later revealed that he understood his objective was to disprove the Labour prediction of 'grave industrial troubles' under a Conservative government (Birkenhead 1969: 256). This assumption was critical to Conservative thinking when placed within the context of Labour electoral strategy of evoking 'fear' about the compatibility of the trade unions and a Conservative government. Macmillan noted: 'if none of those fears have proved reasonable, we may be able to force the opposition to fight on socialism . . . then we can win' (Macmillan 1969: 361).

The price for peace with the trade unions would be inflationary wage settlements as when aspiring to full employment, 'the balance of power lies with a heavily unionised workforce' (Gilmour and Garnett 1998: 82–3). The approach adopted became viewed by critics on the right as industrial appeasement. The emphasis on, and trust in, securing voluntary agreement, rather than the use of legislative intervention meant that policy seemed to be guided by communication and encouragement. It would come to incur the wrath of the right in future decades. This was evident from the comment by

Powell: '[we] came to power without any specific policy on trade union law and practice, and faithfully carried that non-commitment out for thirteen years' (Powell 1968: 5). However, avoiding industrial warfare made political sense as 'nothing would have been more damaging to the Conservatives than the public's realisation that the party could not get on with the unions and the Conservative government spelled industrial trouble' (Gilmour and Garnett 1998: 82).

The evolving conundrum was how to deal with the inflationary pressures flowing from the impact of annual wage increases (Taylor 2005a: 138). The option of addressing this by abandoning the commitment to full employment was rejected, even though this would have placed the emphasis on trade union leaders to demonstrate restraint in order to protect the jobs of their members. They had also refused to consider the option of statutory restrictions being imposed upon the trade unions to compel greater responsibility. They contemplated the use of incomes policies as a means of stipulating the level at which wages could be increased, but this was problematic for two reasons. First, it contravened the Conservative belief in wages being determined by the market rather than the state; and, second, such an imposition could undermine trust with the trade union movement, and what would be the consequence if their compliance could not be achieved? (Dorey 1995a: 49).

By 1957 the credibility of reiterating the importance of moderation and responsibility in wage bargaining was being questioned. Recognizing the dangers of the consequences of inflation, Macmillan sought to defend the record of the Conservatives over the preceding 6 years. In doing so, he delivered his most famous political line:

> Let's be frank about it; most of our people have never had it so good. Go around the country, go to the industrial towns, go to the farms, and you will see a state of prosperity such as we have never had in my lifetime. (Lindsay and Harrington 1974: 202)

The speech could be seen as arrogant, and appealing to the materialistic instincts of the electorate, but it also served as a warning, that is, that inflation was a concern that had to be addressed to avoid the good times coming to an end (Ramsden 1999: 364). On how to address this, Macmillan was to come into open conflict with his chancellor, Peter Thorneycroft, who feared that inflationary pressures within the economy were 'infecting the middle classes as their economic security was [being] undermined' (Evans and Taylor 1996: 112). Thorneycroft, along with fellow Treasury ministers advocated 'bringing public spending under control' so as to create the 'foundations for inflation free growth' (Evans and Taylor 1996: 113). The Thorneycroft strategy implied allowing unemployment to rise as part of an anti-inflationary strategy (Green 2000: 409–30). He argued that by failing to tackle inflation Macmillan was creating both electoral and governing difficulties for the Conservatives. In doing so, he implied that the Macmillan strategy was being dictated by short-term thinking and a desire to avoid losing the next general election (Barnes 1987: 100, 122).

Making the case for a slight increase in unemployment to discipline (and constrain) bargainers would place Thorneycroft (and fellow Treasury ministers Powell and Nigel Birch) on a collision course with Macmillan (Lowe 1989: 505–26). Thorneycroft, Birch and Powell argued that significant cuts to welfare needed to be adopted and proposed that £153 million be removed from the 1958–59 estimates. A specific measure to save £65 million by withdrawing family allowance for the second child was rejected at Cabinet after the Minister for Pensions, John Boyd-Carpenter, threatened to resign (Gilmour and Garnett 1998: 140). The eventual compromise within Cabinet resulted in around £100 million worth of savings being identified, which was unacceptable to Thorneycroft, Birch and Powell, who all resigned in January 1958 (Shepherd 1996: 178–9). Although embarrassing to Macmillan, he recognized that Thorneycroft was in a minority within the Cabinet (Shepherd 1996: 179). Macmillan proceeded to brush aside their collective resignations as 'little local difficulties' that should not detract from the 'wider vision' of what his Government could achieve (Blake 1998: 281). Indeed in resignation they 'raised no banner of revolt' within the party (Butler and Rose 1960: 40). In the battle between alternative priorities in terms of public expenditure, inflation and full employment, Macmillan had won, as evident with the appointment of the more 'compliant' Derick Heathcoat Amory as his new chancellor (Ramsden 1999: 365). Heathcoat Amory delivered an expansionist budget, which provided the stimulus that Macmillan sought to ensure as the date of the next general election drew nearer (Evans and Taylor 1996: 114). However, the conflict showcased how despite their desire to promote domestic economic tranquillity and rising living standards – to demonstrate governing competence – there were underlying weaknesses within the economy (Evans and Taylor 1996: 108).

Regardless, the perception was that by the late 1950s 'the social democratic framework and its constituent institutions' that the Conservatives had inherited 'appeared to be working very well' (Dorey 1995a: 44). The Conservative leadership were therefore perfectly happy to continue pursuing what seemed to be successful policies as they provided them first, with a viable governing approach, and second, provoked a strategic dilemma for Labour (Gamble 1974: 63). The self-confidence of one-nation Conservatism was evident as Macmillan proclaimed after victory in 1959 that 'the class war is over, and we have won' (Macmillan 1972: 15).

From a Labour perspective, losing office in 1951 was a 'critical' defeat. Recovering power is always contingent upon two factors. First, there has to be an electoral perception that the incumbent government is incompetent and thus vulnerable, which did become the case for the Attlee administration. This constitutes the *necessary* precondition for a potential change of government. Second, the necessary aspect may not be *sufficient* – that is, just because a government is vulnerable to the charge of incompetence does not mean that the opposition is going to be automatically swept into power. The party of opposition has to demonstrate that it is credible and worthy of replacing the incumbent administration (Ball 2005: 1–28). The difficulty for Labour in opposition post 1951 was the general policy trajectory of the Conservative governments and their performance. The Conservatives inherited power in an era that was moving towards prosperity and consumerism, and thus were able to present themselves as a party of governing competence and a government that was improving living standards (Turner 1996: 317, 321). In this context Conservative tactics intensified the policy dilemmas facing Labour, as Pugh observes:

> It was in this period that Labour became the *victim* of the political consensus that had sustained it in 1945 . . . [the Conservatives] . . . had calculated that electoral survival required them to uphold the domestic consensus because they were vulnerable to Labour warnings that their return to office would see a higher cost of living, mass unemployment and attacks on the welfare state. Significantly, however, that nightmare vision failed to materialise . . . the new government upheld the fundamentals of the consensus. (Pugh 2010: 305–6)

By choosing to operate within a mixed economy, sustaining the welfare state and by adopting a conciliatory approach to the trade unions, the Churchill administration had minimized the scope of Labour's opposition strategy. That combination of competence and moderation meant that the necessary condition for a change of government referred to earlier was not in place by 1955 or in 1959. For example, in 1955 when Labour sought a return to government in the May 1955 general election, against the newly appointed prime minister, Anthony Eden, they had been critically undermined by the fact that it was

> hard for Labour to argue with any credibility that its achievements had been threatened, and as a result Labour candidates found it difficult to know what line to take at the election; even an internal party report of 1955 identified "the absence of clearly defined differences between the parties" as a cause of Labour's defeat. (Pugh 2010: 307)

The second term in office had, however, provided the Labour opposition with clear evidence of governing incompetence that could be attached to the Conservatives: Suez. This was an opportunity for Labour to score political points and critique the competency, credibility and unity of the Conservatives, albeit with the associated risk of being accused of being unpatriotic. The details of the Suez crisis have been well documented elsewhere (most recently Kyle 2011). From our perspective the critical issue is its impact upon the Conservatives, and how it culminated in Macmillan replacing Eden in January 1957.

For Eden it was a tragedy. He had waited over a decade for Churchill to resign so that he could assume the leadership. As early as 1946 supporters of Eden had manoeuvred and plotted but Churchill clung on (Ball 2004: 279–83). However, when Churchill finally did resign in the face of internal party pressures in early 1955, Eden finally became prime minister (Gilbert 1988: 989–91). His credibility was enhanced by calling a swift general election and increasing his parliamentary majority from 17 to 59, although even during the campaign there was criticism within Conservative ranks about his tendency to make 'speeches and policies on the hoof' (Rhodes-James 1986: 408).

Eden had entered Downing Street from the Foreign Office where he was widely admired for his expertise in foreign policy, yet this was to be his downfall. Relations between Britain and Egypt had deteriorated under the new Egyptian leader, Colonel Nasser, and his subsequent decision to nationalize the Suez Canal (which was partly owned by Britain and France), provoked Eden into action, using the World War II as his point of reference (Ramsden 1999: 333). Eden felt that Nasser was a dictator whom the West needed to stop; an assertion that he held despite the fact that pursuing a military solution would be against the wishes of the United States, and would divide the Commonwealth. To his critics his strategy evolved through his inability to 'adjust his thoughts to the altered world status of Great Britain' (Nutting 1967: 47).

The policy intervention that Eden utilized was constructed on a pretext. Their supposed immediate policy goal was to bring the Canal under international control, but their ultimate purpose was the removal of the Egyptian Government and Nasser (Gilmour and Garnett 1998: 111). To facilitate this objective Israel would invade Egypt, which occurred on 28 October, whereupon France and Britain would intervene (beginning on 31 October) to separate them, while securing their objective of regaining control of the Canal (Davies 1996: 357). The escapade had massive implications for the government not just in economic terms, but with regard to the special relationship. Opinion within the party was divided on the validity of military intervention, and two ministers, Edward Boyle and Anthony Nutting, resigned (Kyle 2011: 566). Eden also faced considerable pressure from the United States to withdraw and accept a ceasefire. What made the position of President Eisenhower so significant was the economic fall-out of their non-support. Sterling had come under massive pressure and the United States refused to provide any support for the pound, and furthermore chose to block funds at the International Monetary Fund (Evans and Taylor 1996: 105). The eventual withdrawal of the British, with the Canal left under the control of the United Nations, left the prestige of the British on the world stage seriously undermined (Thomas 1967: 18). Eden was also seriously undermined by the accusation that he had lied to Parliament when he later implied that he had no forward knowledge that Israel would attack Egypt. However, by this stage his conduct and decision-making was largely being seen in the context of his ill health (Dutton 1997: 424; Owen 2008: 109–40).

With Eden's reputation in tatters and his health a cause for concern, there were clearly doubts about his ability to continue as prime minister. Of even greater consideration was the fact that 'good relations with the United States were crucial for Britain's defence, foreign and economic policies' and moreover 'the restoration of good relations' demanded that Eden be replaced (Evans and Taylor 1996: 105). Eden's ill health between late November and mid-December meant Butler was acting as prime minister, while Eden was convalescing in Jamaica, but further complications with his health (and the knowledge that he was losing the support of his Cabinet) led to his resignation on 9 January 1957.

The choice for the Conservatives as to the next prime minister was between two of the leading advocates of New Conservatism and the one-nation approach – Butler and Macmillan. Butler was assumed to be the favourite to win according to the national press (Fisher 1977: 85). However, their performances in front of the 1922 Committee in November would aid Macmillan and undermine Butler. As acting prime minister, Butler gave a defensive and uninspiring speech, whereas Macmillan offered a campaigning and optimistic (and opportunistic) speech. The subsequent informal processes of consultation that the Conservative Party utilized to find out who was best positioned to succeed Eden suggested the following. Macmillan was felt to be a more unifying presence than Butler, who was regarded with considerably more hostility on the right of the PCP than Macmillan (Bogdanor 1994: 75).

The damage done to the credibility of the Conservatives was largely addressed by the replacement of Eden with Macmillan, who was to be widely praised for the 'inspirational' leadership that he displayed in challenging circumstances (Ramsden 1999: 362). The change of prime ministerial leadership neutralized the Suez issue, leaving Gaitskell and Labour with limited political options and remarkably, despite the evident failure that it was, it had 'little effect on domestic politics' (Evans and Taylor 1996: 107). The dominance that Macmillan was to demonstrate over Gaitskell was at its most evident during the 1959 general election campaign. When Gaitskell implied that significant increases in expenditure on social services could be implemented, but without increases in taxation, Macmillan seized his moment (Butler and Rose 1960: 59). It provided Macmillan with the political ammunition that he needed to confirm the central message of the Conservative campaign – that is, that Labour were financially irresponsible and that Gaitskell was engaging in electoral bribes (Fielding 2007: 311). Exploiting Gaitskell's tortuous relationship with Bevan, Macmillan noted that 'it was his [Gaitskell's] addiction to figures on which he built what seems now a false reputation, that led Mr Bevan to describe him as a desiccated calculating machine. . . . That is now only a half-truth. . . . I think he is still rather desiccated, but his reputation as a calculator has gone' (Butler and Rose 1960: 62).

The 1959 general election was a watershed election as the impact of television changed the dynamics of party projection and increased the emphasis on the image of party leaders. Here, Rowland noted the dominance of Macmillan over Gaitskell. He felt there was irony that it was the aristocratic and older Macmillan who was adapting to this new technique of political communication, as an 'image of Macmillan pruning his rose garden is worth half a dozen solid speeches by Gaitskell' (Rowland 1960: 358).

Degeneration and the exhaustion of the one-nation tradition 1960–1964

During their third term, however, the Conservatives would degenerate in a manner that was indicative of the exhaustion of the one-nation governing approach (Evans and Taylor 1996: 121). Long-serving governments show the following symptoms of degeneration, and these were present in the Conservative administration that fell in October 1964:

1   the appropriateness of their policy objectives and their reputation for governing competence being questioned, especially in the sphere of economic management;

2   increasingly negative perceptions of leadership credibility and thereby electoral appeal within the governing party;

3   increasing evidence of ideological division and mutual suspicion within the governing party;

4   accusations of abuse of power as allegations of sleaze and corruption engulf the governing party;

5   the inability of the governing party to avoid culpability for past mistakes and withstand the time for a change argument;

6   the evolution of an increasingly unified, electorally appealing, politically renewed and credible main opposition party (Heppell 2008a: 580).

By the early 1960s the underlying fragility of the economy was exposed (Turner 1996: 333). There was a 'distinct change in mood' by the early 1960s as the impact of lower growth rates and increasingly industrial unrest became evident (Thorpe 2011: 500). European countries were securing higher levels of growth, whereas Britain seemed to be engaging in stop-go economic cycles. Whereas Britain had a growth rate of 2.5 per cent between 1955 and 1960, these compared unfavourably with France (4.8 per cent), Italy (5.4 per cent) and West Germany (6.4 per cent) (Findley 2001: 336).

To respond to the perception of economic decline, the Macmillan government had advocated a three-pronged renewal strategy, which became defined as a Keynesian plus package (Pemberton 2001: 354). First, the

National Economic Development Council (NEDC) was established and brought together ministers, government officials, employers and trade unionists to identify the obstacles to faster growth (Pemberton 2001: 355). It was thereby established to promote economic growth, and advocated a commitment to 4 per cent growth by 1966, without a clear explanation of how this could be achieved (Turner 1996: 336). However, the NEDC, designed to facilitate economic growth possessed no planning powers, and excluded from its remit were wages and prices (Taylor 2005a: 139). Second, the National Incomes Commission was created to address the concern of keeping wages in line with the growth in production and thus prevent the inflationary spiral (Findley 2001: 333). Finally, entry into the European Economic Community (EEC) was advocated thus recognizing that, relative to the six member states of the EEC, the British economy was in decline (Evans and Taylor 1996: 121).

Within the context of the future direction of Conservative politics the rejection of the application for membership of the EEC requires further consideration. By the beginning of the 1960s it was becoming increasingly evident that the EEC was delivering substantive economic benefits for its member states, and the alternative free trade zone (EFTA) had failed. This was running parallel to the two other dimensions of British foreign policy: first, the need to re-solidify the Anglo-American relationship in the aftermath of Suez; and second, the continuing process of disengagement from Empire. Thus Macmillan had seen EEC entry as a means to secure economic benefits (a governing strategy) and demonstrate party renewal (a political strategy) (Stennis 1998: 61–90). The process of seeking entry was to be a long drawn out and tortuous process, that Macmillan endured from the point of announcement in July 1961 to the eventual rejection in January 1963. During the course of the application it had become evident that seeking entry had the potential to divide the party. When the House divided on the idea of launching a bid for membership nearly 30 Conservative backbenchers rebelled (Crowson 2007: 29). As Evans and Taylor noted, 'the announcement introduced the European virus into the Conservative bloodstream' and produced a furious outcry from the nationalist-imperialist right who saw it as a betrayal of Empire/Commonwealth (Evans and Taylor 1996: 121–2).

The subsequent rejection of their EEC application for membership destroyed the main pillars of the strategy for economic recovery and the future dynamics of foreign policy. Michael Fraser, the director of the Conservative Research Department, acknowledged that it undermined the intended electoral strategy of the Conservatives in seeking a fourth successive term, as Macmillan had hoped to narrate his re-election campaign around the opportunities that could be afforded through membership of EEC. Fraser noted that Europe was meant

> to create a new contemporary political argument with insular Socialism, dish the Liberals by stealing their clothes, give us something new after twelve to thirteen years; act as the catalyst for modernisation, give us a

new place in the international sun. It was Macmillan's ace, and de Gaulle trumped it. The Conservative Party never really recovered. (Butler and King 1965: 79)

The reputation of the Conservatives for governing economic competence had been questioned by economic decline. This competence-based degenerative symptom became tied into the second- and third degenerating symptoms, that is, negative perceptions of leadership competency, and ideological division within the parliamentary party. These degenerating symptoms were clearly evident in the botched Cabinet reshuffle that Macmillan made (July 1962) and by the disputed succession contest through which Lord Home (Alec Douglas-Home) acquired the party leadership and premiership (October 1963).

In an attempt to demonstrate the renewal of his administration Macmillan engaged in a complete reconstruction of his government in July 1962, the so-called 'Night of the Long Knives'. For Macmillan the objective of the reshuffle was fourfold. First, with the Conservatives now trailing in the opinion polls (and suffering at by elections) there was a demand for a 'refurbishing' of the image of the party. A major reshuffle could be used to renew their image in preparation for a general election in 2 years' time (Alderman 1992: 244). Second, many backbenchers (perhaps frustrated at their own lack of advancement) felt that a number of ministers were underperforming, and their limitations were a contributing factor to the increasing difficulties that the Government was experiencing. Macmillan acknowledged that some ministers were 'not up to it' (Horne 1989: 345–6). Third, Macmillan was anxious about the criticism that the 'electorate was getting bored with the old familiar faces' (Rawlinson 1989: 84). Specifically, Macmillan feared that boredom may relate to him as party leader and prime minister (Thorpe 1989: 342–53). Creating a new Cabinet and ministerial team would create the image of a younger and more dynamic administration. Finally, there was a policy dimension. The greatest casualty was to be the chancellor, Selwyn Lloyd, who had replaced Heathcoat Amory in July 1960. Macmillan felt that political popularity was tied to economic performance, and that Lloyd's caution was an obstacle to the expansionist approach that he wanted. Removing Lloyd, whom Macmillan felt had 'lost his grip', and replacing him with Maudling ensured that Macmillan had a more acceptable Chancellor (Macmillan 1973: 93).

With these considerations in his mind Macmillan dismissed seven members of his Cabinet. However, the reaction was not what Macmillan had expected. Maudling later acknowledged that the resentments created by the scale of the reshuffle and its reverberations created more difficulties for Macmillan that it solved (Maudling 1978: 124). For Macmillan himself it would damage his reputation: the butchery of his Cabinet created an indelible image of weakness and mobilized further criticism of his leadership style and party management methods. It failed in one of its objectives as the advancement of younger ministers served paradoxically to highlight the anachronistic image of Macmillan himself (Ramsden 1996: 167). However, in his own memoirs Macmillan justified the whole exercise in terms of replacing Lloyd with Maudling, by concluding: 'we were now definitely set upon an expansionist course, and the whole purpose of the changes at the Treasury was to ensure that this would take place without delay' (Macmillan 1973: 108).

The cumulative effect of these governing difficulties was a decline in public confidence in Macmillan. Speculation about his continuance as prime minister intensified as the Labour opinion polling lead was often in double digits (Butler and King 1965: 205). Eventually ill health forced Macmillan to resign in October 1963. The war of the succession resulted in Lord Home acquiring the party leadership and the premiership in controversial circumstances (Bogdanor 1994: 76).

Macmillan wanted to prevent Butler from succeeding him. He felt that Butler lacked electoral appeal; that he could not unify the party and that he lacked the strength of character to be prime minister (Horne 1989: 471). He also felt that the rising stars within the Conservative ranks – Macleod and Edward Heath – were too young to be considered and that they were candidates for the next succession contest (Thorpe 1996: 283). In his search for a credible non-Butler candidate, Macmillan was initially attracted to Hailsham (Horne 1989: 531). Hailsham was now available due to the recent parliamentary passage of a bill permitting hereditary peers to renounce their peerages and stand for election to the House of Commons (Blake 1998: 291). Hailsham indicated his interest in being considered for the leadership and his willingness to renounce his peerage to this end. The succession process would coincide with the Annual Conference and thus the speeches of the assumed three candidates – Butler, Maudling and Hailsham – acquired a huge significance. Butler was criticized for delivering a pedestrian and mundane speech, while Maudling delivered a content-laden speech on treasury matters without any of the 'rhetorical devices' traditionally associated with great orators and leaders (Baston 2004: 206). However, Hailsham also alienated many Conservatives by attempting to transform the conference into a nomination convention for his candidature. Macmillan quietly abandoned Hailsham as the prospect of Lord Home as an alternative anti-Butler candidate gathered momentum (Fisher 1977: 104).

In order to determine the succession the Cabinet agreed to a series of consultations to assess opinion. Of the consultations it was those within the parliamentary party (by the Chief Whip Martin Redmayne) and within Cabinet (by the Lord Chancellor, Lord Dilhorne) which would be crucial and widely contested (Denham and O'Hara 2008: 17). It was worth noting that Lord Home had indicated at the Cabinet meeting to discuss the succession process that he was willing to canvass opinion in Cabinet. This led to the assumption that he did not consider himself a candidate for the succession.

Both Redmayne and Dilhorne would report back to Macmillan that their soundings suggested that Lord Home was the most acceptable option, and that there was significant concern (opposition) about Butler. However, the concept of one parliamentarian, one vote did not appeal to Redmayne. When identifying the strength of feeling within the parliamentary party, he did not give equal weighting to the opinions of individual Conservative parliamentarians. His calculations were based on the fact that greater consideration was given to 'people on whose opinion one would more strongly rely on than others' and he found experienced parliamentarians tendered towards Home (Redmayne 1963: 101–3). After all, Macmillan told Redmayne at the beginning of their consultations, that: 'I want Home. Somehow or another you have got to devise a way so that I can say the party wants Home' (Stark 1996: 18). Redmayne was able to do so on findings which revealed first preferences (Home leading Butler 87–86 then Hailsham 65 and Maudling 48 plus Macleod 12 and Heath on 10) and then when considering second preferences and factoring in definite aversions (which eliminated Hailsham, Macleod and Heath), his final figures presented to Macmillan showed 113 for Home, 104 for Butler and 66 for Maudling (Baston 2004: 208).

When assessing opinion in Cabinet, Dilhorne claimed that his soundings led him to believe that ten Cabinet ministers endorsed Home, three endorsed Butler, four opted for Maudling and two preferred Hailsham. Macleod, who would later publish a devastating critique of how Home had annexed the leadership by dubious methods, was scathing in his condemnation of the accuracy of the figures produced by Dilhorne. The most notable flaw was that Dilhorne was claiming that Macleod was a Home supporter. If so, why would Macleod subsequently refuse to serve in Home's Government? (Gilmour and Garnett 1998: 199).

On the basis of the aforementioned (and distorted) processes of consultation, Macmillan drafted a memorandum arguing the case for Home and presented it to the Queen. However, at the same time leading Conservative elites – Hailsham, Maudling, Powell and Macleod – had met and agreed that they all wanted to serve in an administration led by Butler not by Home (Punnett 1992: 43). As Macmillan attempted to bounce the Queen into a speedy succession, it was still possible for Butler to stop Home. He could refuse to serve under Home and fight for the process to be reopened. To do this Butler needed all of his fellow Cabinet dissenters to agree not to serve under Home. If they did then Home would have to inform the Queen that he was unable to form an administration. This Butler felt unable to do. He decided to be pragmatic and serve under Home. Maudling and Hailsham agreed to serve as well, but Powell and Macleod refused. Lord Home renounced his peerage and reverted to Alec Douglas-Home to become prime minister. Having obtained a parliamentary seat at a hastily arranged by-election 3weeks later he became the official leader of the Conservative Party.

However, the war of the Macmillan succession was not just a failure of process; it was also a failure of outcome (Punnett 1992: 46). The selection of Douglas-Home was detrimental in two clear ways. First, an image of a party at war with itself was created which worked to the electoral advantage of the Labour Party. That sense of disunity was all encompassing as Powell, the figurehead of the Conservative right, and Macleod, the figurehead of the Tory left, were united in their opposition to him. That Douglas-Home could only unite the extremities of left and right in opposition to him, demonstrated the implausibility of him as a unifier. Second, Douglas-Home was not an electoral asset. The primary responsibility of any leader of the Conservative Party is voter mobilization – the politics of support or the art of winning elections. Douglas-Home failed to retain power for the Conservatives. He singularly failed to present himself to the electorate as a credible politician worthy of re-election. In an increasingly telegenic and meritocratic era, the media savvy intellectual modernizer, Harold Wilson, was able to outmanoeuvre the anachronistic Douglas-Home. Douglas-Home was widely criticized for his ineffectiveness on television and this was a significant impediment to their election campaign in the autumn of 1964. Integrating policy expertise (substance) with communication and presentation (style) Shepherd offered a damning critique of Douglas-Home:

> He was plainly out of his depth on the economy; an earlier self-deprecating confession that he had to do all of his economic calculations with the help of a box of matches seemed all too evidently true. It made a pitiable contrast to Wilson's command of statistics and talk of the white heat of the technological revolution. (Shepherd 1991: 160)

Macmillan would later come to accept that Douglas-Home was not voter-friendly, and admitted to his miscalculation with breathtaking arrogance: 'that illness was a sad blow for me. Without being conceited, it was a catastrophe for the party' (Clark 1998: 399). Difficulties continued in the 1963–64 period, the most notable of which was the 'sensitive issue' of abolishing resale price maintenance (RPM) (Campbell 1993: 150). While some Conservatives viewed RPM as an anachronism and an obstacle to the free market, which 'featherbedded manufacturers by keeping prices high at the expense of the consumer', others saw it as an 'essential safeguard to protect the small shopkeeper from being undercut and put out of business by the new supermarkets' (Campbell 1993: 151). As the president of the Board of Trade, Heath was keen to proceed with this as a symbol of Conservative modernization even though Douglas-Home had misgivings (Ziegler 2010: 146). Critics, such as Hailsham, argued about how this would be viewed by many small businesses who were a natural part of the Conservative constituency; moreover, why proceed in the final months before facing the electorate, when it could be addressed immediately after re-election (Hailsham 1990: 358)? Once Douglas-Home allowed Heath to proceed it caused considerable divisions within the PCP, and indeed within the Cabinet (Findley 2001: 327–8, 344). Moreover, key sections of the Conservative press ran 'fervent' anti-abolition campaigns, such as the

Daily Express, who at the time had a readership of over 11 million or around a quarter of the electorate (Butler and King 1965: 185, 197). The rebellions that its parliamentary passage provoked had an impact on perceptions of the respective parties. By early 1964, 48 per cent of the electorate thought Labour was more united than the Conservatives, and only 22 per cent thought the Conservatives were more united than Labour (Butler and King 1965: 83). Douglas-Home later concluded that 'it certainly cost us quite a lot of votes' and 'it probably cost us seats' (Hennessy 1986: 66). It also demonstrated the limited political antennae of the new prime minister, who later admitted that his limited grasp of domestic politics put him at a disadvantage when entering Downing Street (Home 1976: 184–216).

Therefore, in the final year of their third term the capacity for Conservative renewal was constrained by negative perceptions of leadership legitimacy/ competency and internal division. They were also constrained by the existence of the fourth degenerating tendency, that is, the growth of sleaze. An image of decadence became associated with the Macmillan government in 1963, as a result of numerous scandals. Electoral concerns reached a zenith when John Profumo, the Minister for War, admitted to lying to the House of Commons with regard to his relationship with Christine Keeler, who was also conducting a relationship with a Soviet Naval attache. Labour insinuated that Macmillan had been negligent over national security and that he was gullible for having accepting the original denial of Profumo (Knightly and Kennedy 1987). That Macmillan was so bemused by the unfolding of events, reinforced an image of him as being old, tired and out of touch.

While Macmillan, and his successor Douglas-Home, appeared to be socially unrepresentative of New Britain, Labour had a new party leader in the shape of Wilson. Wilson was able to outshine the anachronistic Douglas-Home in terms of electoral appeal. This observation leads us into the final two aspects of the degenerating tendencies of long-serving governments – that is, the presence of an increasingly unified, electorally appealing, politically renewed and credible main opposition party, which is able to exploit the time for a change argument. Wilson skilfully crafted a narrative based around Labour as the party of modernization, change and the white heat of technological revolution. He cleverly sought to portray himself as a symbol of inclusive modernization. He argued that the harnessing of science and technology for national purposes could remake Britain and transform its economic performance. The visionary rhetoric of new frontiers in New Britain, under a meritocratic leader, was designed as a contrast to the elitist establishment figure of Douglas-Home, and the Conservatives as the custodians of decline. The rhetoric over modernization, and the immediacy of the election, helped to bridge the divides between the socialist left, to whom Wilson was softly associated, and the social democratic revisionist right. While tensions still existed, Labour looked considerably more unified than 5 years earlier; the Conservatives looked considerably more disunited than when Macmillan secured them their third term (Shore 1993: 87–8).

Therefore, the crisis-ridden, third-term Conservative administration demonstrated all of the symptoms of a degenerating long-serving government. Their economic competence was questioned and they suffered from negative perceptions of leadership competence. They also displayed signs of internal division and suffered from accusations of sleaze. Thus when facing an increasingly unified, electorally appealing, politically renewed and credible main opposition party, they found it difficult to undermine the time for a change argument. The consequence was electoral rejection. Their vote fell from 13,749,830 in 1959 to 12,001,396 and their vote share was down from 49.4 per cent to 43.4 as their parliamentary representation was reduced from 365 to 304 (Kavanagh and Cowley 2010: 350).

One-nation statecraft

The one-nation statecraft strategy provided the basis for recovery after 1945 and access to office for a three-term administration. In statecraft terms the Conservatives were not an absolute success, but relative to a Labour movement that turned upon itself after 1951, it was enough to establish that they were the more unified and less factional party. For example, any internal tensions that the Conservatives experienced over Suez in late 1956 or the Thorneycroft resignation in 1958 were dwarfed by Labour's self-inflicted wounds during the late Attlee and Gaitskell eras. Conservative electioneering was aided by the factional feuding between the Bevan inspired left and the Gaitskell aligned social democratic right. The Bevanites felt that defeat in 1951 was a consequence of being insufficiently socialist, whereas the Gaitskellite social democratic right felt that the emphasis on public ownership should be downscaled. The intensity of that factional infighting would see Bevan having the whip withdrawn, and only just avoided expulsion from the party. Between 1951 and 1955 an impotent Attlee struggled to manage his party effectively and was left accused of 'following rather than leading his party' (Theakston 2010: 150). Throughout the early part of the 1950s the divisions were so deep that Attlee was consumed with simply trying to hold his party together, and with this being his 'overriding consideration' it meant that 'returning Labour to power at the next general election became secondary' (Thomas-Symonds 2010: 252). The Conservatives electoral successes in 1955 and 1959 propelled the Labour Party into another bout of ideological soul-searching, notably in the 1959–61 period, where disputes over public ownership and unilateralism, contributed to two challenges to Gaitskell's leadership in 1960 and 1961 (Heppell 2010: 19–38). The Conservatives were somewhat fortunate to have Gaitskell opposing them due to his limitations as a party manager and party leader (Pugh 2010: 299). Between 1955 and 1963 the Conservatives benefitted from the fact that

Gaitskell was as 'well known for the struggles managing a fractious Labour movement as he was for critiquing Government policy and presenting himself as the leader of an alternative administration' (Heppell 2012: 46). He seemed to devote more time to opposing the left of the Labour movement, as he did opposing the Conservatives (Williams 1978: 404). His death and replacement in early 1963 by Wilson was less helpful to the Conservatives. Although a controversial figure, (who had previously been aligned to the Bevanite left), Wilson chose a different and less confrontational party management route than Gaitskell. A gifted communicator Wilson used his speeches in the 1963–64 period to 'tell the left what it wanted to hear' but in reality 'party policy served to reassure the right' (Thompson 2006: 63). With a general election imminent Wilson wanted to blur the differences between the factions and transcend the old ideological factional debates of the 1950s. The next two decades would show this to be a mirage, but for a brief but important period it looked as though Wilson had 'set aside' the 'dismal background of Labour's years of fratricide' (Morgan 1992: 252). As the third-term Conservative government degenerated, the highly effective Wilson presided over an apparently more unified Labour movement was just enough to propel Labour back into office.

The Conservatives could take some comfort in their achievements in office, and their time had become viewed by some as a golden age of economic development (Black and Pemberton 2004: 1). It was a period of unprecedented economic growth which had involved considerable advances in terms of living standards, and in addition there were rising real incomes, and increases in the consumption of goods and services (Pemberton 2004: 108). Even in their final term, so consumed by perceptions of economic decline, unemployment averaged only 1.8 per cent and inflation 3 per cent, while the wages of manual workers were 20 per cent higher (Pinto-Dushinsky 1987: 154–5). The politics of affluence was central to Conservative strategy and was 'conceived politically', that is, promoting suburbia which was a Conservative environment, or advancing property ownership which was a Conservative attribute (Black 2004: 91). Tying their electoral strategy to the concept of affluence was hugely beneficial to the Conservatives in the 1950s, especially as Labour took a 'dim view' of affluence and 'struggled to acknowledge that consumerism mattered' (Black 2004: 92). The Conservatives thus sought to frame party competition as a choice between the redistributive objectives of socialism or becoming better off by individual consumerism (Black 2004: 91).

Affluence was rhetorically tied into the notion of competence. Conservative strategy had been defined by emphasizing how they were better equipped to manage the economy than the socialists (Turner 1996: 320). As Turner notes, it was a strategy designed with an 'overtly political purpose' of managing economic policy to fulfill social objectives while at the same time 'buttressing' the position of the Conservative Party (Turner 1996: 328). Competence thus became critical to their appeal. As Barnes notes of the 1955–59 period, they had made a 'better fist' of 'delivering a combination of economic growth, cuts in taxation, full employment and low inflation' than many other administrations (Barnes 1987: 137). However, as the notion of relative economic decline became prevalent by the early 1960s the Conservatives found that their credibility on the competence label became questioned (Turner 1996: 333). The perception of decline was given further momentum by the focus on international comparisons, and therein is the paradox of how to interpret the age of one-nation Conservative dominance – an age of affluence domestically (although huge regional and class variations existed) but a perception of wider decline economically within the world. Perceptions of decline were not solely economic as their 13 years in office was characterized by a journey from great power status towards greater consideration of co-operation within Europe (Turner 1996: 317). There was a psychological shock of becoming less significant on the world stage and within the world economy and the realization of the loss of influence was a challenge (Pemberton 2004: 112).

While the Conservatives could also take comfort in the fact that Labour had secured a single-figure parliamentary majority, there was a recognition that the climate of opinion had moved to their disadvantage (Gilmour and Garnett 1998: 215). As a multi-term administration a degree of boredom had set in and the time for a change argument was harder to withstand. The increasing emphasis on a meritocratic age chimed with the language and agenda that Wilson offered, and while the underlying tensions existed within Labour, Wilson was far more adept at binding left and right than Gaitskell had been. Indeed the deaths of Gaitskell (1963) and Bevan (1960) seemed to symbolize a reduction in the factional infighting of the mid-1950s. Wilson avoided drawing attention to internal divisions and sought to close down the feuding over nationalization, unilateralism and the EEC, where Gaitskell seemed determined to 'win' the argument at the expense of party unity. Between 1963 and 1964 Wilson was a highly effective leader of the opposition, and certainly more effective than Gaitskell (1955–63), or Attlee (1951–55) had been (Shore 1993: 87–8). The mantra of modernization captured the mood of the early 1960s, and while the Wilson rhetoric of white heat and the national plan would later be exposed, his agenda was chiming in with a view of the Conservatives as the establishment in a decade in which deference would be challenged and the lampooning of authority would become established through such mediums as *That Was the Week That Was* (Turner 1996: 349). The age of Conservative dominance was prolonged and involved considerable stages of change which may have been overstated for political purposes by many protagonists, both at the time and retrospectively. It was the era that moved on from austerity and rationing, through to consumption, prosperity and affluence, and then the notion of relative decline. In this age of change, Turner concludes thus:

> The party existed in a political environment which was constantly changing, and in order to survive it had to change itself. This process

of adaptation was the mark of its political success. Often it was able to change the external environment in order to protect its own interests, and the [early] Macmillan government was particularly successful in this endeavour. But sometimes external change was too fast, and the party's response slightly too slow or indecisive to bring complete success. The year 1964 was one of those occasions, but it was not be any means the end of the party's dominance of post war British politics. (Turner 1996: 352)

2

Adjustment through modernization: The transmission belt to Thatcherism 1964–1975

Defeat in the 1964 general election would act as a prelude to a decade-long struggle to construct a new statecraft strategy that would enable the Conservatives to win elections (the politics of support) and govern competently (the politics of power). The single-figure parliamentary majority that Labour secured in October 1964 would lead to a shorter-than-normal Parliament. Harold Wilson would dissolve Parliament in early 1966 and secured a larger parliamentary majority (of 99) as the Conservative vote fell further (11,418,433 or 41.9 per cent). The Conservatives did secure an unexpected return to office in June 1970 with a 46.4 per cent vote share and 13,145,123 votes, but the turbulence of office would contribute to two defeats in 1974. The February 1974 general election saw them fall back to 11,872,180 votes and the October 1974 general election saw a further reduction to 10,464,817 votes. Critically both contests witnessed a rise in support for other parties – notably the Liberals and Scottish Nationalists – meaning that the Conservative share of the vote fell significantly to 37.9 per cent and then to 35.8 per cent (Kavanagh and Cowley 2010: 350–1).

These events coincided with the leadership tenure of Edward Heath. It may be convenient for some Conservatives to use Heath as the yardstick against which leadership and governing incompetence should be judged, but this is to oversimplify. Heath would lead the party through a period of ideological turbulence. He would have to manage the conflict between progressives in the one-nation mould who believed that the Conservatives should remain situated in the centre ground and those on the right who wanted to pursue a more free market strategy. Heath struggled to manage this divide effectively. In that struggle his political reputation would be damaged (Fry 2005: 211).

His premiership would provoke a number of controversies: how should we interpret his objectives when entering office (is 'Selsdon Man' a myth?)?; how significant were the policy U-turns that his administration implemented (or were they acts of pragmatism?)?; why was the general election of early 1974 called; and what explains Heath's removal from the leadership in 1975 (was it simply that Margaret Thatcher was the only alternative to Heath – i.e. 'anyone but Ted' or an ideological conversion?)? However, before considering the Heath government of 1970–74, it is necessary to consider the period of opposition between 1964 and 1970. This is a critical juncture. It appeared that the party was undertaking a significant strategic reappraisal which 'appeared to herald a direct assault on the post war settlement' and Conservatives post-war statecraft strategy (Taylor 2005a: 140). Retrospectively the Heath era can be viewed as the transmission belt between two traditions – the one-nation accommodation with the politics of consensus and Thatcherism and the politics of conviction. In this interim period, Heath would attempt and fail to construct a new form of Conservative statecraft. His failure can be seen as either the first abortive attempt to implement Thatcherism or an attempt to modernize the existing settlement to make it work more effectively, which failed.

Planning for power: Renewal between 1964 and 1970

The scale of their electoral defeat in October 1964 created a conundrum for the Conservatives. A comfortable Labour victory, and the assumption of a full 5-year parliament, would have provided the Conservatives with time to make decisions on their key questions: leadership succession (and the method of determining the succession) and intellectual and policy renewal (Garnett 2005: 192). However, the timescale in which such deliberations would take place was complicated by the possibility of Wilson dissolving Parliament to obtain a stronger mandate. The question was should the Conservatives seek a new leader before Wilson sought his dissolution?

Alec Douglas-Home lacked leadership credibility. His inability to retain power undermined him, confirming him as a 'stop-gap leader who was bound to give way sooner or later' (Campbell 1993: 166). These arguments carry validity but his subsequent performance as leader of the opposition also drew criticism. His limitations as a parliamentarian 'were now far more damaging than in office' (Blake 1998: 297). More importantly he was disinterested in the task of intellectual and policy renewal, so this process was delegated to Heath (Campbell 1993: 167).

However, Douglas-Home made a critical intervention in the short time that he was leader of the opposition. He recognized that the magic circle was no longer tenable and that it worked to the advantage of candidates from elite backgrounds. What was needed was a meritocratic system which could allow the party to select a more socially representative leader (Fisher 1977: 195–7). However, the new democratic procedures would ensure that the electorate was limited to Conservative parliamentarians, and elections for the leadership would only occur when a vacancy existed. This would be when the incumbent chose to stand down (or died). That no procedure existed to challenge the leader was deliberate (Hutchinson 1970: 138). The new procedures assumed that a discredited leader would voluntarily stand down and therefore no rules on challengers needed to exist (Fisher 1977: 147–8).

The new procedures would involve a series of eliminative ballots up to maximum of three. Within the first ballot the leading candidate would be declared the winner only if they had an overall majority, plus a lead of 15 per cent over the second-placed candidate. If this was not forthcoming a second ballot would be called, in which alternative candidates could enter the contest. If no victor was forthcoming, then the leading three candidates would enter a final ballot in which Conservative parliamentarians could declare a second preference as well, which would ensure that a clear winner could be found once the least popular candidate had been eliminated (Bogdanor 1994: 81).

However, the new procedures did not remove the stain of illegitimacy for Douglas-Home. He knew that a campaign was being mounted to force him to stand down. That campaign was being initiated by allies of Heath. Heath did not actively campaign but he did nothing to discourage his supporters as they set about destabilizing Douglas-Home (Roth 1972: 184). When William Whitelaw (his Chief Whip) informed him that it may be in the best interests of the party for him to step aside, he did so. Upon resigning he informed the 1922 Committee that the party must complete the succession process 'swiftly and efficiently' and 'with dignity and calm' (Home 1976: 221).

The Conservatives were looking for a meritocratic figure who could effectively speak the language of modernization – that is, a Conservative version of Wilson (Butler and King 1966: 53). As R. A. Butler had retired from political life, and with Iain Macleod opting out, it was assumed that it was a straight choice between Heath and Reginald Maudling. Both were identifiable with the one-nation wing. Maudling was the pre-contest favourite due to his seniority and opinion polls showing he was the preferred candidate of floating voters (Roth 1972: 185). However, the succession contest was given greater ideological definition by the unexpected candidature of Enoch Powell. Powell knew that he could not win himself but he was keen to provide a platform for his views. His candidature would constitute a 'foretaste of the alliance Thatcher successfully constructed to win the leadership . . . [through] . . . a combination of free market enthusiasts, [and] traditional right-wingers concerned about immigration' (Evans and Taylor 1996: 145). Powell would secure a poor return of only 15 supporters, which was unrepresentative of the impact of those views within the PCP. What they did represent was the fact that Powell was a 'strange figure' unsuited to leading a political party, or even advancing a political faction. His viewpoints may have gained adherents but he personally showed limited interest (or skill in) translating this into support (Shepherd 1996: 293). Ultimately, his participation in the contest was to be of little consequence, and no second ballot occurred, so his supporters' second preferences were never sought. This was because Maudling decided not to seek a second ballot. Heath had won 150 to 133 on the first ballot, and without the 15 per cent lead over Maudling a second ballot should have been required (Punnett 1992: 60). Maudling realized that he would need all of the Powell supporters (plus the small number of abstainers) to support him to defeat Heath. It was highly unlikely that this would be feasible and a demoralized Maudling understood this (Baston 2004: 255).

Heath's usurping of Maudling was probably aided by the positive impact that Heath made relative to Maudling in the short period of opposition under Douglas-Home. In addition to assuming the more significant role of shadow Chancellor, (with Maudling becoming shadow Foreign Secretary), Heath was appointed to Chair the Advisory Committee on Policy. Heath utilized this position to advance his leadership credentials at the expense of Maudling, and 'went so far as to forbid the Research Department to supply the papers coming out the policy groupings to Maudling' (Campbell 1993: 172).

The process of repackaging policy dominated the opposition era. It would culminate in the much-debated Selsdon agenda that was to shape expectations of what the incoming administration of 1970 would aim to implement. However, it would differ from the process of policy renewal post 1945 in two ways. First, in 1945 the parliamentary arithmetic enabled the Conservatives to engage in that process with increased certainty that policy could be developed in preparation for a 1949 or 1950 general election. Post 1964 they would be forced to face the electorate after only 18 months and the process was still in its embryonic stage. This was the view of Heath who concluded that although defeat in 1966 was disappointing it gave them 'the opportunity of developing the policy review which had been started in 1965' (Heath 1998: 282). The second difference between the renewal processes of 1945–51 and 1965–70 was in the purpose and presentation of renewal. Whereas the Butler-inspired renewal process had been about impressionism and establishing the broad trajectory of the policy agenda, the Heath process was far more detailed with a greater emphasis on the policy specifics. However, policy development was influenced by the need to maintain party unity, that is, to avoid increasing the divide between the free market Conservatives led by Powell, and the welfare state pragmatists led by Maudling (Gilmour and Garnett 1998: 222). As a consequence the policy review, (prior to 1966), became 'a way of avoiding tackling the most fundamental questions' and 'the process lost sight of the wood for the trees' (Ball 2005: 23).

In early 1966 the Labour administration was viewed as reasonably competent and was able to consolidate its appeal on a modernizing platform based around the meritocratic image of Wilson. This helped propel them to a comfortable victory in the March 1966 general election (Ball 2005: 17). By the standards of electoral politics today, the reaction within the Conservative party and within the press was restrained. That restraint reflected an acceptance that the defeat was the continuing 'working out of the unpopularity and decline of the party when they left office in 1964' (Ball 2005: 17). Heath had not had time to establish himself as the new leader and given that there was little expectation that they could win (Heath 1998: 282), there was 'only limited discernable criticism' of him (Rhodes James 1972: 99).

Of the impact of the policy review at this stage, Ball concluded that 'it suffered from the blunderbuss effect – a horde of small shots, but little that really hit the target' (Ball 2005: 17). After all, the policy-review process had to ensure that the programme of policies offered, or the narrative, was attractive enough to the electorate to win back power, while at the same time retaining the unity of the party. It also had to offer a credible governing approach through which policies that were proposed could be implemented. That process had an emphasis on practical solutions to problems rather than being philosophically driven. Those practical remedies were cloaked in the 'language of management consultancy' (Evans and Taylor 1996: 147). The ongoing process, which involved more than 30 groups, would feed into the 1968 statement *Make Life Better* presented at the annual conference of that year. It would then infamously culminate in the meeting at the Selsdon Park Conference in January 1970, that would aim to draw together the various themes and objectives of the process to form the manifesto for the next general election.

In rhetorical terms Heath was careful initially. Modernization implied change, he argued, but it was change that would build upon the achievements of the 1951–64 administrations and was thus within the existing policy framework. For example, he informed the 1965 Annual Conference that greater selectivity in welfare provision was about the 'modernisation' of, not the 'abolition of' the welfare state (Campbell 1993: 203). Thus Heath was acting as a balancer, arguing a line that built upon the one-nation era, rather than repudiating it, but at the same time showing sensitivity to the evolving right. Significantly, Heath tried to avoid discussing incomes policy for this very reason – Maudling was strongly in favour, while Powell and Keith Joseph were against (Campbell 1993: 204). Campbell notes that 'Heath had no strong views on the matter', but his 'prime concern was to avoid open disunity, so for the present he preferred to evade the issue, making no clear commitment either way' (Campbell 1993: 204).

There was to be an interesting comparison between how they dealt with incomes policy and their approach to industrial relations. Here the objective of the 1969 policy document *A Fair Deal at Work* was to address the problem of unofficial strikes which was felt to be the primary issue with regard to industrial relations (Dorey 2001: 114). What was advocated was the creation of legally binding agreements between employers and trade unions, which could be enforced by a new industrial relations court. If it were deemed that disputes were threatening the national interest, then it was proposed to lead into a cooling off period of 2 months and a pre-strike ballot. The Conservative opposition was convinced that their framework was viable and they believed that once the legislation was enacted trade union leaders would regard further resistance as 'futile' (Garnett 2005: 208). This misplaced assumption would explain their position on incomes policy, as senior Conservatives 'assumed that a successful attack on militant trade unionism would in itself reduce much of the inflationary pressure from wage increases' and therefore they could avoid 'the need for tough deflationary measures which might increase unemployment' (Garnett 2005: 209).

The consequence of this approach was twofold. First, it would lead to rhetoric that would come back to undermine them when in office. So convinced were they of the imminent 'success' of their industrial relations policy this would 'obviate' the need for incomes policies. This then led to the following claim in their manifesto: 'we utterly reject the philosophy of compulsory wage control' (Dorey 2001: 112). A gap existed between this apparently clear claim and Heath's own attitude. He was said to be 'doggedly non committal' throughout most of the opposition era (Campbell 1993: 232). However, Heath was pulled towards this position out of 'political opportunism and rhetorical momentum, rather than conviction'. Adopting this rhetorical position (and thus rejecting Maudling's position), did not mean that Heath personally was embracing the position of Joseph (and Powell before his removal from the shadow Cabinet). Rather he had been persuaded by Macleod who considered it 'advantageous to take up the clearest possible anti-socialist cry before the election', even though Macleod personally 'did not mind if he had to reverse himself in government' (Campbell 1993: 232). From this Campbell deduces that this was entirely in tune with Heath's 'approach to politics' – that is, 'rejecting the *philosophy* of compulsion did not say anything about rejecting the *practice*, if in the Government's judgement it should become necessary' (Campbell 1993: 233). Thus the impending 'success' of their industrial relations legislation was inextricably tied to their hope that an incomes policy would not be necessary, and it would provide them with a means of addressing inflationary pressures within the economy (Garnett 2005: 210). Evans and Taylor conclude therefore that the 'entire policy-making process was marred by a serious omission' and that the Conservatives fought 'the general election of 1970 unprepared for the central problem which faced it' thereafter (Evans and Taylor 1996: 150–1).

It is fair to say that the opposition Conservatives were divided on a variety of issues (Fry 2005: 212). These would involve policy disagreements but also personal conflicts. The early period in opposition found Heath and

Whitelaw (his Chief Whip) struggling to contain dissension over Labour's proposed imposition of oil sanctions on the Ian Smith regime in Rhodesia (Garnett 2005: 195). While the leadership instruction was abstention, 50 Conservatives voted against the imposition of sanctions and 31 supported sanctions (Campbell 1993: 205). Nigel Fisher, who was a front-bench spokesperson on Commonwealth affairs, refused to abstain and supported the imposition of sanctions, and was thus forced to retreat to the backbenchers (Ziegler 2010: 196). As 80 Conservative parliamentarians rebelled against the instructions of the leadership, Wilson ruthlessly exploited the divisions within the PCP. The accusation that Heath was sacrificing principles in an attempt to preserve party unity (and then failing to do so) delighted the Labour benches (Campbell 1993: 204). Tony Benn recorded in his diaries that 'Heath is a pathetic figure, kicked this way and that, and is incapable of giving firm leadership'; the Conservatives are 'splintering before our eyes' (Benn 1987: 354).

Within months of this humiliation Heath was undermined by his own spokesperson on Colonial Affairs, Angus Maude. Writing in the *Spectator* in January 1966 Maude implied that Heath was a 'dry technocrat' and that the party had 'completely lost the political initiative' (Butler and King 1966: 20). Heath dismissed Maude. Within 18 months as party leader other significant figures from their governing years – Selwyn Lloyd, Duncan Sandys and John Boyd-Carpenter – were no longer within the shadow Cabinet. This caused considerable resentment. That Heath was also advancing younger and inexperienced Conservatives, such as Anthony Barber, Geoffrey Rippon and Peter Walker, aroused 'dissatisfaction among more seasoned representatives who thought that they had been overlooked' (Garnett 2012: 85). As a consequence his allies became dubbed the 'Heathmen' 'as if they constituted a specific faction within the party', an accusation that was compounded by the perception that Heath himself 'habitually treated Conservatives outside the new magic circle in a dismissive fashion' (Garnett 2012: 85). For example, when considering how Heath treated Edward du Cann (whom he dismissed as Party Chair in 1967), Wright suggested that it showed that Heath was a man who nursed grudges (du Cann had not backed Heath over RPM when at the Board of Trade) (Wright 1970: 387).

However, the primary internal party problem for Heath was the issue of immigration, which was becoming an increasingly salient issue within British politics. How should he respond to Labour's Race Relations legislation, which was designed to outlaw any kind of racial discrimination? The shadow Cabinet decided to accept the *principle* of the legislation but sought to *oppose* the legislation on the grounds of whether it could be effectively implemented. However, from the left Edward Boyle argued that the shadow Cabinet should back the legislation, fearing that opposition might allow Labour to portray them as racist (Ziegler 2010: 206–7). This is where Powell intervened with his infamous 'Rivers of Blood' speech. Noting the projected growth of the immigrant population, Powell observed that his constituents feared that 'in this country in fifteen or twenty years, the black man will have the whip hand over the white man' (Shepherd 1996: 346–7). And to those who sought legislation 'against discrimination' Powell argued that they 'had got it exactly and diametrically wrong', as the real 'discrimination and sense of alarm and of resentment lies not with the immigrant population but with those among whom they have come and are still coming' (Shepherd 1996: 348). The Powell intervention caused anger within the shadow Cabinet. They believed that Powell had accepted the negotiated compromise (Whitelaw 1989: 80–2). Heath was appalled at Powell and his open defiance of his authority and the agreed position of the shadow Cabinet (Heffer 1998: 456). Powell 'had overstepped the rational limits of dissent' and Heath was 'outraged, not least because Powell had caused embarrassment' and 'now seemed to think that he was licensed to speak out without fear of dismissal' (Garnett 2012: 86). Heath wanted to dismiss Powell and informed a reticent Thatcher (who was arguing for delay) 'he absolutely must go' (Thatcher 1995: 146–7). Dismissal became inevitable when his shadow Chancellor (Macleod), shadow Home Secretary (Quintin Hogg, formerly Lord Hailsham), employment spokesperson (Robert Carr) and education spokesperson (Boyle) threatened to resign if Powell remained (Shepherd 1994: 500). Heath dismissed Powell on the grounds that his speech was 'racialist in tone and liable to exacerbate racial tensions' (Shepherd 1996: 351).

The furore that Powell created over immigration has come to historically overshadow the wider contribution that he was trying to make to the debates on the future of Conservatism. Powell would advance 'clear alternatives' to the policies that have been deemed to have failed by 1964; and his combination of free market ideas and hostility to immigration appealed to sections of both the middle and working classes (Gamble 1974: 115). Powell was the first prominent post war Conservative to advocate the doctrine of the free economy which was to dominate Conservative discourse in the 1970s and 1980s (Gamble 1988: 70–3). Indeed, Joseph claims that it was 'Powell who converted both Thatcher and himself' and there is some legitimacy to the argument that 'Powellism was a precursor to Thatcherism' (Evans and Taylor 1996: 162). Thus the impact of Powell was that he showed that 'there was an intellectual alternative to the modernisation of the social democratic state' and it was an alternative narrative for the Conservatives (Gamble 1988: 73). However, the timing of his advance and the controversy and distraction away from the economic arguments that flowed from his attitudes on immigration created a fear within Conservative elites that Powell's attitudes would alienate uncommitted voters and disrupt party unity (Brittan 1968: 145–55).

The culmination of their review of policy in opposition was to be a weekend meeting at Selsdon Park Conference (January 1970), which aimed to pull together the review process into a coherent package of policies for the next general election. In reality the meetings at Selsdon failed to address the central policy concern that would face an incoming Heath government: inflation (Gilmour and Garnett 1998: 242). However, despite the ambiguity of this central issue Selsdon would acquire a significant influence upon the psyche of Conservatives over the next two decades. Of the five legislative priorities reported as agreed at Selsdon (tax cuts, trade union reform, law and order, immigration control, and higher pensions for the over-eighties), only three could be described as 'aggressively right wing'. But an impression of a substantive shift to the right was established in the press reporting (Campbell 1993: 265). The fact that the press briefings afterwards emphasized law and order so much, when it had hardly been covered during the policy discussions at the conference, was illuminating. This was a consequence of an ill-thought through and cynical intervention by Macleod. Heath was apparently worried about what to say to the awaiting press. Macleod advised: 'It's quite easy, Ted. Just tell them we believe in law and order that always goes down well' (Gilmour and Garnett 1998: 242). Therefore, although Heath did not really share the right-wing instincts that were being associated with him, the fact that the media made the link was partly his own fault as Heath 'compensated for rejecting the views of *laissez-faire* radicals by using their language' (Butler and Pinto-Duschinsky 1971: 46).

The politician that ensured that Selsdon entered the minds of the electorate was ironically Wilson. He attempted to exploit the suggestion that the Conservatives had lurched to the right by suggesting that they were planning to dismantle the welfare state. Wilson 'invented a composite model of the new breed of hard faced Tory – economically liberal but socially authoritarian' and christened this type of Conservative (and Heath) as 'Selsdon Man'. Wilson said that the Conservatives had 'an atavistic desire to reverse the course of 25 years of social revolution; what they are planning is a wanton, calculated and deliberate return to greater inequality' (Campbell 1993: 265). Campbell notes that

> "Selsdon Man" was a brilliant phrase, but it rebounded on Wilson, first because it lent the opposition's earnest catalogue of humdrum policies precisely the cloak of philosophic unity and political impact that they had hitherto lacked, and second because it turned out that the electorate was at least as much attracted as repelled by them. At a stroke Wilson had succeeded, as Heath and all his advisors had consistently failed to do, in sharpening the Tories' image and opening up the appearance of a clear political choice between Labour and Conservative. (Campbell 1993: 265)

The difficulties that the Wilson administration had experienced had already contributed to an improving opinion polling position for the Conservatives in the 1968–69 period (Garnett 2005: 193). Their national plan, and the institutional apparatus designed to facilitate this – the Department for Economic Affairs – had failed to hit the predetermined growth target of 4 per cent. Their economic credibility had been undermined by the humiliation of devaluation. This had occurred after the implementation of deflationary measures including expenditure cuts and a statutory 6-month wage freeze, which had been designed to stave off devaluation. The Wilson administration also struggled to grapple with the rise of trade union militancy, and more damagingly proposals advanced within the famous *In Place of Strife* (1969), which aimed to manage industrial relations more effectively, had to be withdrawn. With the PLP and the Cabinet divided on the proposals, a humiliated Wilson backed down (Tyler 2006: 462). These governing failings and internal party divisions should have provided opportunities for Heath as leader of the opposition to exploit, but doubts about his ability to propel the Conservatives to victory existed. Within Conservative Central Office concerns about his skills at campaigning were openly discussed (Garnett 2012: 84).

As the lead in the opinion polls that the Conservatives possessed began to narrow and then disappear, those doubts about Heath's 'stiff, odd, tense and humourless' public personality became more magnified (Campbell 1993: 189). The May 1970 local elections were particularly worrying because if they were replicated in a general election then Wilson would have a 50-seat majority. Shortly after those elections Labour pushed their lead up to 7.5 per cent in the opinion polls (Campbell 1993: 269). The opportunistic Wilson chose to dissolve Parliament almost a year earlier than necessary in order to exploit the current environment. There was a palpable fear of defeat within Conservative ranks (Ziegler 2010: 219).

A genuine concern among some Conservative elites was how to ensure that Powell would not assume the leadership after Heath was forced to stand down after the inevitable defeat (Carrington 1988: 214). Maudling and Whitelaw were so fearful of this prospect that plans were made for a meeting with Douglas-Home for immediately after the general election to discuss the leadership (Ziegler 2010: 219). However, Heath remained convinced that they would win, and despite doubts about his personal appeal the Conservative campaign was strongly focused around him as leader and alternative prime minister (Ziegler 2010: 219) With Labour doing likewise it contributed to highly personalized coverage to what was an 'unusually presidential campaign' (Butler and Pinto-Duschinsky 1971: 343–5). Personalizing the campaign in this way appeared to aid Wilson and not Heath, as the Labour lead increased to 12.4 per cent, whereupon Powell intervened (Hurd 1979: 18). Powell reintroduced the issue of immigration. Heath was now forced to answer questions on whether Powell could be a future Conservative leader, and whether he wanted to expel him from the party (Campbell 1993: 277).

However, with days to go before the electorate went to the polls, the supposedly smooth progress to re-election for Labour was undermined by worrying balance of payments figures. Senior Labour figures began to show their reservations. Barbara Castle doubted the size and durability of the opinion polling lead: 'I wish there weren't another five days before the election!' she wrote in her diaries 'although Heath is making such a pathetic showing personally and is getting such a bad press, I have a haunting feeling that there is a silent majority sitting behind its lace curtains, waiting to come out and vote Tory' (Castle 1984: 805). The doubts that Castle had in the accuracy of the opinion polls proved to be justified. Against expectations Heath was victorious. He took great 'satisfaction that the experts, the know-alls and the trend setters had been confounded' (Hurd 1979: 26). There was a swing of 4.8 per cent which produced a total vote of 13,145,123 (and a vote share of 46.4 per cent) for the Conservatives, providing them with 330 parliamentarians and a working majority of 31.

Powell claimed his interventions on immigration contributed to the election victory (Shepherd 1996: 400–3). He was certainly a dominant personality within the campaigning period. The press association assigned two reporters to him as opposed to one for Heath, Wilson and Jeremy Thorpe, creating an impression that it was a virtual four-party campaign, as Powell (or reaction to Powell) took up about 20 per cent of all election coverage on television (Shepherd 1996: 392, 401). Whether Powell wanted the Conservatives to win was another question (Hurd 1979: 22). Due to his conduct in opposition and his difficult relationship with Heath, victory he admitted had 'sealed my exile' (Shepherd 1996: 403). With Powell marginalized, the Conservatives were back in office and appeared well placed to resume their role as the natural party of government. It was seen as a personal triumph for Heath, and a justification for the meticulous preparation that had been made while in opposition.

From the Quiet Revolution to who governs? The Heath government 1970–1974

The allocation of senior portfolios was predictable as Douglas-Home went to the Foreign Office, Maudling to the Home Office and Macleod to the Treasury. Douglas-Home would no longer be seen as an alternative prime minister, but Maudling and Macleod could have been seen (either by themselves, their supporters, or the media) as threats to Heath. However, these two heavyweights were to be removed from the equation. Macleod tragically died in July 1970. Maudling, meanwhile, became engulfed in scandal (alongside accusations of excessive drinking) and had to resign from the Home Office in 1972, despite protesting his innocence (Maudling 1978: 193–205).

When Macleod died Heath appointed Barber to the Treasury (a 'promotion too far' according to Fry 2005: 222), and when Maudling was forced to resign he appointed Carr to the Home Office. Walker, Rippon, Barber, Carr and James Prior were Cabinet ministers who could be described as 'Heath's protégés if not creations' (Ziegler 2010: 242). Roth was more scathing in his appraisal. He noted that they 'seemed chosen favourites rather than obvious choices', and that their promotions indicated that Heath was keen to surround himself with those whose positions 'depended more on loyalty to him than to proven ability' (Roth 1972: 210). King felt that this meant that Heath had a 'weak Cabinet' because he liked to be 'surrounded by his friends rather than the most able members of the party'. King concluded, however, that this was because Heath was 'very suspicious and had good reason to doubt the loyalty of many serious members of his party' (King 1975: 9, 56). Heath sought the moral high ground by arguing that he could have 'bought support by giving places to potential trouble makers' but this was 'not the purpose of a modern government' (Heath 1998: 311). However, the Cabinet of Cronies accusation has to be tempered by the acknowledgement that both Thatcher and Joseph were members of the Heath Cabinet.

Despite high expectations when entering office, the Heath era would become remembered for its governing difficulties, that is, 'the record number of work days lost due to strikes, some of which severely dislocated life for millions of ordinary people, states of emergency, double digit inflation, a three-day working week, blank television screens, lawlessness and vandalism and, at the end, a crisis general election which the government lost' (Kavanagh 1996a: 360). These had not been the expectations when the Conservatives gathered for the 1970 Annual Conference. Here, Heath informed the party faithful that they had been 'returned to office to change the course and the history of this nation, nothing else' (Butler and Kavanagh 1974: 10).

This rhetoric built upon the assumptions that had underpinned the policy review in opposition. There was thus an expectation that his administration would reduce state intervention in the economy and lower public expenditure and income tax. Alongside the assumed pursuit of greater freedom in the economic sphere and greater competition with improved efficiency and greater productivity, was to be trade union reform, avoidance of formal prices and incomes policy, and increased selectivity in the allocation of welfare entitlements. The cumulative effect was that the incoming Heath administration was to challenge consensus politics. The logic underpinning these changes was that these measures would encourage enterprise and initiative, they would promote economic growth, and modernize the British economy, thus arresting decline (Dorey 2011: 92).

Their earlier rhetoric appeared to leave limited scope for ambiguity and would include numerous hostages to fortune. When promising a new style of government, Heath had emphasized in their manifesto his belief in securing 'long term objectives' as against 'short term gain' (the Wilson approach), and claimed:

I want to see a fresh approach to the taking of decisions. The Government should seek the best advice and listen carefully to it. It should not rush into decisions, it should use up to date techniques for assessing the situation, it should be deliberate and thorough . . . *once a decision is made, once a policy is established, the Prime Minister and his colleagues should have the courage to stick to it* . . . courage and intellectual honesty are essential qualities in politics, and in the interests of our country it is high time we saw them again. (Campbell 1993: 271)

Claiming that the 'gap between the politician's promises and the government's performance will be closed' was naive (Kavanagh 1987b: 222). Nonetheless it could be argued that they set off with a clear set of objectives in order to modernize Britain, and that they pursued these with rigour in the initial months of government. Implementing the Selsdon agenda would mean, among other things, that they would

1   seek entry into the EEC
2   refuse to provide state assistance for 'lame duck' companies
3   create a statutory framework to regulate industrial relations
4   not introduce a compulsory incomes policy.

The most important objective was securing entry into the EEC (Turner 2000: 64). This position was held despite the fact that while negotiations were ongoing Conservative whips had calculated only 194 Conservative MPs were in favour of entry, 70 were undecided and 62 were hostile (Norton 1978: 67). Once negotiations were completed, the publication of the White Paper (in June 1971) would 'signal the beginnings of a drawn out parliamentary battle' (Crowson 2007: 38). On the advice of Francis Pym, his Chief Whip, Heath postponed until after the summer recess any parliamentary division on the principle of entry (Garnett and Aitken 2002: 96–7). However, Heath hoped that opinion within the PCP would be influenced by the fact that the majority of constituencies and activists favoured entry and that the 1971 Annual Conference accepted the terms upon which entry had been secured by 2,474 to 324 (Kelly 1994: 250). He also was to benefit from the position, and divisions around this, that the Labour opposition adopted. By officially opposing the terms of entry, Ball argues, Wilson put the question on a 'partisan basis' and this meant that it pushed the undecided within the PCP towards 'loyalty' to the party, even if they remained unenthusiastic about the principle of entry (Ball 1996: 317).

Exploiting the awareness of a significant body of pro-European Labour MPs (who they were confident would vote for the terms of entry), Pym and a reluctant Heath granted a free vote for the October 1971 parliamentary division on the principle of entry (Norton 1978: 70). Heath later admitted that he wanted a three-line whip, but that Pym (and Whitelaw) had persuaded him that a free vote would be 'healthier for the party' (Heath 1998: 378–9). It resulted in a majority of 112 for entry (356–244), with the number of

Conservative 'rebels' (39) outweighed by the number of Labour rebels (69) who defied a three-line whip imposed by the shadow Cabinet (Meredith 2008: 85–8). By the time the Bill received its final approval in June 1972 Heath had managed to win all 104 divisions, although 20 Conservatives rebelled at second reading, 31 rebelled on a pro-referendum amendment and 16 rebelled on the final reading which was won by 301 to 284. After the division, Pym announced that 'it has been a terrific battle, full of tension and drama, the determination and patience of the Conservative Party has been remarkable' (Norton 1978: 79). That Pym was 'relieved that it was over' was understandable as it had been the 'most persistent' example of backbench dissent that the PCP had experienced in the post-war period (Norton 1978: 79–80).

Entry was to be the primary legacy of the Heath government. That the Conservatives would within a few decades become overwhelmingly Euro-sceptic has caused further damage to Heath's reputation. The argument that the political implications of entry were 'disguised' during the parliamentary passage of the European Communities Act has been increasingly made (Young 1998: 246–51). In reality the passage of the parliamentary legislation would encapsulate the poolers/absolutists distinction that would come to dominate the debate in forthcoming decades. The Heath frontbench would argue that sovereignty would not be eroded, and rather it would be shared and enhanced as membership would increase the range of choices open to the British state. The attitude of Heath was that they should not obsess about institutional dynamics as there was 'no need to specify' on the 'theological principles of arrangements' (Lord 1994: 37–9). This ambiguity, and the resultant difficulties in securing parliamentary ratification, would contribute to the Heath European strategy suffering from a legitimization problem. Due to this Gifford concludes that Heath's government 'failed to articulate or institutionalise a coherent European project' that would persuade either the party or the electorate of the benefits of membership (Gifford 2008: 54).

Beyond successfully securing European entry the Heath government would experience a number of governing difficulties that would make a mockery of the rhetorical flourishes of their early months of power. A month after Heath delivered his famous Quiet Revolution speech to the October Annual Party Conference, his Secretary of State for Trade and Industry John Davies made an equally memorable intervention. Davies was the former director general of the CBI (1965–69), and within months of entering Parliament in 1970 he was put in charge of the new super ministry of Trade and Industry. Here he was to demonstrate the 'disadvantage of inexperience' (Gilmour and Garnett 1998: 248). That November he told the House of Commons that the government was determined to make 'industry stand on its own two feet or go to the wall', and that the 'consequence of treating the whole country as lame ducks was national decadence'. He concluded that the vast majority 'live and thrive in a bracing climate and not in a soft, sodden morass of subsidised incompetence' (Bell 2004: 66).

Heath would later lament that Davies 'was trying too hard to prove his credentials' (Heath 1998: 330). As Campbell notes, it is less well remembered that Davies was more interventionist than his rhetoric in Parliament suggested. His comments to the Annual Conference a month earlier, about not bolstering or bailing out companies 'where I can see no end to the process of propping them up' had an important sentence before it. Here Davies did acknowledge that the consequences of abandoning 'great sectors of our productive community at their moment of maximum weakness', suggests he was more moderate than the 'lame ducks' rhetoric would imply (Campbell 1993: 310). But as Ziegler notes, Davies had given 'several hostages to fortune which fortune, as is its way, was in due course to deploy with some brutality' (Ziegler 2010: 333).

A considerable amount of time had been devoted to the industrial relations in the policy review in opposition. Once in government, Heath sought through the Industrial Relations Act of 1971 to change the climate of confrontation, and provide both new rights but also new responsibilities for trade unions as institutions. In his memoirs he was at pains to emphasize the 'fundamental difference' between his and Thatcher's later trade union reforms, in that his were done in the 'spirit of one nation Conservatism', as 'we had nothing against the trade unions as such' (Heath 1998: 409). The legislation would come into force in August 1971 and would involve the creation of a Registrar of Trade Unions and Employers' Association and the establishment of the National Industrial Relations Court which had the status of a High Court. However, the act was misconceived, as Gamble notes:

> It was designed to deal with the problem of unofficial strikes and the growing power of shop stewards in some major industries, and it sought to do this by giving greater authority to the national union leaderships. The refusal of the trade unions, however, to trade some loss of their privileges for greater authority over their members destroyed the plan and soured relations between unions and Government. (Gamble 1988: 75)

By the time Heath departed Downing Street the legislation was deemed to have failed, and was seen to have harmed, rather than aided, industrial relations. Its non-viability would contribute in time to its 'tacit abandonment' and its inclusion in the list of U-turns that would be associated with the Heath era (Ball 1996: 329). It was naive to assume that if the trade unions would not accept a Labour administration legislating on trade union power (through the aborted *In Place of Strife*), that they would accept a 'Tory version' (Fry 2005: 221). Upon reflection a more astute political move would have been for the Heath government to have implemented Labour 1969 *In Place of Strife* proposals, because politically it would have been problematic for Labour to oppose (Prior 1986: 72). While this may have been a tactical miscalculation, the wider strategic calculation that underpinned the Industrial Relations Act was flawed. Their commitment to operate without an incomes policy meant that containing inflation was dependent on the industrial relations legislation working. Its failure would contribute to the momentum that would lead to the infamous U-turns.

The difficulties for the Heath government started quickly. There was 'no honeymoon' and quickly the 'unprecedented combination of rising unemployment and rising prices produced an alarming and perplexing situation' (Ball 1996: 320). In the first year of office many of the commitments identified in opposition began to be implemented. In addition to commencing the legislative process on industrial relations, and beginning negotiations to enter the EEC, the government announced cuts (in the mini-budget of October 1970 and the budget of March 1971) in public spending, income tax and corporation tax (Kavanagh 1996a: 373). However, concerns began to develop about the fear that what they were trying to achieve was 'not understood or appreciated by the public' (Ball 1996: 321).

Although there was a growing feeling that the government had no 'idea of how to control inflation' (Ball 1996: 327), the root cause of the policy adaptations, or U-turns of 1971–72 stemmed from concerns about unemployment. By the beginning of 1972 unemployment hit the highest level since the winter of 1947 (Kavanagh 1996a: 373). Permitting a high level was 'counter to everything Ted believed in' (Prior 1986: 73). During the winter of 1971–72 unemployment rose above one million – a figure which Heath feared would be politically unacceptable to permit when seeking re-election. As a consequence their governing approach morphed back to the traditional corporatist and interventionist ways of the post-war era. In time, however, Ball argues the language of 'U-turn' would become 'impressed into the national consciousness' to such an extent that it would fatally undermine the 'credibility' of the government and Heath himself (Ball 1996: 328). The process of policy adaptations occurred at many levels and involved:

The rescuing of 'lame duck' companies

Having entered office with a firm commitment to have a 'hands off' approach to industry, and not use the state to bail out so-called lame duck companies making big losses, the Heath government proceeded to intervene and nationalize Rolls Royce in late 1971. Fear about social and political unrest eventually led to the rescue of the Upper Clyde Shipbuilders in early 1972. The Rolls Royce intervention could initially be viewed as an 'exceptional expedient' which was 'dictated by international obligations and defence considerations which in no way invalidated the principle of not propping up lame ducks' (Campbell 1993: 442). After all, Rolls Royce was the 'standard-bearer for British industry', and if it failed it would 'damage national prestige' (Ziegler 2010: 343). However, the rescuing of the Upper Clyde

Shipbuilders was different as Heath (and Davies) had earlier suggested that this was 'precisely the sort of company they were determined not to rescue' (Campbell 1993: 442). As it stood on the brink of going into liquidation a report, in which Nicholas Ridley (junior minister in the Department of Trade and Industry) advocated complete closure, was leaked. As the threat of civil disorder escalated Heath informed the Cabinet that 'it would be necessary to suspend, for the time being, the application of the established policy of accepting that, when concerns ceased to be viable, they should be allowed to go into receivership' (Ziegler 2010: 345). This bailing out of companies in financial difficulties 'caused much unease among government backbenchers and the contrast between words and action was commented on by supporters and political opponents' (Kavanagh 1996a: 370).

Adopting state-directed economic planning and regional development

Through the formulation and implementation of the 1972 Industry Act the government further contradicted their commitment to disengage. The Bill was fuelled by a view that the advantages of EEC membership could only be fully exploited if industrial capacity was strengthened. The Bill therefore made provision for two types of state assistance for industry – first there was to be financial incentives for investment in new plant and machinery; and, second, was the restoration of regional investment grants for areas suffering from high unemployment (Kavanagh 1996a: 373). Within Cabinet, Thatcher and Joseph publically accepted it while privately having reservations, but Conservative backbenchers were clearly unhappy especially as Wilson 'offered barbed congratulations to Heath on his belated conversion to sound socialist principles' (Ziegler 2010: 357). The scale of unease of the Conservative backbenchers was evident when Sir Harry Legge-Bourke, Chair of the 1922 Committee described the legislation as a 'socialist bill by ethic and philosophy' (Bell 2004: 73).

The abandonment of the industrial relations legislation and the search for a tripartite consensus

The Industrial Relations Act failed in the sense that the number of working days lost to strikes increased. In the first year of its operation (1972) Britain lost over 23 million man days in stoppages, which was the largest number since 1926 (Kavanagh 1987b: 222). It became virtually inoperable when the TUC decided that they would expel any union that registered under the Act, an action which 'effectively crippled' the policy (Kavanagh 1987b: 225). The National Union of Mineworkers (NUM) called a national strike for January 1972 demanding a 47 per cent pay rise for their members (Taylor 1996: 177). The Cabinet agreed not to refer it to the new institution – the

National Industrial Relations Court – fearing this would further alienate the NUM (Ziegler 2010: 350). Taylor suggests that instead the Cabinet, 'raised the white flag' by setting up a public inquiry under Lord Wilberforce (Taylor 1996: 177). Commenting on the scale of the crisis at the time, Hurd recalled that 'the government is now vainly wandering over the battlefield looking for someone to surrender to and being massacred all the time' (Hurd 1979: 103). The resulting report (produced within 3 days) offered the Government a way out, but a humiliating one at that with the offer of a 32 per cent pay increase being recommended (Kavanagh 1996a: 368–9). The 'authority' of the Government was badly undermined and it smacked of 'surrendering to industrial muscle' (Kavanagh 1996a: 369). In the aftermath, Heath informed the nation that 'we must find a more sensible way to settle our differences' (Campbell 1993: 420–1).

This apparent surrender to the NUM did tremendous damage to the self-confidence and standing of the Heath government, and undermined morale within all sections of the party (Whitelaw 1989: 124). There was a tacit abandoning of the Industrial Relations Act in the face of its non-viability, as the Heath government sought stability and growth through a 'tripartite consensus' (Ball 1996: 329). The objective through 1972 was to acquire agreement on a policy of voluntary pay restraint through inclusive talks involving the Government, the TUC and the CBI. It was a 'clumsy though probably sincere' attempt but it constituted a U-turn, and its eventual failure by the autumn would contribute to the fourth identifiable U-turn on incomes policy (Bulpitt 1983: 179).

The adoption of a compulsory prices and incomes policy

Gamble argues that the 'biggest change of all', and the 'one which excited the loudest shouts of betrayal, was incomes policy' (Gamble 1988: 76). As was mentioned earlier in the chapter, the manifesto for the 1970 general election had made it clear that the leadership opposed the philosophy of incomes policy. However, after the failure to secure a voluntary agreement for pay restraint involving the CBI and the TUC, the Government intervened in November 1972 to impose a statutory incomes policy. It should be noted that the demand for an incomes policy was 'intensified' by a severe run on the reserves which had increased inflation and concerns about a balance of payments deficit, leading to the government deciding to float the pound. This in turn would leave 'them with no alternative to the restoration of wage discipline' (Evans and Taylor 1996: 200–1). Indeed, Heath would later argue that by this time he 'did not really believe it was practicable to fight on without statutory backing' (Heath 1998: 414). However, the jettisoning of the 1970 manifesto commitment prompted Powell to ask whether Heath 'had taken leave of his senses' (Dorey 2001: 128). Stage 1 (a complete freeze) and 2 (a phase of an egalitarian increases across the board) of the statutory incomes policy were successful, but the policy came unstuck at stage 3 (an increase of 7 per cent) when negotiating with the NUM in the winter of 1973–74. A year earlier when rebelling against the imposition of a statutory incomes policy Ridley claimed that Thatcher congratulated him for his stance, but was unable to join him (Evans and Taylor 1996: 201–2).

Increases in public expenditure

Between July 1971 and March 1973 the Heath government adopted classic Keynesian reflationary methods by increasing public expenditure (Kavanagh 1996a: 373). This contradicted their aforementioned commitment to holding down or reducing public expenditure, but it was deemed to be necessary in order to boost output and stimulate growth (Gamble 1988: 76). The reflating of the economy in 1972, in the eyes of Heath's critics, was the 'cause of the rampant inflation' of 1974 and 1975 (Evans and Taylor 1996: 201). It was done in an effort to 'spend its way back to full employment', and they were 'able to do so because the constraint afforded by fixed exchange rates had disappeared' (Gamble 1988: 79). However, Gamble notes that to 'keep the momentum of the expansion going' meant that the Heath government 'found itself obliged to intervene in markets more and more, and to try to control wages and prices directly' (Gamble 1988: 79). The experience of the Heath government was 'thought to prove the monetarist critique of Keynesianism' (Evans and Taylor 1996: 201). Anyway, the growth strategy, which was now described in Conservative 'demonology' as the 'Barber boom', was not sustained (Evans and Taylor 1996: 202). By early 1973 there were increasing fears among Conservatives that the economy was overheating. Moreover, the inflationary pressures created in late 1973 by the rise in oil prices 'removed any credibility' from the dash for growth strategy, and made 'some measure of deflation inescapable' (Gilmour and Garnett 1998: 282). The expenditure cuts of May and December 1973 were welcomed by many Conservative MPs, notably du Cann, who had been so vocal in his criticism about the rising level of expenditure (Ball 1996: 330). However, while Heath loyalists described these adjustments in economic strategy as 'pragmatic', to his critics they smacked of 'inconsistency'. More generally it could be said, however, that the Conservatives were giving the impression of 'confusion' with regard to their strategy (Ball 1996: 330).

Given the ideological turbulence maintaining party unity was an ongoing challenge. The Heath Government would experience a remarkably high level of backbench parliamentary rebellions. For example, while the last Conservative Parliament (1959–64) had experienced a rebellion rate of 11 per cent, the 1970–74 parliament would see government dissent rise to 18 per cent, and the 1971–72 session would have a dissension rate of 29 per cent (Norton 1978: 40). At the end of the rebellious year that was 1972, there was a 'growing conviction' among Conservative parliamentarians that they were 'regarded as servants of a leader who has little regard for their affection, or their principles, and who considers them as cattle to be driven through the gates of the lobby' (Cosgrave 1972: 878).

Campbell concludes that 'it is easy in retrospect to trace the parliamentary party's rejection of Heath back to before 1974–75' (Campbell 1993: 510). There were clear 'warning signs' in 1972, as known critics of Heath were elected to positions of significance (Kavanagh 1996a: 375). Having left his junior ministerial role within the Department of Trade, Ridley was elected as chair of the backbench finance committee. Another critic of the economic policy reversals, John Biffen, was elected as chair of the backbench industry committee (Norton 1978: 241). Of perhaps greater retrospective significance was the election of du Cann as the new Chair of the 1922 Executive Committee. They had a relationship based on mutual distrust (Ziegler 2010: 354). Heath disliked du Cann for having voted for Maudling in the 1965 party leadership election, and Heath repaid him by dismissing him as Party Chair (in 1967) and then excluding him from ministerial ranks when the party returned to power in 1970 (Clark 1998: 457). Upon his election du Cann assured Heath 'You will have my full support, and I want you to know that I mean it,' but as Ziegler notes, 'he did not mean it, and the Prime Minister knew that he did not mean it' (Ziegler 2010: 354–5).

The perception that the Heath government had been humiliated by the 1972 miners' strike had created a view 'that it should never happen again', as their 'authority could not survive another such defeat' (Campbell 1993: 421). This mentality would put them on a collision course with the NUM in the autumn of 1973, as in party terms a 'second surrender to the NUM was out of the question' (Ball 1996: 345). The emerging crisis was initiated when the National Coal Board offered a pay increase of 13 per cent to the miners, which was within the parameters of the incomes policy that the Heath government had set down. Given that the NUM was seeking an increase of 40 per cent, they began an overtime ban in November 1973. Their claim coincided with the Yom Kippur war in the Middle East and thus their bargaining positioning was enhanced by the impending energy crisis created by OPEC imposing a fourfold increase in oil prices. Coinciding with this was a work to rule by engineers in the electricity industry, and action by train drivers, which created the cumulative impact of diminishing coal supplies and electricity power cuts. The subsequent imposition of a 3-day week to conserve energy supplies contributed to a heightened sense of national crisis and political impotence (Dorey 1995a: 124).

Ramsden concludes that Heath was left with two alternatives. Option one was pay whatever was required to get the miners to return to work, and 'fight another day'. Option two involved Heath appealing for the support of the people in the hope that a renewed and enlarged mandate could exert pressure on the miners where 'arguments had failed' (Ramsden 1999: 410). Option one was problematic for Heath in party terms as he was under 'pressure from backbenchers who would not countenance another sell out to the miners' (Kavanagh 1996b: 363). Option two was also problematic for Heath as he was personally deeply reluctant to engage in a confrontation that a 'Who Governs' style campaign would necessarily generate (Ramsden 1999: 412). The Cabinet was divided on which option to select and prevaricated. Carrington, Prior, Walker and Geoffrey Howe felt that a renewed mandate was the only way to defeat the miners. Polls suggested that they possessed a small lead and if they won a second election and had the prospect of five further years in office (till early 1979), they would be in a stronger position to take on the miners than continuing to the end of their current mandate. However, Pym and Whitelaw opposed the idea of an earlier election, feeling that it was unnecessary (Butler and Kavanagh 1974: 35). Taylor argues that Heath felt that he could avoid an early election as he (for too long) retained hope that he could persuade the miners to compromise, a view which was a 'remarkable testimony to Heath's self confidence; a self-confidence bordering on delusion' (Taylor 2005b: 97).

Press speculation began to mount that a general election would be called for the 7 February, but leading up to the 17 January (the last day at which Parliament could be dissolved for this to occur) Heath was gripped by indecision. Ziegler concludes that 'dithering had unfortunate consequences for the party', as it was claimed by some political commentators that they had 'considered holding an election, but had run away from the possibility because they thought that they would lose' (Ziegler 2010: 423). Had Heath gone then (by 17 January) it would have been a campaign against the miners' overtime ban, not a strike, but a week after deciding not to seek a new mandate the NUM voted for a strike (Kavanagh 1996b: 362–3). A reluctant Heath now felt compelled to go for option two, and called a general election for 28 February. In what would be his final broadcast as prime minister he informed the electorate that

> the issue before you is a simple one. . . . Do you want a strong Government which has clear authority for the future to take the decisions that will be needed? (Clark 1998: 426)

That part of the statement created as many questions as answers – if the electorate needed a strong Government, did that mean the present one was weak? In what way was the authority of the current Government requiring a reconfirmation? After all, there was one and half years of the Parliament left. And what 'decisions' did Heath think 'needed' to be made? (Clark 1998: 426). The election 'was held in inauspicious circumstances, during deep winter, a three-day week, petrol rationing and a coal miners' strike' (Kavanagh 1996b: 351). Despite this Heath was remarkably confident of being re-elected and this was a widespread view. As Ziegler notes 'at the onset of the campaign it was taken for granted by almost everyone that the Conservatives would win' and 'in a time of emergency, the country was bound to rally behind the established authority: patriotism would blend with self interest to produce a swing away from anarchy to security and stability' (Ziegler 2010: 432).

The prospect of the Conservatives being re-elected was not aided by Powell intervening and encouraging Conservatives supporters to vote Labour as this at least provided a route map out of the EEC (Powell was not seeking re-election as a Conservative.) (Shepherd 1996: 433–6). Moreover, there was a contradiction at the heart of the Conservatives request for a second term – that is, 4 years earlier they had emphasized how governments needed to stand aside from wage negotiations, arguing that this should be left to trade unions and employers, and yet now there were arguing that a statutory prices and incomes policy was necessary in the fight against inflation (Kavanagh 1996b: 351). The re-election campaign was further undermined when the director general of the CBI, Campbell Adamson, described the Industrial Relations Act as a 'disaster' and that it should be 'repealed' (Ziegler 2010: 433). If business was of this view it made it harder to defend and justify the approach that Heath had been adopting. It was an intervention that Heath regarded as unforgivable (Heath 1998: 516).

The answer to Heath's question 'who governs Britain' was inconclusive. The hoped for response of 'you and not the miners' did not materialize (Ziegler 2010: 435). The final opinion polls had given Conservatives confidence. Gallup had them up by 2 per cent; NOP, Harris and OPC had them up by between 4 and 5 per cent, and ORC projected a Conservative majority of between 60 and 80 (Campbell 1993: 612–3). However, once all of the results were confirmed, the Conservatives had the largest share of the vote at 37.9 per cent to Labour on 37.1, although Labour had more seats at 301 to 297. The Liberal surge in vote share at 19.3 per cent (and 14 seats) was a considerable advance on their 1970 share of 7.5 per cent. For Heath the deduction in the Conservative vote share (at 8.5 per cent from the 46.4 per cent in 1970) was a 'devastating rebuff' (Campbell 1993: 615).

Heath called a Cabinet meeting and noted that the Conservatives had secured the majority of the votes cast, and where 6 million votes had been for the Liberals, 'the nation would expect him to attempt the formation of a right-centre coalition before handing power to the Labour Party' (Ziegler 2010: 436–7). Heath felt that Thorpe was 'keen to enter a coalition' (Heath 1998: 518). However, Thorpe had significant reservations about serving under Heath, as he was sceptical when Heath informed him that senior Conservatives 'wished to continue to serve under his leadership' (Thorpe 1999: 114–16). However, the Liberals wanted a commitment to proportional representation. The Heath Cabinet was only willing to go as far as offering a Speaker's convention on electoral reform. Of the Cabinet meeting to discuss the Liberals terms for forming a coalition, Bogdanor notes the following: when Heath mentioned proportional representation, Thatcher responded with 'oh, no we couldn't' (Bogdanor 1996: 373). Bogdanor concludes that it 'was at this point that her hostility to Heath as a traitor to

Conservatism crystallised', in that he was 'prepared to sacrifice any chance of the Conservatives ever again achieving an overall majority on their own for the mere temporary renewal of power' (Bogdanor 1996: 373).

The idea of any arrangement with the Liberals crumbled when both Heath and Thorpe realized that they could not take their parties with them. The Conservatives were forced back into opposition. Before evaluating the endgame for Heath in the 12 months between March 1974 and February 1975, it is worth reflecting upon how his three-and-half-year government has been viewed. The Heath government is open to two interpretations.

The first interpretation is the right-wing critique that views 1970–74 as a failure, and that Heath personally must shoulder the responsibility as it was due to weak leadership (Bruce-Gardyne 1974; Holmes 1995). For them the success of Thatcherism a decade later 'made Heath's government look wrong-headed and indecisive' (Seldon 1996: 2), and thus the Heath era has to be defined as a failure as 'its initial right wing objectives' were 'abandoned in the face of difficulties' (Seldon 1996: 2). Thatcher concluded that 'the poisoned legacy of our U-turns was that we had no firm principles, let alone much of a record' to defend (Thatcher 1995: 240). However, such firm convictions have to be seen alongside Thatcher's own admission as to why she did not resign from the Heath Cabinet. She admits that 'those of us who disliked what was happening had not yet either fully analysed the situation or worked out an alternative approach' (Thatcher 1995: 220).

It is not just a charge of betrayal that fuels the Thatcherite critique. It is the charge of incompetence (Gamble 1988: 78). The performance of the economy under their stewardship had deteriorated rather than improved. Union power had appeared to have intensified rather than diminished, and with legislation to improve industrial relations being easily resisted, an image of Britain being 'ungovernable' gathered momentum (Gamble 1988: 78). Kavanagh notes that 'contrary to its 1970 manifesto the government at the end of its term presided over record levels of inflation and balance of payments deficits, public spending had increased by nearly 50 per cent in real terms, inefficient firms were propped up and a record number of days had been lost due to strikes' (Kavanagh 1996a: 363). Moreover, an 'effective' administration would secure re-election, and due to the above-mentioned reason, Heath led the only post-war administration to last only a single term, and they suffered a massive reduction in their vote share between entering and departing office. The 8.6 per cent difference between June 1970 and February 1974 was only bettered in the post-war period by the gap between Major's victory in April 1992 and his defeat in May 1997.

The second interpretation is that Heath was a pragmatist operating in difficult circumstances. This Heath loyalist position would counter the above Thatcherite critique by arguing that the government was a 'success, implementing most of its manifesto pledges', and 'showing flexibility in the face of great difficulties' (Seldon 1996: 2). The memoirs of Heath present the defence case, as do those of insiders such as Walker, Prior and Gilmour, but these are interpretations in which the term 'U-turn' is hardly mentioned (Heath 1998; Walker 1991; Prior 1986; Gilmour 1992). The central plank to the loyalist argument is to stress the great achievement of the Heath era, entry into the EEC, although this argument becomes dependent upon your view on the merits of the European project. Hennessy suggests that rather than view Heath as a proto-Thatcherite, it is better to view his Quiet Revolution as an attempt to 'breathe new life, economic vitality especially, into the post-war settlement' (Hennessy 2000: 356). In that context, Hennessy argues Heath is not

> so much a compulsive U-turner but more of a somersaulting moderniser – a premier prepared to execute great leaps of policy for the purpose of continuing to move more effectively in the same direction with its trio of interlocked signposts: full employment and a modernised economy well placed to take full advantage of the other great Heath ambition, membership of the EEC. (Hennessy 2000: 336)

Thus the ambition of Heath was a better consensus. He wanted to preserve the essentials of the post-war settlement (Hennessy 2000: 336). However, his capacity to achieve this was to be fatally undermined by circumstances beyond his control. There is a need to acknowledge the destabilizing impact of international economic trends. The ending of the Bretton Wood system of fixed exchange rates intensified the uncertainty, while the weakened economy was in 'no position to cope' with the outbreak of the Yom Kippur War between Israel and Arab states (October 1973), which 'led to the quadrupling of oil prices by OPEC countries' (Kavanagh 1996a: 380). Heath also had to devote considerable amounts of his time to the escalating conflict within Northern Ireland and this interfered with the time devoted to other governing difficulties. By March 1972 the decision was made to suspend the Stormont Parliament and impose direct rule from Westminster. The suspension of Stormont contributed to a 'loosening of the traditional Conservative links with the Ulster Unionist MPs' (Kavanagh 1996a: 369).

The Thatcherite critique in part rests on an 'exaggeration of the right-wing intent' of the incoming 1970 administration. Seldon argues that 'Heath and the shadow Cabinet allowed the [Selsdon] conference and subsequent pronouncements to be invested with a right-wing ideological coherence that was neither intended nor deserved' (Seldon 1996: 13). Seldon concludes that Heath was

> never a believer in laissez faire, but was a traditional Tory who saw the state as an essential deliverer of economic and social policy . . . so while some policies advocated at the 1970 general election, such as the rejection of an incomes policy and tax and spending cuts were more right wing

then offered by the party at any general election since 1945, the motives for the policies were *instrumentalism* and *opportunism*, not *ideology*. (Seldon 1996: 14)

Kavanagh suggests that the Selsdon Man image associated with Heath, and used against him by his critics, stemmed therefore not from his ideological beliefs but from his electioneering rhetoric. He was not an ideologue; rather he was 'consistent about ends, flexible about means: he was a pragmatist, concerned with pursuing the best means to achieving economic growth and greater personal freedom' (Kavanagh 1996a: 367). Building on the communicative dimension, Garnett offers a similar critique:

> At a 1970 election press conference he read out a brief which promised that a specific Conservative policy would "at a stroke, reduce the rise in prices." The phrase had been carefully crafted: the abolition of Labour's Selective Employment Tax (SET) would make prices rise *more slowly*, rather than reducing them overnight. But the words "at a stroke" had been chosen deliberately, to create the impression that Conservative policies would have an immediate impact on the rate of inflation; and if that persisted at a high level after the election, the Conservatives could hardly complain that the overall meaning of Heath's declaration had been distorted when Labour critics used it against him. The 1970 manifesto contained an unwise repudiation of the "philosophy" behind the use of incomes policy as a means of containing inflation. This meant what it said – that is that Heath disliked the idea of incomes policy, not that he would never resort to such measures if they seemed unavoidable. But to his critics (especially on the right) such *semantics* were irrelevant; in their eyes it looked as if Heath had ruled out the prospect of an incomes policy, and when his government felt constrained to implement such a policy they bitterly resented this "U-turn." (Garnett 2012: 88–9)

The Peasants Revolt 1974–1975

Resentment at losing power meant that it was inevitable that speculation would gather about whether Heath should retain the leadership. Heath wanted to remain and circumstances meant that this would be possible in the short term. He remained resolute even if he 'seemed almost physically diminished' by the impact of defeat, according to Cecil Parkinson, who concluded that 'one just felt sorry for this desolate and lonely figure' (Parkinson 1992: 48). He would retain the leadership (for the time being) for two reasons. First, the existing procedures for selecting the party leader only referred to when a vacancy existed – that is, there were no rules permitting a challenge to take place. Second, given that Wilson was leading a minority administration, it was possible that he could seek a new mandate at very short notice. This was a significant factor for many Conservatives as Ziegler notes: 'to fight another election with Heath still leader might seem unpromising', but to 'fight it with a divided party and an unproven replacement at its head could be disastrous' (Ziegler 2010: 448). So, paradoxically, due to these circumstances Heath was 'impregnable but weak' (Ziegler 2010: 448).

The limited reshuffle that Heath conducted to his shadow Cabinet proved to be significant. With Barber wanting to stand down from frontline politics, Heath needed to appoint a shadow Chancellor. Rather than appoint Joseph he played it safe by promoting the more loyalist Carr. Thatcher concluded that Carr was 'committed to the interventionist approach that had got us into so much trouble'. By rejecting Joseph it was clear that Heath had 'set his face against any policy rethinking' that would acknowledge that their 'economic and industrial policy had been seriously flawed' (Thatcher 1995: 241–2). Denied the shadow Chancellorship, Joseph remained within the shadow Cabinet but without any portfolio. Heath acquiesced to this request from Joseph so that the latter was free to intellectually consider long-term economic thinking. To facilitate this Heath also agreed to allow Joseph to set up the Centre for Policy Studies (CPS). This was a naive move by Heath. Later Heath was said to 'feel betrayed when the CPS turned out to be an intellectual springboard for a determined challenge to his leadership' (Campbell 1993: 627).

Joseph was at his most provocative when he delivered a speech in September where he 'turned an open secret into open warfare' (Ziegler 2010: 452). In what was an 'unequivocal challenge' to the authority of Heath, Joseph questioned the prioritization of unemployment over inflation. He argued that by believing that we must overheat the economy to try to prevent unemployment at any cost simply fuels inflation, which in the long run only creates more unemployment. Keynesian thinking must be abandoned and the only cure for inflation is to control the money supply – that is, by government being more disciplined in terms of printing money (Denham and Garnett 2001: 259). Given the close proximity of the general election, Heath was unable to dismiss Joseph (Howe 1994: 168).

It is not surprising that the meetings of the shadow Cabinet were acrimonious as the differences between Heath and Joseph intensified. As a newly promoted member, Michael Heseltine observed that 'my first doubts as to Ted's ability to hold the party together stemmed from the brusqueness and brutality he displayed in the conflict' between himself and Joseph (Heseltine 2000: 157). Similar doubts about his unifying capabilities and political judgement were growing within the PCP (Behrens 1980: 32–3).

After defeat in October 1974 Heath was increasingly viewed as a three-time loser and thus an electoral liability (Wickham-Jones 1997: 74). His eventual successor felt that this reaction to another electoral reversal was delusional. She could not accept his analysis of the election campaign which was that it had been a good containment exercise and that the mechanics had worked well. Thatcher felt that Heath 'could not change' as 'he was too defensive of his own past record to see that a fundamental change of policies was needed'. She concluded that 'everyone except Ted knew that the main problem was the fact that he was still leader' (Thatcher 1995: 261, 263). However, critics still faced the same conundrum that they faced in March – that is, the rules did not permit challengers and the contests for the succession could only take place when a vacancy exists, and Heath was 'too truculent' to resign (Baker 1993: 43). This was despite the fact that some, not commonly identified as enemies, were encouraging him to do so. Kenneth Baker told Heath: 'you had better resign now as leader if you don't want to be hurt, there are many people in the party who are out to destroy you – the malicious, the malcontents, the sacked, the ignored and overlooked, are all blaming you' (Baker 1993: 43–4). Heath could have chosen the option of voluntarily submitting himself for re-election to secure a renewed mandate. On this option Ramsden notes that Heath had decided 'with the convoluted logic of a trapped man' that 'he did not intend to fight a leadership contest because he wanted to stay on to resist the right wing'. But this 'only made sense if he thought he would *lose* a contest' (Ramsden 1996: 435).

If he would not resign, then his critics concluded that the rules would have to be changed so that a challenge could be initiated. Heath was now on a collision course with his old nemesis, du Cann, Chair of the 1922 Executive Committee. Heath did realize the danger that du Cann now was and offered him a place within the shadow Cabinet, which was rejected, presumably as du Cann felt Heath was attempting to 'neutralise me' (du Cann 1995: 204). Heath later condemned du Cann for 'undermining my attempt to unify the party' (Heath 1998: 529). In the aftermath of defeat du Cann informed Heath that the view of the 1922 Executive Committee was that Heath should resign and that if he did not then the rules governing the election of the leader of the Conservative Party needed to be revised (du Cann 1995: 200–2). Heath lacked the political authority to withstand the demand to review the party leadership selection procedures. Should that review require that Heath stand for re-election (i.e. permit a challenge), then Heath remained determined to stand (Critchley 1994: 143).

Ironically it was Douglas-Home who was put in charge of the committee that would re-examine how leaders of the party were elected. (The committee convened in November, and reported back in early December.) Their findings became known as 'Alec's revenge', given the assumption that Heath supporters had campaigned against Douglas-Home in 1965 (Ramsden 1996: 440). The committee would argue that there should be provision for annual elections for the party leadership. This would thus solve the dilemma of an unpopular party leader refusing to resign. If there was no challenge to the incumbent leader, then they were re-elected unopposed. However, if someone wished to initiate a challenge, they would need the support of a proposer and a seconder, and challenges would be permitted within the first 3–6 months of a new Parliament, or during the first 28 days of a parliamentary session. Also built into the new provisions was a proviso that the 15 per cent surcharge should be of the whole electorate of Conservative MPs, rather than of those actually voting. This would make it more difficult for an incumbent to retain the party leadership, as abstentions would undermine the leading candidate almost as much as votes for an alternative candidate could. Due to this provision it was impossible for anyone to be elected on the first ballot, even if there was only one candidate, if half of the Conservative MPs abstained (Denham and O'Hara 2008: 21).

There is little doubt that the new procedures were designed with the explicit purpose of removing Heath. Given that the procedures permitted annual challenges, it meant that even if Heath were to survive a challenge in the first 3–6 months of the new Parliament, he would still be vulnerable (and more vulnerable than a new leader not tainted by defeat) to a challenge in the autumns of 1975–78, assuming that the Labour administration lasted a full 5 years. In the short term, however, speculation on who could challenge Heath centred on Whitelaw, Joseph and du Cann. Loyalty prevented Whitelaw from initiating a formal challenge, but his supporters worked on the assumption that their man could enter at the second ballot stage after an inconclusive first ballot had forced Heath to resign (Clark 1998: 454–5).

The rumoured challenges of Joseph and du Cann failed to materialize. Joseph undermined his prospects even before the new procedures had been agreed (Denham and Garnett 2001: 275). In October 1974 he delivered a speech that was designed to argue that the Conservative Party needed to construct a social policy platform that was geared towards the re-moralization of society (Clark 1998: 461). Specifically Joseph suggested that social deprivation was caused by the increasing proportion of children being born to working-class adolescent girls. He appeared to be arguing that stricter birth control (i.e. promoting contraception) should be applied to girls of lower socio-economic groupings, whereupon he became denounced as a mad eugenicist (Blake 1998: 319). The negative publicity surrounding Joseph caused him to reassess whether he wanted to challenge Heath (Denham and Garnett 2001: 265–75). The du Cann candidacy was not forthcoming in part due to speculative innuendo that began to circulate about his financial circumstances, with the implication being that this could cause embarrassment in the future (Fisher 1977: 160–3).

With Joseph and du Cann now out of the equation, Thatcher decided that she would stand. She made her decision before the new procedures had been confirmed, and took the time to inform Heath of her intentions (Thatcher 1995: 266). Thatcher recalled that 'he looked at me coldly, turned his back, shrugged his shoulders and said "If you must"' (Thatcher 1995: 267). Heath recalls thanking her politely for warning him in advance (Heath 1998: 530). She was not deemed a serious threat to him and most felt that she was not seen as a conventional leadership aspirant. Her candidacy appeared to be 'indicative of the trouble Heath's critics had found in finding a potential alternative leader' (Wickham-Jones 1997: 75). Thatcher would later claim that her primary motive was ensuring that Heath was removed from the leadership. In her memoirs she noted that 'it seemed to me most unlikely that I *would* win', but 'I did think that by entering the race I would draw in other stronger candidates who would be open to persuasion about changing the disastrous course on which the Party was set' (Thatcher 1995: 267).

As the first ballot approached (including a third maverick candidate, Hugh Fraser), it was widely assumed that Heath would win. The Heath camp believed that they had 129 firm supporters, plus an additional 10–15 who they thought would probably support him, meaning that they were expecting a return of around 139–44 (Ramsden 1996: 450). That their canvassing proved to be so inaccurate flowed from the ineptitude of the Heath campaign. Heath did little to try and persuade potential supporters (Baker 1993: 44), and in fact managed to alienate 'even those who should have ranked amongst his loyal supporters' (Cowley and Bailey 2000: 600).

When Thatcher secured 130 (47.1 per cent) to Heath 119 (43.1 per cent) with 16 voting for Fraser and ten spoiling their ballot papers, it was inevitable that Heath would resign and not proceed to the second ballot (Heppell 2008b: 62). With Heath now removed the best option for one nation Conservatives was to ensure that only one candidate went forward – that is, Whitelaw. However, his ability to carry all the Heath vote and extend it by sweeping up the abstainers, or those who voted for Thatcher or Fraser as protest votes, was undermined by the emergence of a bloated field of other new candidates, including Prior, Howe and also John Peyton. The fracturing of the non-Thatcher vote, and the fact that Thatcher was able to capture the Fraser vote, propelled her to the leadership with 146 votes to Whitelaw on 79, with Prior and Howe both on 19, Peyton on 11 and two ballot papers being spoilt (Heppell 2008b: 63).

The key question when evaluating the events of October 1974 to February 1975 is whether Thatcher should be viewed as an accidental leader. The accident thesis suggests her first ballot showing was a by-product of negative votes from parliamentarians willing to do whatever it took to remove Heath – that is, it was more a rejection of Heath, rather an endorsement of Thatcher (Gilmour and Garnett 1998: 298). Crewe and Searing subscribe to this point of view and conclude that many of her negatively induced supporters 'had no idea that she was about to hatch a new ideology and behind it march the party off to the right' (Crewe and Searing 1988: 371). However, alongside this anti-Heath personality-based argument we need to acknowledge an ideological explanation that challenges the Crewe and Searing interpretation. Research by Cowley and Bailey suggests that there was an ideological explanation to her victory (Cowley and Bailey 2000: 599–629). They managed to determine the voting behaviour of all but a handful of Conservative parliamentarians who participated in the 1975 leadership ballots. They then listed all of them on the Norton typology of Conservative thought – which identifies parliamentarians as being on the economic right (critics of one-nation Conservatism), or on the economic left (defenders of one-nation Conservatism) – and cross-referenced this to their voting choices (Norton 1990: 41–58). From this they were able to conclude that 'ideology was a key determinant of voting in both rounds of the contest. . . . The right – however defined – strongly supported Thatcher; the left – however defined supported Heath and then Whitelaw' (Cowley and Bailey 2000: 628–9). This suggests that a significant body of opinion within the PCP was looking for not just a change of leader, but a change of direction (Ramsden 1996: 453).

Heathite modernization as statecraft

The party leadership tenure of Heath was a turbulent period for the Conservatives. They were engaging in a disputed process of adaptation that failed to provide a viable statecraft strategy for them. Although Heathite modernization managed the politics of support aspect and provided access to power by regaining office in 1970, it failed to demonstrate governing competence and political argument hegemony. As a consequence they were the only post-war administration that the electorate removed from office at the first opportunity. As the unravelling of the dimensions of statecraft evolved Heath struggled to effectively manage the party.

Heath had been interested in a managerial reform of the state. However, a small and growing band of neoliberals believed that the Selsdon agenda should commit the party to reducing the state. By advocating a managerial reform of the state within the contours of the post-war settlement, Heath was attempting to construct a new narration of Conservatism. It sought to transcend the waning appeal of the approaches that had defined the immediate post-war period which were associated with the one-nation narrative of Macmillan. But the Heathite approach struggled to withstand the surge of neo-liberal thinking over this period. At the beginning of Heath's leadership this right-wing challenge was limited in number but by making limited concessions to their thinking, and using rhetoric that suggested more than limited concessions, Heath set himself on a collision course with this evolving faction.

Despite his own background as a successful Chief Whip under Eden and Macmillan, Heath proved to be a poor party manager. He did not communicate effectively with his own backbenchers and this led to an increase in parliamentary rebellions and an image of party disharmony. He was determined to avoid the 'embarrassment' of 'compromises' and 'concessions', as he wanted to get his legislation through 'unchanged' (Seldon and Sanklecha 2004: 55). As Conservative backbenchers could not influence policy through informal meetings with ministers (designed to secure compromises and then support), then if they disagreed with government policy, the only 'available outlet for their frustration' was parliamentary rebellion (Seldon and Sanklecha 2004: 55). Cabinet critics, such as Joseph and Thatcher, remained publicly loyal whatever their private reservations.

However, once in opposition these rebellious critics of Heath would provide the potential votes to remove him from office, and propel Thatcher in as his replacement.

Thus, the Heath Government of 1970–74 has to be viewed as a 'critical' period in the subsequent emergence of Thatcherism (Gamble 1988: 73). The contradictory policy choices that were pursued were a reflection of the difficulties of governing at that time. But they also reflected an internal battle within the party. It was an 'intriguing' Conservative Government for it was a transmission belt between two eras of Conservatism, as Seldon concludes:

> It promoted elements of both the old and new worlds and was trapped uneasily as one paradigm was beginning to lose its hold, but the other model had yet to secure intellectual credibility or popular backing. (Seldon 1996: 1)

The performance of the Heath government discredited 'adjustment through modernisation' in the eyes of enough Conservatives to ensure the election of a new leader who would espouse a new narration of Conservatism. The failure of the Heath government would help 'precipitate the birth of Thatcherism' (Gamble 1988: 69). Later on Thatcherites would imply that the Selsdon agenda was the correct remedy, and that it was the U-turn which was the great failing of the Heath government. This would be to oversimplify. For Thatcherites the real lesson of the Heath era was the need to protect the autonomy of central government, and that this had been 'seriously compromised by Heath's search for agreement on incomes policy with the trade unions' (Kavanagh 1987b: 236). Thatcherism would seek a 'new method of controlling inflation without bargaining with trade unions' and in doing so would restore 'some autonomy to the centre' – that is, a new narration of Conservatism through a new statecraft strategy. In this pursuit Thatcher would be more fortunate than Heath, as

> the trade unions and the left wing of the Labour Party were more powerful and obstructive between 1970 and 1974 than they were after 1979 . . . [the Labour] . . . government's resort to the IMF in 1976, the subsequent winter of discontent and collapse of the social contract, and the economic record of the Callaghan government had all discredited Labour and the unions by 1979. (Kavanagh 1996a: 385)

3

The free economy and the strong state: The pursuit of Thatcherism 1975–1992

Margaret Thatcher would lead the Conservatives for over 15 years and her three successive general election victories ensured that she was prime minister for 11 years between 1979 and 1990. Given the turbulence of the decade prior to her leadership – four defeats out of five general elections between October 1964 and October 1974 – it is not surprising that she was held in such high regard by many Conservatives. However, what is really intriguing about her era is the gap between the retrospective and positive interpretations of her leadership by her supporters, and the reality of her vulnerability in opposition between 1975 and 1979 and the evolutionary nature of her agenda once in power. This chapter charts the impact of Thatcherism upon the Conservatives in four sections. First, it observes the difficulties that she faced in *establishing* 'Thatcherism' as a new and unexpected leader of the opposition with limited support within her shadow Cabinet. Second, it considers how her administrations went about *implementing* Thatcherism as she set about imposing conviction politics in place of consensus politics. Third, it considers how the Thatcher governments set about *justifying* Thatcherism and how they attempted to persuade the electorate of the merits of their policy choices. Fourth, it considers how the shift from Thatcher to John Major contributed to *consolidating* Thatcherism as the Conservatives won an unprecedented fourth successive term in 1992.

Establishing Thatcherism? The era of opposition 1975–1979

The opposition period under Thatcher was characterized by 'hesitancy' (Cosgrave 1978: 183). Many of the political press 'continued to believe that some ghastly and nightmarish mistake had been made, and that time would see a reversal to the natural state of affairs' (Cosgrave 1978: 171). However, her greatest doubters were among those Conservative parliamentarians who had not voted for her in either of the leadership ballots. Many of them found it 'hard to adjust to the idea of such a naive and unsophisticated politician in the role of leader' (Campbell 2000: 312–13).

Her problems were compounded by the evidence that she was not an electoral asset (Campbell 2000: 317). For much of the opposition period she trailed Harold Wilson and then James Callaghan as the leader who would 'make the best Prime Minister' (Kavanagh 2005: 225). One opinion poll in 1978 suggested the Conservatives would 'gain more support' if Edward Heath was their leader (Harris 1988: 81). Heath himself saw 'no possibility of his inexperienced successor growing into the job which she had inappropriately snatched' from him (Campbell 1993: 689). His attitude was 'I'm in reserve' (Ziegler 2010: 491). Relations when she replaced him were poor and they deteriorated. For example, they briefed against each other on the question of whether Thatcher had offered him a place in the shadow Cabinet in 1975. He would claim that no offer was made. She would claim that an offer was made, but that she was relieved that it was not accepted (Heath 1998: 536–7; Thatcher 1995: 282–3). The hostility between them was widely noted within and beyond Parliament. For example, when Thatcher suffered a torrid parliamentary debate over immigration in early 1978, the Labour MP Denis Skinner shouted across the floor 'she's having a rough time, isn't she, Ted?', whereupon many noted Heath's response: 'a grin, and a huge meaningful wink' (Behrens 1980: 105).

Upon acquiring the leadership she retained many of those most closely associated with Heath, such as Francis Pym, James Prior, Iain Gilmour, Lord Carrington and, of course, William Whitelaw. Her most surprising appointment was that of Reginald Maudling, who was 'staggered' to be offered the post of shadow Foreign Secretary (which he held briefly until 1976). Not only was Maudling the 'most consensus minded' of Conservatives, he was also deeply critical of Thatcher and Keith Joseph. He (privately) viewed Joseph as 'nutty as a fruitcake', and when Heath was defeated by Thatcher he told Heath: 'this is the worst day in the history of the Tory Party . . . the party's taken leave of its senses' (Baston 2004: 467–9). The inclusion of Pym, Prior, Gilmour, Carrington, Whitelaw, Maudling and that of Michael Heseltine (a 'man of interventionist if not corporatist inclinations') was offset by the removal of not only Peter Walker (who nonetheless returned in 1979), but also Robert Carr (previously shadow Chancellor) and Geoffrey Rippon (previously shadow Foreign Secretary) (Kavanagh 2005: 224).

Thatcher was slow to advance her own supporters like Norman Tebbit, John Nott, Nicholas Ridley, Cecil Parkinson and Nigel Lawson. Her caution was also evident by her decision to promote the centrist Mark Carlisle (to Education in 1978) rather than her ideological bedfellow, Rhodes Boyson (Kavanagh 2005: 224). Caution was also evident in her decision to appoint Geoffrey Howe to the Treasury brief, rather than Joseph. Whitelaw had insisted that as a precondition of his future support she must not appoint

Joseph as shadow Chancellor (Bale 2012a: 221). In the event, Howe was increasingly moving onside in terms of the economic agenda that she wanted to advocate, that is, abandoning incomes policies and relying on control of the money supply, alongside reductions in taxation and public expenditure, even if this resulted in higher levels of unemployment (Bale 2012a: 187–8).

However, the most eye-catching appointment was that of Peter Thorney-croft as the new Party Chair (best known for his resignation from the Treasury in 1958), and as his deputy Angus Maude (an old nemesis of Heath) (Behrens 1980: 62–3). The surprise advancement of Thorneycroft offered 'potent symbolism' given his well-established concerns about the growth in the public sector (Ramsden 1980: 154–5). Although Chris Patten remained as Director of the Conservative Research Department, Gilmour was replaced as Chair by the more like-minded Maude (Kavanagh 2005: 226).

Increasingly, however, the Conservative Research Department was 'circumvented', allowing her to 'draw from the ideas of right wing think tanks, such as the Centre for Policy Studies' (Evans 1999: 40). Thatcher would later argue that the Centre for Policy Studies, under the guidance of Alfred Sherman, was a 'powerhouse of alternative Conservative thinking on economic and social matters' (Thatcher 1995: 251). This was an era in which increasingly 'the party's own policy-making structures lost their near monopolist role with a more crowded and competitive market growing to influence the leader of the Conservative Party'. Thatcher 'proved a willing target' as in addition to the Centre for Policy Studies, her outlook was increasingly shaped by other think tanks such as the Institute for Economic Affairs and the newly formed Adam Smith Institute (Norton 2012: 101–2).

Although it is too simplistic to say that a coherent and electorally viable programme that was to be Thatcherism was established between 1975 and 1979, one should nonetheless acknowledge that Thatcher was widely understood at the time to be to the right of the party. As Denham and O'Hara have noted, 'she stood, more clearly than Heath, for lower taxes and less state intervention in the economy'. Unlike Heath, she saw the state 'not as the principal instrument of economic modernisation' but as the 'key obstacle to achieving the same objective' (Denham and O'Hara 2007: 177). This was evident during her leadership campaign when she stated (in January 1975) that 'one of the many reasons for our electoral failure is that people believe too many Conservatives have become Socialists already' (Kavanagh 2005: 224).

Thatcher was open about stating the disappointments created by the previous Conservative administrations. She felt that they 'had lost the initiative' in the battle with the advocates of 'collectivist, egalitarian and anti-capitalist values'. She concluded that the 'left had captured the vocabulary of political and social debate' and that there was 'no authoritative Conservative response' (Kavanagh 2005: 231). To be effective in opposition she concluded that 'argument was everything' and that the Conservatives must have a 'clear philosophy and a coherent set of beliefs from which the party's arguments and policies should follow' (Kavanagh 2005: 231). This mindset was most famously captured in 1975 by her comment that 'we must have an ideology . . . the other side have an ideology that they can test their policies against, [and] we must have one as well' (Young 1990: 406). Thatcher was thus advocating conviction not consensus politics. She felt that the previous three decades had created a socialist ratchet effect – that is, every time Labour was in office the succeeding Conservative administration had accepted much of their socialist impact in the name of consensus and continuity (Joseph 1976: 20).

However, Thatcher 'constantly had to curb her instincts' for both internal party and electioneering reasons (Evans 1999: 42). There was an anxiety about how far to the right the party could move without intensifying internal divisions or alienating the electorate. As one frustrated Conservative right-wing backbencher at the time noted, she was using her 'skill to avoid translating her beliefs into clear commitments until the party and the people have caught up with her'. This would explain the 'tension between her militant and value-laden speeches on the one hand, and her lack of detailed policy statements on the other' (Evans 1999: 42–3). Clearly between 1975 and 1979 her PCP had not caught up with her. Behrens concluded that at this time the PCP could be subdivided into two camps. First, there were the diehards who embraced the arguments that Thatcher and Joseph were making on economic strategy. Second, there were the ditchers who believed that principles should reflect circumstances, and pragmatically the Conservatives should be willing to intervene in the economy where necessary to protect social harmony. Many of the ditchers simply felt that the stance that Thatcher was beginning to articulate would not be politically feasible (Behrens 1980: 3). Their continued belief in the importance of a non-dogmatic form of Conservatism was best encapsulated by Gilmour, who was still inside the shadow Cabinet when he published *Inside Right* in 1977 (Gilmour 1977).

However, at this juncture Thatcher's objective was to set the agenda by outlining her principles rather than detailed policies (Bale 2012a: 223). She came to believe that the policy reappraisal undertaken by Heath in the 1960s created too many detailed policy pledges, and it was better to rely on principles through which policies could be developed and applied (Thatcher 1995: 295). This was her instruction to the raft of policy-review groups that were established, which fed into a sub-committee of the shadow Cabinet (chaired by Joseph), who then presented feedback to the shadow Cabinet (Patten 1980: 20). There is a tendency to simply state that the opposition era was defined by two documents which outlined their evolving principles: *The Right Approach* (1976) and *The Right Approach for the Economy* (1977) and to assess their content. However, what is perhaps more illuminating is to try and get beyond their desire to outline principles and see if we can detect significant developments in policy. This can be achieved by considering three policy arenas that had defined (and disfigured) the party under Heath: inflation, incomes policy and industrial relations.

For Thatcher tackling inflation became the priority – this rather than full employment was the new quandary (Taylor 2005a: 140–3). The solution would be informed primarily by the thinking of Milton Friedman who argued that creating targets with regard to money supply would curb inflation, but also by the thinking of Friedrich Hayek who felt that immediate and substantial public expenditure cuts was the best way to cure inflation (Evans 1999: 45). However, Heath from the outside, and Gilmour and later Prior from the inside, would all express their reservations about the unacceptable levels of unemployment flowing from the proposed solutions (Prior 1986: 109). The monetarist emphasis on controlling the money supply, and their commitment to controlling public expenditure, was tied into a desire to remove 'obstacles to free competition' and 'addressing the network of corporatist institutions which were encroaching on the functioning of free markets' (Gamble 1988: 92). This led to the need to address two hugely contentious issues: incomes policy and industrial relations.

Those associated with the moderate Tory Reform Group attempted to argue the case for a Conservative version of the Social Contract – combining commitments on industrial democracy and urban deprivation with understandings on wages (Russell 1978: 78). They outlined their concerns about 'abandoning attempts to secure understandings with the trade unions' and the shift to 'relying on the disciplines of bankruptcy and unemployment to curb prices' (Gamble 1988: 93). However, Thatcher withstood their criticism and denunciated statutory incomes policies. This ensured that the party was 'committed to a return to free collective bargaining and therefore to curbing trade union power by other means' (Gamble 1988: 93).

Initially Thatcher showed caution on industrial relations matters. Given the experience of the unworkable Industrial Relations Act, caution was understandable. Her shadow Employment Secretary, Prior, was keen to engage with moderate trade union leaders in the hope that he could gain their support for an incomes policy (which he still argued for against the instincts of his leader). To begin with Thatcher restricted herself to denunciating excessive trade union power, without offering proposals on how to curb such power. However, their commitment to operating without an incomes policy and their desire to reduce the level of intervention within the economy made the 'need to weaken trade union power' an 'inescapable necessity' (Gamble 1988: 94). Between October 1978 and March 1979 the drafting of the section of the manifesto on industrial relations evolved considerably, and the Winter of Discontent politically meant that the Conservatives could now seek a mandate to address the problem of excessive trade union power (Taylor 2001: 124).

This was because the Winter of Discontent provided the opportunity for Thatcher to engage with the Stepping Stones strategy which had previously been hugely contentious. It was a communications strategy formulated by two outsiders – John Hoskyns and Norman Strauss – which was designed to outline the means by which to persuade the electorate of the necessity of change. Central to this strategy was the need to show the electorate that it was the trade unions that were responsible for economic decline (Taylor 2001: 116). The resistance that Prior had to this strategy was diluted by the Winter of Discontent, and the manifesto of 1979 had significant differences to that of the 1974 general elections. For example, in 1974 there was no mention of picketing but 1979 included a commitment to review and amend legislation in this regard; in 1974 they had been supportive of the corporatist NEDC, but now this was not mentioned; in 1974 there was no mention of the closed shop, but in 1979 there was a commitment to legislate to restrict it. This was a more 'assertive approach' than the one in 1974 (Bale 2012a: 210).

Although the primary focus should be on inflation, incomes policy and industrial relations, our understanding of the Conservatives in opposition also requires an appreciation of other policy areas, notably foreign policy, European policy, devolution and immigration. Gamble notes that it was not Thatcher's apparent repudiation of consensus politics at domestic level that provided the first real evidence of a shift in style and content. Rather it was her views of foreign policy. Her attacks on detente and her desire to initiate an ideological crusade against communism (requiring a major build-up of arms among NATO countries) led the Soviet media to label her the Iron Lady. This sobriquet was a 'bonus' for the Conservatives as it gave a potentially positive image that 'a then untried female leader needed' (Fry 1998: 141). Tied into these attitudes was her strong support for the Atlantic Alliance and her doubts about the EEC (Gamble 1988: 87–9). That membership was accepted by Thatcher, rather than passionately advocated, was evident from a comparison between the manifestos of 1974 and 1979. For Heath it was argued that membership provided the 'opportunity to reverse our political and economic decline', but for Thatcher while decline remained a concern, Europe was no longer stated as the means of reversal. Her emphasis became shaped by defending British interests within Europe and finding ways to correct the shortcomings of the EEC (Bale 2012a: 207).

These concerns about national identity were also tied into two domestic policy concerns: devolution and immigration. Had Heath been re-elected in 1974 it was his intention to create a Scottish Assembly, in tune with the recommendations of a Royal Commission which had reported back in autumn 1973. However, although Thatcher initially backed the position of her predecessor, she had reservations. She felt that the promise had done little to withstand the rise of the Scottish National Party, and longer term she feared that agreeing to an assembly would lead to the breaking up of the United Kingdom (Bale 2012a: 207, 225). She calculated that as support for a devolved assembly was not particularly high, and as Labour were 'hopelessly divided' over it, then the 'tactical balance of advantage' meant changing their position was appropriate (Thatcher 1995: 324). Her demand that Conservatives vote against the Labour legislation on this (December 1976) would result in five rebels voting with Labour (and nearly 30 abstaining including Heath), and would lead to the resignations of her shadow Secretary of State, Alick Buchannan-Smith, and his deputy, a young Malcolm Rifkind (Bale 2012a: 225).

Just as Thatcher 'personally drove' the change to the policy position with regard to devolution, so she did likewise on the issue of immigration (Bale 2012a: 225). Despite the reservations of Whitelaw (shadow Home Secretary), Thatcher sought to exploit 'popular anxieties' when she noted that she 'understood' the electorate's fears about being 'swamped by people of a different culture' and promised to deal with their 'worries' (Evans 1999: 47). Promising to deal with their worries meant stating what those worries were – an assumed influx of immigrants unless a tougher line on immigration was established (Bale 2012a: 224). Constructing their harder line meant, claimed Thatcher, 'we had a comprehensive and agreed approach which satisfied all but the die-hard advocates of repatriation' (Thatcher 1995: 407).

In opposition Thatcher achieved the minimal requirement of a leader of the opposition: she ensured that her party were viewed as credible and electable. Beyond that she was dependent on circumstances and timing. Had Callaghan dissolved Parliament in the autumn of 1978, when the opinion polls had the parties running neck and neck, then the Conservatives could have been defeated. However, the Conservatives were to benefit as inflation and unemployment increased and the incomes policy that Callaghan was relying upon collapsed during a wave of public sector strikes (Dorey 2001: 166). It created two benefits for Thatcher and the Conservatives: first, for Thatcher it vindicated her decision to oppose a statutory incomes policy; and second, industrial militancy during the winter undermined the claim that Labour could work harmoniously with the trade unions (Gamble 1988: 93).

The Conservatives successfully persuaded enough of the electorate that the Winter of Discontent was symbolic of the failure of Keynesianism and symptomatic of the consequences of excessive trade union power and an overextended state (Hay 2010: 465). In establishing this narrative the Conservatives were aided by the fact that their electioneering efforts and communications strategy was so well developed. Their approach was influenced by the decision to appoint Gordon Reece in early 1978 and then the move towards using Saatchi and Saatchi as their advertising agency (Bale 2012a: 195). They 'took negative campaigning to a new level', and their advertisements were certainly 'eye-catching', notably the infamous 'Labour Isn't Working' poster (Kavanagh 2005: 228). Target groups were identified, such as working-class housewives and first-time voters, and strategies were designed to get the Conservative message across to them – this involved bypassing the so-called opinion formers within the so-called prestige press and finding ways to communicate more directly with ordinary people (Bale 2012a: 195). Appearances were scheduled on television and radio in which Conservative elites were told to focus in on brevity and repetition within nine-word sentences. The press campaign concentrated on mid-market popular newspapers such as the *Express* and the *Mail*, and tabloids like the *News of the World* and the *Sun*, whose readership was predominantly the skilled working class, many of whom were dissatisfied with Labour (Bale 2012a: 193–5).

The Conservatives secured a comfortable parliamentary majority of 43. They secured 2 million more votes than Labour, and had increased their vote by 3 million from October 1974. The swing from Labour to Conservative was 5.2 per cent, and the 7 per cent gap between the two main parties was the biggest since 1945. However, on the significance of their victory Norton concludes that the electorate 'were voting on the basis of retrospective rather than prospective evaluations: that is, they were voting against Labour rather than for the Conservatives' (Norton 2012: 108).

Implementing Thatcherism: From consensus to conviction 1979–1990

Thatcherism was an evolutionary governing strategy. It was a 'constantly changing dynamic process, driven by political learning [and] adaptation' (Kerr and Marsh 1999: 169). Not only was it characterized by 'improvisation, muddle and opportunism' (Gamble 1996: 23) but it was a strategy that evolved within a party that was not 'Thatcherite'. It would be wrong to think that she 'transformed' the Conservatives at a parliamentary level from a 'Tory consensual' to a 'loyal Thatcherite body' by changing the 'composition' and 'thought of the party' (Norton 1990: 43). The 'Thatcherites' – that is, the advocates of economic liberalism and social conservatism – were a minority within parliamentary ranks (Norton 1990: 44, 55). It should also be noted that although it was true that many known economic 'wets' were eased out of the Cabinet – (e.g. Gilmour and Carlisle in 1981, and later Pym in 1983 and Prior in 1984), her ministerial ranks retained a significant number who were not her natural ideological bedfellows. Acting as a bridge between the dries and wets was Whitelaw (1979–88) and she maintained throughout her premiership a Cabinet role for Walker. Nor did she allow dampness to preclude the promotion of talented ministers to Cabinet, as illustrated for example by Douglas Hurd (1984) and Kenneth Clarke (1985). In her memoirs her justification seemed initially pragmatic as she argued that Cabinet must 'reflect the varying views' in the parliamentary party, before adding (with Walker in mind) that there were 'some people that it is better to bring in because they would cause more trouble outside' (Thatcher 1993: 418).

The paternalistic wing was numerically dominant in her first Cabinet, with Carrington in the Foreign Office, supported by Gilmour; Pym at Defence; Whitelaw at the Home Office; Carlisle at Education; Heseltine at Environment, and Walker at Agriculture (Doherty 1988: 53). However, she saved the key economic portfolios for those who she felt were, in her infamous words, 'one of us' (Young 1990). Howe as Chancellor, his deputy, John Biffen (Chief Secretary), Joseph at Industry, and Nott at Trade, comprised an 'inner core' of dries (Hennessy 2000: 409). Prior at Employment was the only member with a direct impact upon the economic strategy who did not share the view of the dries. The lower ministerial ranks were 'well stocked' with candidates for Thatcher to advance – e.g. Lawson, Ridley, Parkinson and Tebbit. However, many of her leading supporters would in the later stages of her tenure become detached from her due to disagreements over her leadership approach and ideological commitments with regard to Europe, notably Lawson and Howe (Bale 2012a: 284).

The origins for interpreting Thatcherism stem from how we interpret the pre-Thatcherite era. The consensus thesis has become a relatively well-established theory to explain continuity (pre-Thatcherism) and change (through Thatcherism), and remains a useful analytical tool through which to interpret Thatcherism (Kavanagh 1987a). This is because the pillars that exist within the consensus thesis enable us to compare and contrast the policy objectives (and political style) of the Thatcher administrations, with the previous Conservative administrations of the post-war era – that is, 1951–64 and 1970–74.

The pillars embraced a range of economic, social and foreign policy objectives. The pillars include the pursuit of full employment; an adherence to the mixed economy; an approach to industrial relations that incorporates the trade unions into policy-making or is conciliatory towards them; a belief in active government and justifying an expanding of the responsibilities of the state; the continuance of the welfare state; and finally, a foreign policy stance underpinned by nuclear capability and the Atlantic alliance (Kerr 1999: 68). Thatcher bemoaned the timidity of post-war Conservative administrations and their acceptance that they had to 'retreat gracefully' in the face of the 'inevitable advance' of the left. Managing that process and presiding over the Attlee settlement had created the governing overload and crisis of the 1970s, and the Conservatism that had accepted this had to be repudiated (Thatcher 1993: 104).

From Keynesianism to monetarism: Full employment or low inflation

Thatcherism would challenge the consensus pillars of the mixed economy – accommodating the trade unions and full employment. Inflation replaced full employment as the dominant concern as Keynesianism was replaced by a monetarist emphasis on controlling inflation. The June 1979 budget involved the imposition of a fiscal squeeze with cuts in public expenditure and an attempt to restructure taxation. Income tax was lowered from 33 to 30 per cent and alongside this the top rate of income tax was reduced from 83 to 60 per cent, while value-added tax was increased from 8 to 15 per cent to pay for this. Alongside a determination to hit money supply targets and reduce the rate of government borrowing, the objective was to signal the government's commitment to increase incentives and its faith in the private sector (Gamble 1988: 98–9).

Economic thinking was consolidated through the Medium Term Financial Strategy in early 1980, which made controlling the supply of money in the economy a key target alongside reducing the Public Sector Borrowing Requirement (PSBR). This strategy reflected the Thatcherite view that 'governments could not directly affect real economic variables (especially growth and unemployment), but only financial variables, above all the inflation rate, by controlling the money supply, and public borrowing which was seen as contributing to the growth of that supply' (Tomlinson 2007: 6–7). Evans argues that the resulting increase in unemployment was expected and acceptable, even if it was to make their attacks on Labour's record on unemployment seem dubious. He argues that Thatcher and Howe 'were prepared to create an economic slump in order to kill inflation' and weaken trade union influence, and 'resurrect the simple notion of proper money for the benefit of the British people' (Evans 2013: 23). Unemployment did rise steadily reaching 2.4 million in 1981 and then 3.5 in 1985. However, although leading Conservatives expected their anti-inflationary monetary strategy to lead to a rise in unemployment, they did not anticipate the scale of the increase that would occur (Tomlinson 2007: 2; Green 2006: 66–8).

Inflation stood at 10.3 per cent when they entered power, and increased to 21.9 per cent a year later. However, their objective of reducing inflation was achieved as it hit 3.6 per cent in time for the 1983 general election (Thompson 1996: 169). However, Bale questions the extent to which its reduction was the consequence of the monetarist experiment. He argues that it was a by-product of the boost to sterling created through North Sea Oil, alongside high interest rates, the aforementioned squeeze on public spending and borrowing, and due to the fact that rising unemployment was reducing expectations with regard to wage rises (Bale 2012a: 265). Indeed, monetarism would be gradually abandoned between 1983 and 1986 as indicators on money supply proved to be unreliable. More significantly, it was the revenues flowing from privatization which would fund the restructuring of taxation for the better off which would create the incentives to promote entrepreneurialism (Hay and Farrell 2011: 447).

Challenging the mixed economy: The politics of privatization

Although privatization would become the flagship policy of Thatcherism, it only became an integral feature of her administrations after 1983 (Johnson 1991: 144). The shift in the vocabulary from 'denationalisation' to 'privatisation' developed incrementally once in office, and thus the idea that privatization was part of a coherent and ideologically driven blueprint, as argued by Wolfe, is overstated (Wolfe 1991: 237–52). Any commitment to privatize in the first term was 'dwarfed' by the emphasis placed on monetarism and the embracing of privatization was in part a consequence of the limited success of monetarism (Marsh 1995: 600).

The increased focus on privatization flowed from the realization that it would provide a number of overlapping benefits for the Conservatives. First, for an administration attracted to the idea of reducing public expenditure, transferring state-owned firms and industries to the private sector acted as an incentive for these nationalized entities to seek efficiencies as they could no longer rely on the state to subsidize them. Second, by transferring such activity to the private sector it removed from the state the responsibility for wage determination. The experience of both predecessor administrations in the 1970s had demonstrated how wage determination was politicized and intensified conflict between the government and the trade unions. Transferring this conflict to market forces and the profit motive was an attempt to depoliticize this area of conflict. Third, it generated another revenue stream through the sale of shares, which could cover the loss of revenues from cutting income tax rates. Fourth, privatization created a political and electoral conundrum for Labour. Could Labour win while continuing to adhere to their commitment to nationalization which would necessitate increasing taxation? Ultimately, the Conservative commitment to privatization, and within that the sale of council houses, had created a time-specific electoral strategy. The extent of its popularity would not be sustainable by the Major era, but the Conservatives were calculated to have gained an electoral benefit of 0.9 per cent in 1983 from the council house sales, and by 1987 the wider share sell-offs from privatization increased their vote by 1.6 per cent (McAlister and Studlar 1989: 176).

Thatcher would talk about creating a 'share owing democracy' and redistributing wealth to ordinary working people (to annoy the political left), as well as aligning it to the Eden notion of a 'property own democracy' (to the irritation of the conservative left). And irritation was an accurate way to describe the attitude of traditional paternalistic Conservatives, who now found one nation being used as a critical term, alongside a new label for them – 'wets'. The one-nation paternalists questioned the Conservatism that Thatcher was espousing, which they regarded as an alien import into the Conservative tradition (Evans and Taylor 1996: 229). Gilmour would later lament on the unsavoury aspects of the campaigns by the government to encourage the electorate to buy shares in the nationalized industries. He argued that the 'expensive advertising associated with each sale' was poorly 'disguised party propaganda' (Gilmour 1992: 103). Perhaps the most memorable critique of privatization was from Harold Macmillan. Between 1984 and 1986 he was increasingly vocal in his questioning of Thatcherism, made clear from his 'selling off the family silver' speech to the Tory Reform Group (Evans 1998: 24–31).

The inability of the one-nation wing to withstand the Thatcherite onslaught is one of the more intriguing aspects of the Thatcher era. As identified earlier in the chapter, the Thatcherites did not constitute a majority within the PCP or within ministerial ranks. However, this does not mean that the one-nation left were the majority. As Norton identified, there was a significant body of agnostics or instinctive party loyalists within the PCP, who were willing to accept the Thatcherite agenda when it produced electoral dividends (Norton 1990: 41–58). For reasons of personal advancement (i.e. ministerial office) or loyalty, many damp Conservatives would make an accommodation with Thatcherism. Those critics of Thatcherism who were in office lacked organizational structures to challenge her agenda (Bale 2012a: 283). Many of their leading advocates were compromised by office in the early years of Thatcherism (e.g. Gilmour, Pym and Prior) and when they did publicly voice their scepticism after leaving office, their arguments were easier to dismiss as the bitterness of politicians deprived of power (Evans 2013: 50). Their alternative strategy was also easy to dismiss as a return to the failed consensus style solutions undermined by the crisis of the 1970s. As a consequence their attempt to create an anti-Thatcher grouping – named Conservative Centre Forward and launched under the leadership of Pym in 1985 – did not make any significant impact (Evans 2010: 208–28).

Industrial relations: 'The Enemy Within'

Pym wanted to re-establish a 'partnership' between government, industrial management and trade unions (Pym 1985: 160–2). However, this corporatist mentality was incompatible with the Thatcherite thinking with regard to industrial relations. The Thatcher years were characterized by rhetoric which demonized the trade unions as the cause of economic decline due to the crippling effects of their strike action and the inflationary impact of their wage demands (Rosamond 1996: 185–6). What was intriguing about their approach to industrial relations was the gap between their manifesto commitments and their subsequent conduct. This was because at the time of entering power they were in agreement on the need to address the trade union problem, but they disagreed on the best way of achieving their objective. Prior (her first Employment secretary) felt that the trade unions should and could play a constructive role in sustaining an efficient and stable form of capitalism. Thus his instincts were towards persuasion and minimizing conflict and confrontation. He wanted to keep the level of legislative measures to a minimum and hoped that the 1980 Employment Act would be sufficient on its own to encourage responsible and moderate trade unionism (Dorey 1995b: 155–6). In contrast Thatcher regarded the trade unions, or more specifically the miners, as the enemy within (Thatcher 1984) and thus she felt that further legislative interventions would be necessary. To facilitate this she removed Prior from Employment and replaced him with Tebbit in the 1981 reshuffle.

Her approach reflected a fear of a repeat of the 1971 Industrial Relations Act where non-compliance left their large-scale legislative intervention non-viable (Marsh 1992: 74–80). A gradualist approach made it harder for the trade union movement to mobilize their opposition (Moon 1995: 7). Thus the Employment Act of 1980 was followed with further acts in 1982 and 1984, and the Trade Union Act of 1984. Their cumulative impact led to the 'progressive restriction of trade union immunities, the gradual erosion of the lawfulness of the closed shop and secondary action and the ongoing tightening of union ballot regulations' (Rosamond 1996: 190).

The Miners' Strike of 1984–85 was hugely significant for Thatcher, who had a strong desire to win. For in order for Thatcherism to take root within British politics and society she felt it was necessary to defeat the National Union of Mineworkers (NUM), as they were the ultimate symbols of union power, and their President Arthur Scargill was the living embodiment of the militant trade union leader. Second, for the party victory was essential for their political self confidence. The scars of 1973–74 and the fall of the Heath government needed to be overcome (Taylor 2005b: 174). They were on collision course as the Thatcher government was determined to close down uneconomic collieries in preparation for privatization, while the NUM were equally determined to take industrial action and resist any closures (Taylor 2005b: 173). However, Scargill played into Thatcher's hands. The NUM refused to conduct a ballot to ascertain support for strike action. The rationale for this move was Scargill's fear that areas where pits might be deemed viable and thus safe would vote against strike action, but by securing their own futures they would condemn fellow miners' elsewhere to unemployment. The fragmentation of the NUM and its inability to mobilize its membership as a whole was ruthlessly exploited by Thatcher. Scargill was portrayed as bypassing internal democracy out of necessity. Action was not about economic viability but about Scargill's Marxist motives – that is, the aim was political and it was to break down the Thatcher administration. A decade made a difference in terms of popular sentiment. In 1974 support for the employers stood at 24 per cent, with 52 per cent of the electorate sympathizing with the plight of the miners (and 24 per cent in the undecided category). In August 1984 those figures were 40 per cent, 33 per cent and 27 per cent, respectively; and within 5 months of the conflict, a shift away from the miners was detectable – by the end of the year the figures were 51 per cent, 26 per cent and 23 per cent, respectively (Taylor 2005b: 205). However, although Thatcher eventually secured the victory that she craved, there was to be no bounce in the polls as there had been with Falklands (Taylor 2005b: 206–7). Nonetheless, the breaking of the industrial relations pillar of the consensus era was complete.

An active state: Poverty, individual responsibility and social (dis-)harmony

Associated with the pillars of consensus had also been the notion of active government and the pursuit of greater equality as an objective within social policy. The one-nation wing of the Conservative Party was deemed to have made an accommodation with this aspect of the Attlee settlement partly due to their paternalistic instincts. However, Thatcherites were somewhat contemptuous of the idea that those with wealth should be so concerned about the poor or the gap between the richest and poorest within society (Dorey 2011: 130). The new meritocratic Conservatives from the lower middle classes were encouraged by Thatcher to attribute their achievements to hard work and individual effort. The promotion of individual responsibility encouraged social mobility. It created incentives, but also condemnation. Those that did succeed within the lower middle classes were encouraged by Thatcherite thinking to believe that others could as well if only they worked harder (Dorey 2011: 132).

Whereas the previous generation of Conservative elites had been concerned about social inequality, Thatcherites regarded it not as simply unavoidable but necessary. This was because the pursuit of equality as a governing objective was part of the problem that Thatcherism was trying to reverse. Inequality was justified on the following grounds. First, they tried to outline to those in paid employment that 'residual poverty' was the consequence of the 'dysfunctional' character of the welfare state. This undermined the work ethic and encouraged a culture of dependency creating a burden on the overloaded state. Second, by arguing that the egalitarianism that underpins universal welfare created disincentives and dependency, Thatcherites argued that it also undermined economic growth and national prosperity (Dorey 2011: 132–41).

However, Thatcher was unwilling to acknowledge a correlation between poverty caused through unemployment and the violence and riots that engulfed the communities of Brixton and Liverpool in 1981. Indeed, the response to the riots captured the divergence between wets and dries on economic *and* social policy. While both one-nation wets and Thatcherite dries justified inequality and thus divergences in income and wealth, they had conflicting views on poverty. The wets argued that collective action through the welfare state was a necessary and suitable means through which to seek to reduce poverty. From their perspective poverty was *relative* to the existing distribution of income and wealth within society at that moment in time. To Thatcherite dries poverty was *absolute*. This then justified a minimal safety net state, and that poverty was best addressed by the market through the trickle effect flowing from wealth creation. Here incentives towards material gain were critical. The wealth-creating capacity of a freer market, characterized by entrepreneurial activity, would create improvements in living standards, and that would include improving incomes at the lowest end. It was egalitarianism that was fuelling the enlargement of the welfare state, whereas Thatcherism was promoting 'popular capitalism' to showcase how the market had the capacity to improve the living standards of all. For Thatcherite dries there should be no agonizing over the fact that the gap in incomes and wealth – that is, relative poverty – would increase. The gap between the richest and poorest in society would increase significantly, but this did not matter as the position of the poorest would improve even if their relative position fell (Hickson 2009: 347–52).

Welfare: Modification rather than reversal

Gilmour and Garnett argue that Thatcher was pursuing a 'two nations' philosophy as many communities within the inner cities regarded dependence on the state as a way of life (Gilmour and Garnett 1998: 323). However, the welfare strategy of the Thatcher administrations may not have reversed the welfare pillar of the consensus thesis, but it certainly modified it. Even her leading advocates question the overall success of her social policy strategy. If the objective was to cut (or even control) expenditure on public services then they failed according to Ridley (Ridley 1991: 85). Of course this was an immensely difficult task given the massive increase in unemployment, which had inflated the social security budget (Gilmour and Garnett 1998: 321). Attempts at reform were 'incremental' and not that 'innovative' until the third term (Pierson 1996: 214). In addition to redesigning the means testing of housing benefit and income support, the Thatcher era would involve the freezing of Child Benefit. Money-saving objectives underpinned the decision to break the link between pensions and average earnings, and incentives were offered to encourage people to contract out into private pension plans (Bale 2012a: 266).

What of the NHS? This was not necessarily a contentious issue within the party but became an increasing electoral concern. The Thatcher administration was routinely criticized by the electorate who held a view that the NHS was suffering from under investment. A negative image of shortages, longer waiting lists, bed closures and postponed operations gave credence to opposition claims of 'Tory cuts'. There was real evidence of public disenchantment about the performance of the NHS (Bosanquet 1988). And yet the Thatcherites would keep emphasizing that there was a real terms increase in spending on the NHS during their first two terms in office, but neglected to acknowledge that with an ageing population a 2 per cent increase per year was needed just to stand still (Pierson 1996: 210). She was 'cautious' during their first two terms in office, and she felt the need to reassure the electorate the NHS was 'safe in their hands' to 'soothe their anxieties' (Campbell 2003: 509). Her caution reflected her fear that the NHS was Labour territory and it was not possible to 'win' on this ground, and thus it was too politically 'dangerous' to take it on (Campbell 2003: 169–70). However, in her third term, as the negative reporting on the performance of the NHS intensified, she felt compelled to reform. Her imposition in 1989 of the 'internal market' (creating a split between GP fund holders who purchased care for their patients, and health authorities) was to be highly controversial (Webster 1991). The attempt to introduce market disciplines to drive up standards by enhancing efficiency fed the Labour narrative that the Thatcherites were hatching a plot to privatize the NHS. Reform intensified public concern. By 1990 73 per cent of the electorate disagreed with her claim that the NHS was safe in Conservative hands (Campbell 2003: 552–3). Significantly for Conservative backbenchers worried about holding onto their seats, the fact that it was so unpopular was a significant concern (Gilmour and Garnett 1998: 341).

Foreign policy: Reasserting British prestige and influence

In terms of foreign policy it is clear that upon entering power Thatcher recognized that Britain was a middle-ranking power that had been weakened by 'economic decline' (Thatcher 1993: 9). Her strategy was to project herself as a 'cold war warrior' (Fry 2008: 182) and to adhere to fixed principles based on opposition to communism and national independence within the EEC. A more sceptical and aggressive stance was adopted with regard to the Soviet Union. She offered virulent anti-communist rhetoric and questioned the emphasis on detente that had characterized the approach of the 1970s (Thatcher 1993: 65). She felt that although the language of detente was admirable it could not mask the fact that during the pursuit of detente the numeric strength of the Soviet armed forces had increased (Young 1989: 170). Reiterating the need for nuclear capability also created political benefits as it enabled them to exploit the defence issue at elections. This was notable during the 1983 general election, where 77 per cent of the electorate disagreed with Labour's unilateralist position (Butler and Kavanagh 1984: 282).

She understood that 'prestige was a form of power' (Reynolds 2000: 256), and she famously 'exploited the Falklands triumph as a symbol of Britain's rebirth under her leadership' (Campbell 2003: 254). The Falklands experience was traumatic for the Conservatives (forcing the resignation of Carrington from the Foreign Office for failing to foresee the imminent invasion), even if it provided a significant turning point for the government after the economic difficulties of the 1979–82 period. Thatcher quickly framed the debate as being between 'British virtue' and 'aggression' on behalf of Argentina. The military option would be necessary, even if Carrington's replacement, Pym, was more diplomatically minded (Thatcher 1993: 179–81). The Falklands War proved to be a triumph for Thatcher. Her strident cry of 'rejoice, rejoice' may have 'grated' with some, but she captured the jingoistic mood of a significant proportion of the electorate who took pride in a 'brief revival of imperial glory' (Butler and Kavanagh 1984: 27).

One of the intriguing aspects of the Falklands War was its impact upon the popularity of the government. Academic debate followed thereafter about the extent of this 'Falklands factor'. Clarke et al. argued that the impact was longer term and led to an increase in government popularity of over 7 percentage points and that this was a significant factor in explaining their re-election in 1983 (Clarke et al. 1986: 123–41; see also Clarke et al. 1990: 63–81). Although Sanders et al. would argue that the extent of the Falklands factor was being overstated, and that its impact was at most only 3 percentage points, they do not deny the existence of it being a positive benefit to the Conservatives (Sanders et al. 1987: 281–313).

Securing electoral dividends on the European issue would be more problematic. When Thatcher entered Downing Street she supported inter-governmental cooperation with the EEC with regard to economic, foreign and defence policies. This confederalist position was the mainstream position within the Conservatives, and on either side were a small band associated with the European cause who could countenance a federalist agenda, and an equally small grouping of anti-marketeers (Ashford 1980: 110). During their time in office these configurations of opinion would alter and the dominant confederalist grouping would fracture. However, European issues would not be a source of conflict in the early years of Conservative governance post 1979. But the European issue would in some way be linked to the loss from cabinet of Heseltine in 1986; Lawson in 1989; Ridley and Howe in 1990, and of course it was a contributing factor in the downfall of Thatcher herself (Ludlam 1996: 109). The Thatcher era would see an evolutionary wave of debates about first, financial considerations and the budgetary contribution; second, the economic benefits that could be accrued from market liberalization on a pan-European Community scale; and third, the institutional debates on the direction of the European project in which entry into the Exchange Rate Mechanism (ERM) became a source of disagreement.

The first wave to address was the budgetary battle. The net financial contribution that Britain was expected to make had risen steeply under the previous Labour government. This meant that despite being the third poorest member they were the second largest contributor. Thatcher was determined to address this and calling to account an 'overspending bureaucracy' fitted in nicely within her ideological convictions, as the weakness of the British economy meant that the costs of membership were 'politically significant' (Crowson 2007: 48; Gifford 2008: 91). The budgetary issue 'both inaugurated and signalled the Thatcherite way' of operating within Europe, as she eschewed consensus and coalition building associated with conventional diplomacy (Gifford 2008: 91). She was confrontational and her 'handbagging' methods were summed up after the Dublin European Council meeting in November 1979 when she said: 'we are asking for a very large amount of *our own money back*' (Thatcher 1979). The issue was not addressed until June 1984 at Fontainebleu when it was agreed that Britain should be given an ad hoc refund on its contributions alongside an annual rebate (Gifford 2008: 87). Gilmour would question her motives. He felt that she thought she could 'win some kudos and popularity' by standing up against the 'foreigners', and not only was a 'running row with our European partners the next best thing to a war [for her], it would divert public attention from the disasters at home' (Gilmour 1992: 240).

The second European wave related to the creation of the single market was accepted 'relatively harmoniously' (Seawright 2004: 143). George notes that the Thatcher governments were keen to turn 'the direction of discussion' within the EEC towards 'the practical achievement of a free internal market' and 'away from discussions' about institutional developments (George 1990: 177). Thatcher was a 'willing participant' in the moves towards a single market, but failed to appreciate that it was an 'acceleration of the unification process' (Crowson 2007: 51). At the time the claim was that this was the

implementation of 'Thatcherism on a European scale' (Young 1998: 333). It
enabled them to 'entrench neo-liberalism as a global hegemonic project', having
appeared to demonstrate an 'apparent convergence of economic policy across
Europe with that of the British Conservative party', thus 'establishing the
British government as a leading player' (Gifford 2008: 89, 95). Buller provides
an interpretation that suggests that this was evidence of a Thatcherite attempt
at the 'Europeanisation' of the British political economy (Buller 2000), which
would 'bring external pressure to bear on supply side issues, secure domestic
autonomy and have free market ideas accepted' (Crowson 2007: 51).

However, while 1986 is the year of the Single European Act (SEA) leading
to a single market in 1992 and thus a high point for Thatcher on Europe,
it is also the year when real evidence starts to emerge of a split within the
Thatcherite faction of economic dries over the merits of membership of
the ERM. The debates over the merits of ERM membership would operate
in tandem with the realization that the SEA was 'not the end in itself' as
Thatcher thought, but a 'means to an end' for the new European Commission
President, Jacques Delors (Geddes 2005: 123). Delors used the SEA to 'create
the basis for future spillover initiatives' and 'by playing to Thatcherite neo-
liberalism, the British guard was lowered' which 'enabled suggestions of
further integration to be put on the Community agenda'. Thus, Thatcher
'underestimated the expansionist elements' of the SEA because she 'believed
that her free market agenda had been victorious' (Gifford 2008: 89–94).

Confirmation of Thatcher's 'awakening to the European threat' (Crowson
2007: 53) was evident in her Bruges Speech of 1988. The speech is best
remembered for her comment that 'we have not successfully rolled back the
frontiers of the state in Britain, only to see them reimposed at a European super-
state exercising a new dominance from Brussels' (Campbell 2003: 607). It
was a response to her growing realization that for Delors the SEA represented
the 'rejuvenation of the European project and the integration in other areas
linked to the single market such as social, economic, fiscal, monetary and
regional policies' (Geddes 2005: 123). However, her intervention rejected
the approach that her administration had been adopting and it appeared to
be an admission of failure – that is, that her government had been unable
to find a viable position within Europe (Crowson 2007: 53). For the rest of
her tenure her discourse on Europe would be framed by four factors. First,
other member states had 'reneged' on the adherence to free market principles
as adopted in the SEA; second, the legal, political, social and economic
institutions of Britain and the EEC were 'incompatible'; third, that British
sovereignty was being threatened by autonomous European institutions;
and fourth, that the spillover consequences of the SEA into social, fiscal,
economic and monetary policy were 'unacceptable' (Geddes 2005: 125).

Her rhetoric legitimized Euroscepticism. It also intensified the divisions
at the top of the party (and within the Thatcherite economic dry faction)
as she implied that pro-European Conservatives were 'complicit' with the
Delors project (Gifford 2008: 96). ERM membership would become the

battleground. Traditional pro-European Conservatives would now find allies amongst arch economic Thatcherites in the shape of Howe and to a lesser extent Lawson (Lawson was pro-ERM but less accepting of EMU than Howe) (Seawright 2004: 148). Pragmatically, Howe and Lawson saw further integration within Europe as an essentially limited project but one which could aid domestic statecraft (Gifford 2008: 96–7). Howe and Lawson believed that the ERM could provide an external anchor and address the damaging effects on the domestic economy caused by the impact of fluctuating exchange rates and provide the basis for a viable anti-inflationary strategy (Lawson 1992: 647–57, 923; Howe 1994: 448). As a prelude, Chancellor Lawson had since 1986, (against the instincts of Thatcher), begun to shadow the deutschmark as a means of facilitating entry into the ERM (Lawson 1992: 647). The Madrid European Council of June 1989 would see Thatcher bounced into agreeing to set a timetable for entry into the ERM by 1992. If no commitment to do so was made by Thatcher, then both Howe and Lawson would resign (Lawson 1992: 933).

The threat of a joint resignation and the decision to set up a timetable for entry into the ERM (achieved in August 1990) was to have implications for the future of the Conservatives, although the consequences would not become apparent until their fourth term. By the time of their humiliating ejection from the ERM on Black Wednesday in September 1992, Thatcher, Howe and Lawson would all have left office. Lawson would resign from the Treasury in October 1989. Howe would be removed from the Foreign Office in June 1989 and, after a humiliating year serving as Leader of the House and Deputy Prime Minister, his resignation would be the trigger for the removal of Thatcher herself. The primary reason for her removal would be fear that she would lead the Conservatives to defeat. Lawson feared that she would seek a fourth term on the basis of 'crude populist anti-Euroscepticism' (Lawson 1992: 922). This was a valid conclusion for Lawson to make. After all, her strategy for the 1989 European Elections was 'bring Conservative voters – so many of whom were thoroughly disillusioned with the Community – out to vote' (Thatcher 1993: 749). The Conservatives lost in 1989 and many feared a repeat in 1991 or 1992. After a decade of pursuing Thatcherism, breaking down many of the pillars of consensus and repudiating the trajectory of post-war Conservatism, real doubts existed about her persuasive capabilities moving forward. She was leading, but did the Conservatives, and enough of the electorate want to follow?

Justifying Thatcherism: Persuasion and electioneering

The governing strategy identified above demonstrates that Thatcher believed that her mission was to save Britain (and the Conservatives) from the politics of the consensus era. This would involve educating the public in order to change public expectations about the role of the state (Crewe and Searing 1988: 375). The most notable aspect of this was the attempt to persuade the electorate that full employment was not part of the proper role of government. (Moon 1995: 6). That they managed to secure re-election when unemployment had increased challenged a key assumption of post-war British politics – that is, that excessive unemployment would result in electoral defeat. Thatcherism thereby contradicted the spatial theory advocated by Downs. This implied that rational politicians operating within two party systems need to eschew ideology and dilute their message in order to appeal to the floating voter located within the centre ground (Downs 1957: 96–101; 132–6). Thatcherism was the antithesis of this. Instead of moving herself and her party towards the prevailing attitudes of the voters, she attempted to reshape the attitudes of voters – politician-driven politics, as opposed to voter driven (Crewe and Searing 1988: 375).

Through her oratory she sought to justify her policy choices and governing strategy. She would attempt to relate to the electorate by emphasizing her affinity with their concerns and aspirations. This appeal was directed not just at the middle class, but also towards the aspiring working class, for whom her emphasis would be on the possibility of social mobility through adherence to shared British values – family values, individual responsibility, self-reliance and property ownership (Crewe 1988: 31). Tied into this rhetorical appeal to shared interests was to be the search for scapegoats for the crisis of the 1970s, be that the destructiveness and undemocratic nature of trade unionism; the punitive taxation and high inflation associated with Labour governments; the threat to family life created by the permissive generation; the undermining of the work ethic created by excessive social security payments; the desire of the left to understand the causes of crime rather than the need for deterrent and punishment; and coded references to difficulties of assimilating the high volumes of immigrants in the post-war era (Dorey 2014). Such a rhetorical approach reflected her tendency towards black-and-white thinking (Dyson 2009: 38) and her way of seeing the political world as being 'divided into friends and enemies, goodies and baddies' (King 1985 132). However, by such confrontational rhetoric Thatcher was seeking to harness support through fear and by identifying enemies.

To what extent did the politics of Thatcherism change the character of the electorate – how deep was the shift to Thatcherite values? Thatcherism was the beneficiary of social change and they utilized power to accelerate those processes of social change to their advantage (Crewe 1988: 29). Social trends within the 1980s worked to the advantage of the Conservatives and to the disadvantage of Old Labour. Between 1974 and 1987 the Conservatives secured an overall swing of 2.2 per cent, but that rate of swing was zero among the middle classes, but 4 per cent among the working class, which was declining as a proportion of the electorate. The Conservatives used power to diminish the size of Labour's core vote, while simultaneously challenging working-class loyalty and party alignment (Crewe 1988: 32).

For example, the number of shareholders increased (from 7 per cent in 1979 to 22 per cent by 1992) as trade union membership declined (from 13.2 to 7.8 million between 1979 and 1997). Home ownership increased from 57.2 per cent in 1979 to 71.0 per cent by 1987 and council tenants declined in the same period from 31.4 to 22.9 per cent (Pattie and Johnston 1996: 45–6). Voting theories based around class alignment became challenged, and new cleavages emerged around voters reliant on the state for employment and services, and those dependent upon the market, with those in the first bracket inclining towards Labour, and those in the latter tilting to the Conservatives. This provided an electoral incentive for the Conservatives to reduce the state (Pattie and Johnston 1996: 51).

However, when it comes to analysing the extent of ideological change there is evidence to suggest that the pursuit of Thatcherism did not create a Thatcherite nation (Crewe 1988: 25–50). Over the period of Thatcherite governance, the indicators with regard to the prioritization of inflation over unemployment moved away from Thatcherite thinking. In 1980 52 per cent wanted inflation to be the priority and only 42 per cent unemployment, but by the latter part of the decade, 75 per cent identified unemployment as the priority. Equally the balance between spending on public services and tax cuts moved away from Thatcherite solutions. These figures were 37 per cent on each when Thatcher entered Downing Street, but 66 per cent wanted increased spending on public services and only 11 per cent further tax cuts by her third term (Crewe 1988: 34–9).

Therefore, the electorate did not necessarily endorse the governing strategy that Thatcher had imposed upon them. The dominance of the Conservatives in the age of Thatcher was not necessarily a reflection of the 'strength' of Thatcherism. By historical standards her parliamentary majorities were impressive, but if we consider vote share, the victories of 1979, 1983 and 1987 look somewhat less impressive. At between 42.3 and 43.9 per cent of the electorate these are lower vote shares than the victories of 1951 (48.0), 1955 (49.7), 1959 (49.4) and 1970 (46.4), and the landslide parliamentary victories of 1983 (42.4) and 1987 (42.3) were lower in vote share than the 1964 defeat on 43.4 (Crewe 1988: 26). Thus the primary reason for the success of Thatcherism is the lack of a credible alternative. The election victory of 1979 was a by-product of the discrediting of Labour as a party of government due to the cumulative impact of the IMF crisis and the Winter of Discontent. The fracturing of Labour and the formation of the Social Democratic Party (SDP) in 1981 contributed to a more even split between the Labour and third-party vote in 1983 than in previous post-war elections. That Labour secured 27.6 per cent and the SDP and Liberals were combined on 25.4 per cent explains why Thatcher (on 42.4 per cent) secured a parliamentary majority of 144. Thirteen years earlier Heath secured a far smaller majority (31) from 46.4 per cent of the vote, but the gap between Labour on 43.0 and the Liberals on 7.5 per cent was far smaller. Therefore, the self-destructive infighting within Labour in the aftermath of defeat in 1979 was central to the longevity of the Conservatives in office thereafter. Their reaction to defeat and the policy and institutional changes that they fought over created an image of extremism and division, which meant that they were viewed as being unworthy of office. That Labour leaders such as Michael Foot and Neil Kinnock were so widely lampooned by the Conservative-dominated press was another advantage that aided the Conservatives throughout the Thatcher years (Pattie and Johnston 1996: 41–2).

Thatcher had done what the Conservatives asked of her after the traumas of the 1970s. She had provided them with a means to obtain and retain office. Thatcherism appeared to have enabled the Conservatives to once again dominate British government and politics. Thatcher 'wanted to create a new consensus informed by [the] values of economic individualism, national independence and conservative morality' which meant 'that even if the Conservatives lost office in the future any successor government would be obliged to govern within the new constraints which [Thatcherism] had established' (Gamble 1996: 28). However, the Conservatives had to recognize that they needed to solve the puzzle of the post-Thatcher era, either due to loss of office (and constraining a future Labour administration as implied above), or by changing leader while remaining in power. Thatcher herself did not seem to be planning for a defeat or an early succession while in office.

Consolidating Thatcherism:
From Thatcher to Major 1990–1992

As her tenth anniversary as prime minister in May 1989 passed, Thatcher announced that her intention was to lead the Conservatives into the next general election, and that she intended to serve through the majority of that fourth term, possibly stepping down in 1994 or 1995 (Thatcher 1993: 755; 832).

However, the 18 months that followed her tenth anniversary as prime minister saw the Conservative opinion polling position slip due to a combination of factors. First, voters were increasingly concerned about the state of the economy, particularly resurgent inflation, increased interest rates and negative equity. Second, there was the impact of the poll tax, which was introduced in 1989–90 to replace the domestic rating system for funding local services. Its controversy stemmed from the fixed charge element for all adults with only a few exceptions or rebates. The new system was deemed to be unfair and in the event many refused to pay. For Thatcher the rationale was clear. Labour local councils were prone to charging more (not because they represented communities in more inner city areas, but because they were Labour) (Gilmour and Garnett 1998: 343–4). If voters had an incentive to understand the cost of their local services, it was assumed that they would turn to the Conservatives as the party best equipped to charge them the least at local level (Gove 1995: 175). Initially the PCP had been 'obedient', but when it led to protests in London in March 1990 (that led to rioting), concerns began to intensify. By the summer of 1990 approaching 70 per cent of the electorate opposed the poll tax, and nearly 100 Conservative backbenchers (especially those in marginal constituencies) had 'reservations' (Gilmour and Garnett 1998: 343).

The third factor undermining the Conservatives was the divisions within the Cabinet. Specifically, as mentioned earlier, the working relationship between Thatcher and Howe had all but collapsed, leading to his removal from the Foreign Office in June 1989 and his redeployment as Leader of the House of Commons and Deputy Prime Minister. Then Lawson resigned as Chancellor in October 1989. Irritated by her reliance on the advice of her own economic policy advisor, Alan Walters, and the perception that this undermined him, Lawson decided he could not continue (Gilmour and Garnett 1998: 342–5). The resignation of Lawson, so shortly after the demotion of Howe, undermined Thatcher. Lawson's resignation coincided with the timetable for the annual election of the party leader (Campbell 2003: 691). Anthony Meyer, an obscure backbencher, decided he would dispute her re-election. Meyer stood on behalf of the economic damp, Europhile wing of the PCP. Although he was not a heavyweight candidate, the fact that he stood was serious, as he gave all of those who had been dismissed, disappointed or disenchanted by Thatcher an outlet through which to begin the process of undermining her and eventually removing her (Baker 1993: 320).

Thatcher scored an overwhelming victory over Meyer, but psychologically the process was immensely damaging. The mere fact that a challenge was launched was a warning. If a candidate such as Meyer could garner nearly 30 protest votes, and allow around 30 more to register their disapproval, then what might happen if a heavyweight candidate emerged? Many assumed that this could be first of a number of leadership challenges that could occur between now and the general election (Campbell 2003: 696).

Twelve months later Heseltine emerged as that heavyweight challenger. He had served under her as Environment Secretary (1979–83) and then Defence Secretary (1983–86). He had resigned from the Cabinet in January 1986 over a dispute about the future of the Westland Helicopter company. On resigning he was to be strongly critical of her leadership style notably her handling of Cabinet. His differences with Thatcher went beyond stylistics. He was pro-European, economically damp and socially liberal. Ever since his departure from Cabinet it was assumed that Heseltine was positioning himself to succeed her, but to do so after her defeat at the polls, or after someone else had challenged her without winning but had forced her resignation and created a vacancy (Crick 1997: 344).

However, his strategy was to be undermined by the unexpected resignation of Howe. The timing of his resignation (1 November) was critical. It dovetailed neatly into the annual re-election of the leader. In his parliamentary resignation speech Howe, with hitherto unknown passion, outlined the policy disagreements that had existed between himself and Thatcher and the problems associated with her leadership style. He concluded with a non-too-subtle coded message: 'the time has come for others to consider their own response to the tragic conflict of loyalties with which I myself have wrestled with for perhaps too long' (Shepherd 1991: 1). In offering an appraisal of the impact of Howe speech, Miller concluded that he had never seen

> a demolition job done with such meticulous artistry. . . . In content, timing and delivery, it was a killer of the highest class, in turn, witty, factual, regretful and lethal. . . . He had not come to praise Margaret, but to bury her, and in eighteen minutes he had dug her political grave, filled it in beyond possibility of exhumation and conducted an autopsy while the victim was still alive and listening. (Miller 1993: 349)

The Howe speech forced Heseltine to declare his candidacy, with only one day remaining before the deadline for nominations (Heseltine 2000: 355). Heseltine constructed his campaigning approach around three issues: first, reforming the poll tax; second, a new approach to Europe; and third, by citing opinion polling data that demonstrated that if he led the Conservatives, they would lead Labour in the opinion polls, reversing the large deficit under Thatcher. While Heseltine fought a proactive campaign, Thatcher was inactive. She gave few media interviews, made no attempt to persuade wavering backbenchers and chose to attend a European Summit in Paris on the day of the ballot rather than remain in London (Heppell 2008b: 81).

Thatcher would pay for her inactive campaigning approach. She had secured 52 more votes than Heseltine (204 to 152), but failed to pass the necessary majority and 15 per cent threshold: she was four votes short (Watkins 1991: 2). Although Thatcher initially intended to fight on, the damage to her authority was irreversible. Even if she did defeat Heseltine in the 'rematch' second ballot it would be a pyrrhic victory. The question of the succession would remain unresolved, as if she waited until 1992 then unless there was a dramatic change in the opinion polls another leadership challenge might occur in the autumn of 1991 (Heppell 2008b: 82). That evening she met individually with the majority of her Cabinet. Her Cabinet colleagues believed that support was ebbing away from her and that she could not win. As such they informed her that the best interests of the party would be served by allowing a non-Thatcher, non-Heseltine, compromise candidate to emerge (Shepherd 1991: 37).

Thatcher chose to resign and became consumed by bitterness about the method of her removal (Campbell 2003: 738). Major (Chancellor) and Hurd (Foreign Secretary) entered the contest to block Heseltine. Momentum swung towards Major. If Heseltine was disloyal and Hurd elitist, then Major was a unifier whose humble background could be exploited electorally. Major secured the backing of Thatcherites as Thatcher endorsed him, even though Major announced he would reconsider the poll tax. Major defeated Heseltine by 185 votes to 131 with Hurd coming last with 56 votes. Although technically another ballot should have followed under the existing rules, both Hurd and Heseltine withdrew (Shepherd 1991: 78). However, the method through which Major acquired the leadership would explain many of the difficulties he would subsequently experience. He was made leader on the behest of the Thatcherites, but the Thatcherites would rather she had remained in office and furthermore, although he was more right wing than Heseltine and Hurd, he was not really a fully blown Thatcherite. Questions about his legitimacy would remain throughout his leadership tenure (Heppell 2007: 471–90).

There was some confusion on what Major's selection meant. Although Thatcher's removal stemmed from her becoming an electoral liability, the question was whether she was a political liability because of issues of substance (policy) or style (presentation). Those who had voted for her removal by endorsing Heseltine, or then Heseltine or Hurd in the second ballot could have been motivated by substance and style. Those who endorsed Major presumably did so because he was the anointed candidate of Thatcher, and thereby Major would provide the perfect combination of continuity in policy (i.e. Thatcherism) but with a different style. That Major was the candidate of the Thatcherites was just one of many constraints that he inherited. The legacy of Thatcherism and Thatcher was complex: Major had the difficult balancing act of demonstrating that he was a duplicate of Thatcher, without antagonizing the Thatcherites (Evans 1999: 139). Thatcherism was difficult to manage in the immediate post-Thatcher era for the following reasons.

First, Thatcherism had created misplaced expectations among some Conservatives. Their guilt over the manner of her removal contributed towards a revisionist account of the Thatcher years. They began to mythologize Thatcherism. From the vantage point of the new decade, Thatcherism was retrospectively viewed by them as coherent and the golden age of Conservative politics. This was to become the yardstick against which the Major era would be evaluated. Second, Thatcherism was a time-specific governing philosophy. The political climate was turning against the politics of Thatcherism. Non-Thatcherite concerns such as unemployment, social dislocation and inequality were increasing as was concern about the quality of public services. The values of Thatcherism, which were less pronounced than some Conservatives realized, had peaked before her removal (Evans 1999: 139).

This left Major with a conundrum. The first factor demonstrated that Major needed to satisfy the demands for undiluted Thatcherism, and that the revolution should continue. The second factor suggested that Major should soften the excesses of Thatcherism. In the interim period between acquiring the leadership and the general election, Major appeared to be inclined towards the pragmatism of the second option (Evans and Taylor 1996: 247).

Major had to reverse the symptoms of decline that had engulfed their third term. If he failed, electoral rejection beckoned. If he succeeded and secured his own mandate, he could escape the shadows of Thatcher, the individual, and Thatcherism, the philosophy. Those who condemn Major should consider what faced him when he succeeded Thatcher. His inbox included the following:

1   the crisis in the Gulf following the Iraqi invasion of Kuwait
2   the problem of the poll tax
3   the problem of creating a unifying approach to European policy and
4   the problem of the ongoing economic recession.

The immediate concern was the Iraqi invasion of Kuwait in August 1990. The United Nations condemned the invasion of the oil-rich Arab kingdom, and a powerful coalition of forces mobilized to condemn Saddam Hussein. Thatcher had committed British forces to the Gulf War, under US tactical command, in preparation for war if the diplomatic routes failed. Operation Desert Storm was launched in January 1991, by which time Major had been prime minister for only 7 weeks. Kuwait was liberated by March 1991. Iraq accepted unconditionally the outstanding UN resolutions, and military action by allied forces ceased immediately. One big problem remained, however. The British and American dominated allied forces had won the war, but Saddam still remained in Iraq. While there was the hope that the humiliation of defeat might precipitate a coup against Saddam, the danger was that the decision to end the war then would enable the remnants of his army to survive and re-establish dominance in Iraq. From a partisan perspective, the Gulf War had provided Major with an opportunity to showcase his leadership credentials and to look statesmanlike. His reputation was enhanced, as he was widely praised for offering calm and dignified leadership. Shortly thereafter, opinion polling revealed that he was the most popular prime minister for over 30 years, with approval ratings of over 60 per cent (Newton 1992: 136).

The Gulf War dominated the first few months of the Major premiership, alongside the need to reform the poll tax. Identifying and implementing a more acceptable, and voter-friendly, means of financing local government was an essential precursor to securing re-election (Blake 1998: 389). There was a divergence of views between the Tory left and the Thatcherite right on how to deal with the poll tax. Heseltine, newly appointed as Environment Secretary, was initially interested in returning to the old rating system which was an anathema to Thatcherites. After years of attacking the rating system many Conservatives were keen to retain a personal element in whatever system was adopted to replace the poll tax. Despite its contribution to her downfall, some Thatcherites believed that the poll tax was the litmus test for Major. To continue with it implied that the Thatcher revolution was ongoing; to change suggested that Major was abandoning the radicalism that had defined Thatcherism (Evans 1999: 154). Eventually the Cabinet accepted a proposal to replace the poll tax with a council tax which involved both property and personal elements (Walsh 1992: 57). It involved every household paying a two-person tax, which was to be based on a sliding seven band scale of property value. A discount was made available for single occupiers. The new council tax passed through Parliament before the 1992 general election and came into effect from March 1993 but provoked none of the disharmony that its predecessor had (Seldon 1997: 179). Major had demonstrated considerable skill by navigating his way through these difficulties and manufacturing a more practical and affordable scheme, which 'diffused' some of the public anger (Hayton 2012a: 22).

Europe would be even more challenging. Major realized that the European schism had the potential to split the Conservatives and thus he adopted a tactical rather than a strategic approach (Young 1998: 278). Major recognized that relations with European partners had been damaged in the late-Thatcher era by her antagonistic and confrontational approach. In an attempt to usher in a new era of engagement, Major let it be known that he wanted to situate Britain at 'the heart of Europe' (Seldon 1997: 55). The heart of Europe rhetoric reassured Europhiles made uneasy by the phobia of the late-Thatcher era. He believed, however, that by rejecting the federalist vision shared by some European partners he would be able to placate the Eurosceptics (Evans 1999: 147).

The viability of the Major strategy of blurring the differences would be put to the test at the Intergovernmental Conference of European leaders scheduled for Maastricht in December 1991. The Maastricht summit would be critical to determining the future direction of Europe. The other 11-member states were determined to make progress towards a more integrated community. Particularly problematic would be negotiations surrounding Economic and Monetary Union and the Social Chapter. Major had to be sensitive to the fact that many Conservatives feared the Trojan horse symbolism of the construction of a timetable for economic union. Such Eurosceptics argued that the establishment of a single currency and a European Central Bank would be the essential precursor to political union. Resentment was also evident with regard to the Social Chapter, which could aim to secure harmonized minimum wages and maximum hours, which according to Thatcherite dries would undermine British economic competitiveness (Crowson 2007: 55). Given such reservations, the significance to Major of Maastricht was immense.

Major was to secure a triple success. First, he negotiated the right for Britain to opt out of joining the single European currency scheduled for 1999. The opt-out should have placated Eurosceptics, but the fact that the possibility of opting in at a later date remained should have satisfied Europhiles. Second, Major negotiated the right for Britain to opt out of the Social Chapter. Third, Major also secured a symbolic concession. The draft version of the Treaty of European Union made reference to the ultimate aim of a 'Union with a federal goal'. Major negotiated that the emphasis on federalism be removed. A vaguer statement on decision-making being taken as close to the citizens as is possible was inserted in its place. Alongside his single currency and social chapter opt-outs, Major argued that the principle of subsidiarity was being accepted and that federalism had been stalled (Evans 1999: 149).

Irrespective of the subsequent civil war over Europe, what cannot be denied is the positive reaction to the negotiated settlement that Major had secured at the time (Young 1998: 433). Maastricht had been a personal triumph for Major. Given his success, his press office with atypical triumphalism, described it as 'game, set and match' to Major (Seldon 1997: 248). Thatcher was less impressed. She felt that Major had been gullible in assuming that Britain could constructively engage within Europe and he had been duped into the federalist strategy. She argued that it amounted to a 'ruinous straightjacket' which put Britain 'on the conveyor belt to a single currency' (Seldon 1997: 251, 328).

Given the size of the majority and the minimal scale of Conservative dissent, Major could have piloted it through the House of Commons before dissolution. However, he chose to delay seeking parliamentary approval before the general election, as he feared providing the opposition and the media with evidence of Conservative divisions. Better to wait until the new parliament as Thatcher was not standing for re-election. Tragically for Major the delay would maximize the perception of division. By then Major led an increasingly Eurosceptic PCP (the new intake being predominantly Eurosceptic) and faced a smaller majority. Moreover, after Black Wednesday the game, set and match claim seemed rather presumptuous (Crowson 2007: 57).

However, in terms of electoral preparations for 1992, Major had temporarily addressed the European dilemma, as well as the poll tax, as electoral issues. The state of the economy was the main obstacle to re-election. In the late-Thatcher era, the economy had entered recession, and support for the Conservatives dipped as national income declined, manufacturing output fell and house prices collapsed. What was particularly problematic for the Conservatives was where the recession was impacting. Early recessions had impacted primarily on the Labour heartlands and thus the electoral consequences were less pronounced. The late-Thatcher, early-Major recession was hitting Conservative heartlands with potentially devastating electoral consequences (Seldon 1997: 238).

That the recession proved to be more enduring than Conservatives had anticipated was compounded by the structural bind that they found themselves in through ERM membership (entered into in September 1990). To stimulate activity and restore confidence, Major and his new Chancellor

Norman Lamont could have cut interest rates. However, the stability of sterling within the ERM did not permit this course of action (Seldon 1997: 238). This self-imposed constraint designed as a mechanism to bear down on inflation, left two options. First, attempt to delude the electorate by refusing to acknowledge the existence of recession, and talk up the economy. This would result in the infamous Lamont quote in October 1991 that 'the green shoots of economic spring are appearing' (Hogg and Hill 1995: 157). Second, they could adopt a political and electoral approach to economic management in the short term to secure a further mandate, and deal with the economic consequences later. Maintaining public spending prior to an election meant that the PSBR ballooned up over £30 million, much to the chagrin of Thatcherites. Critics assumed that Major and Lamont were cynically trying to court approval. Their profligate pre-election spending, compounded by falling tax yields flowing from increased unemployment, would have to be clawed back when they were re-elected through tax increases (Evans 1999: 152).

Electioneering was driven by an aggressive negative advertising blitz to stimulate alarm about the economic competence of Labour. This consisted of the unveiling of one thousand poster sites displaying a World War II bombshell, labelled 'Labour's Tax bombshell', with the slogan underneath stating 'You'd Pay £1,000 More Tax under Labour'. This tax bombshell poster was then followed up with another poster campaign featuring two red boxing gloves. The right glove had more taxes written on it, and the left glove had higher prices written on it. This poster campaign, entitled Labour's double whammy, attempted to imply the knockout impact for average voters of Labour in power. Their objective was to demonstrate how Labour policies would 'fuel inflation, raise unemployment, increase interest rates, make mortgages expensive and difficult to get, cause financial chaos and bring back the winter of discontent'(Newton 1992: 139).

The success of the Conservatives propaganda campaign was thus clearly evident as they framed the contest around the economic incompetence of Labour and taxation (Sanders 1992: 171). But not only did Major manage to imply that the economic plight would be worse if Labour acquired office, but he also succeeded in disassociating himself from blame for the recession. When the electorate was asked to apportion blame for the current economic crisis, 47 per cent blamed the worldwide recession, 46 per cent blamed the Thatcher administrations, and only 5 per cent blamed the Major administration. That such economic woes were associated more with the Thatcher administrations than with the Major administration demonstrated that some of the electorate believed that the transition from Thatcher to Major had constituted a change of government (Crewe 1992: 25–8). In the event, the Conservatives secured 336 seats and Labour 271, with the Conservative percentage lead being seven points and the Conservatives securing 42 per cent to Labour on 35 per cent (Dorey 1995a: 242).

Thatcherism as statecraft

Was Thatcherism a success? Was it helpful to the Conservatives? The answers to these two questions are dependent upon when they are answered. If these were questions asked in 1988, the answer would have to be yes. They were a year into a third term in office, with a parliamentary majority of over one hundred, their primary political opponents were engulfed in a debilitating, distracting and protracted leadership election (between Kinnock and Tony Benn), and they had a commanding double-digit lead in the opinion polls (Butler and Kavanagh 1988: 23). The Conservatives had thus been seen to have won the 'battle of ideas' and the arguments of her wet critics within the party seemed to have been pushed to the margins (Dorey et al. 2011: 11). However, that year Andrew Gamble published his seminal account of Thatcherism and their pursuit of a free economy and a strong state. Here he implied that it may be a time-specific form of statecraft for the Conservatives and that it may not be sustainable over the longer term (Gamble 1988).

Thatcher had come to the leadership of the Conservatives at a crossroads. For nearly three decades the party had identified their core belief around the need to provide full employment and thus an acceptance of Keynesianism. Thatcher attempted to challenge this: Keynesianism was not the solution, it was the problem (Taylor 2005a: 136–42). The new core belief was the control of inflation through the pursuit of initially monetarism. This challenge to the traditional assumptions that had defined the party for a generation provoked disquiet. It opened up new labels within the party – her critics and defenders of the status quo were to be derided as wets (a term which was to become associated with one nation) and her advocates were dries. In due course as the Thatcherite emphasis on the free economy and national independence seemed threatened by (or could be facilitated by?) the process of European integration, new divisive labels – Europhiles and Eurosceptic – evolved. That Thatcher was so willing to lead the party from a dry and (later) sceptic position embedded a 'one-of-us' or 'one-of-them' mentality that was to create longer-term party management difficulties (Foley 2002: 27–30).

The traditional one-nation Conservatives, now derided as wets, struggled to adapt to the new core belief of prioritizing inflation at the expense of unemployment. For wets their concerns were both governmental and electoral. They assumed that rising unemployment would undermine any claim to governing competence (McLean 2001: 222). This assumption was disproved in the 1980s, and the Thatcherite method would create the necessary level political argument hegemony to retain office through the politics of deflection (Tomlinson 2007: 12–13). Thatcher attempted to persuade the electorate as to the causes of economic decline which had culminated in the governing crises of the 1970s. Thus any increases in unemployment once the Conservatives were in office were a consequence of addressing the governing failures of the 1970s. Past errors, which had provided the dominance of self-interested and unrepresentative trade union leaders, were the cause as opposed to current policies (Stevens 2002: 120).

Deflecting blame onto the trade unions tied into their positioning of Labour in a negative light. The Labour movement as a whole was depicted as 'sectional' rather than 'national' in terms of their interest, and the Winter of Discontent and the Miners' Strike showcased the implications of producer-dominated power. Such sectional producer-dominated interests had 'hijacked' the economic system as they wanted to solidify 'archaic production strategies'. Conversely the Conservatives were on the side of the consumers and representing the national interest. These new rules of the game forced Labour to defend the increasingly less popular trade union movement, or irritate them by challenging them thus creating internal tactical and strategic dilemmas for Kinnock. A similar logic applied to the Conservative pursuit of privatization in the context of Labour's continuing adherence to public ownership as decreed through clause IV (Stevens 2002: 126–7).

However, perceptions of the Conservatives as unified, competent and thus having argument hegemony flowed from the negatives of Labour. Conservative strengths were relative to the crises from the last Labour administration and the factional infighting thereafter. Thatcherite strategy was partly dependent on Labour's continuing commitment to 'old' Labour and internal infighting, a fact that they could not have anticipated would be so successfully overcome by the emergence of New Labour.

4

Obstacles to adaptation: Continued adherence to Thatcherism 1992–2005

John Major was to face immensely difficult circumstances between 1992 and 1997. McAnulla suggests that he suffered from a 'ghost of the past' in the shape of Thatcher, as well as the 'grim reaper' of being forced to operate with a small and dwindling parliamentary majority (McAnulla 1999: 193–4). For example, Thatcher celebrated Major's general election victory by arguing that 'I don't accept the idea that all of a sudden Major is his own man.' She then concluded that 'Thatcherism will live' and that 'there is no such thing as Majorism' (Thatcher 1992). That combination of dealing with the divisive legacy of Thatcherism, while operating with a small parliamentary majority, prompted Major's outburst in his accidently recorded comments to ITN's Michael Brunson in July 1993. Major commented that

> the real problem is one of a tiny majority. Don't overlook that. I could have done all these clever decisive things which people wanted me to do – but I would have split the Conservative Party into smithereens. And you would have said that I acted like a ham-fisted leader. (Major 1999: 343)

After 1992 Major was unable to exploit the mandate that he had secured. He later admitted 'there was much I hoped to do after the election, but which, as things turned out, I would not achieve' and 'I shall regret this all my days' (Major 1999: 214). Given the scale and speed within which his fourth-term administration was to unravel, Major would later speculate:

> I sometimes wonder what would have happened if we had lost in 1992. Labour, not the Conservatives, would have had to face Black Wednesday

and a Eurosceptic attitude as rife in its ranks as it was in our own. Faced with these troubles, Neil Kinnock would have been hard pressed to keep the left wing of his party at bay. On form, the Conservatives would have won any election that followed a one-term small majority Labour government. Assuming this, some Tories have argued that 1992 was the election we should have lost. What the Tories needed was not another spell in power, but the cold, sharp shock of opposition, an ideological cleansing of the palate. . . . Despite our defeat in 1997, I disagree . . . our victory in 1992 killed socialism in Britain. It also, I must conclude, made the world safe for Tony Blair. Our win meant that between 1992 and 1997 Labour had to change. (Major 1999: 310–11)

From Black Wednesday to Black Thursday 1992–1997

The Major administration descended into chaos in the early stages of their fourth term and never recovered. Their claim to governing competence was shattered by their ejection from the ERM in 1992. Their claim to be unified was shattered during the parliamentary ratification of the Maastricht Treaty during 1992–93, by the withdrawal of the Conservative whip from eight MPs (1994–95), by an unnecessary and futile party leadership contest in 1995 and by the constant infighting over the single European currency. Their claim to govern in the public interest was undermined by a series of sex and financial scandals. Their claim to effective leadership was lost as Major seemed consumed by the demands of leading his fractious party rather than leading the nation (Norton 1998: 77–8).

Of these difficulties the most significant was the lost claim to governing competence. The ERM proved to be a 'political crisis of gargantuan proportions' (Hayton 2012a: 22). Entry had been expected to provide 'a credible framework for economic management' that would serve both an economic and a political purpose. Economically it would 'impose tight monetary discipline on the British economy'. Politically it would shift the responsibility for economic management to 'an externally constituted regime' and a 'system of policy rules bound up with broader European commitments' (Kettell 2008: 631, 637). Thus it would provide an external anchor to aid domestic economic management, with potentially the added benefit of improving relations within Europe.

Britain had entered the ERM in October 1990 when Major was Chancellor and Thatcher was still prime minister. As the previous chapter identified, Thatcher was against entry but she was too weakened to withstand the clamour for entry. In justifying entry Major felt that aligning sterling to the Deutschmark, which was the most inflation-resistant currency within Europe, would limit the impact of inflation within the British economy in the future. However, during the summer of 1992 the position of sterling within the ERM became perilous. The value of sterling declined from DM 2.91 in May to DM 2.81 in July and to DM 2.80 in August which was close to the ceiling of DM 2.778. Options such as seeking a realignment or devaluation of sterling within the ERM, or withdrawal, were deemed to be unacceptable (Lamont 2000: 225). Major chose to defend sterling and its position within the ERM and use reserves to prop up its value (Young 1998: 438). Major left no ambiguity as to the importance that he attached to remaining within the ERM. He staked his reputation on remaining within in a speech to the Scottish CBI just days before withdrawal. Those who questioned the merit of membership were dismissed as 'quack doctors peddling their wares', as 'miracle cures simply don't work – never have, never will'. He ended with words that would humiliate him within days:

> All my adult life I have seen British governments driven off their virtuous pursuit of low inflation by market problems or political pressures. I was under no illusion when I took Britain into the ERM. I said at the time that membership was no soft option. The soft option, the devaluers' option, the inflationary option, would be a betrayal of our future. (Major 1999: 326)

Currency speculators did not believe that there was a prospect of economic recovery without devaluation. Massive instability in the currency markets followed involving heavy speculative activity against the weaker currencies. A wave of selling resulted in sterling sliding to the floor of the ERM. Interest rates were increased from 10 to 12 per cent in an attempt to arrest the slide. No market impact was detectable. So interest rates were increased further to 15 per cent. Again no impact was evident (Lamont 2000: 249). An administration that had repeatedly ruled out devaluation had had a devaluation effectively imposed upon it against its will. It was an expensive failure and cost the taxpayer £3–4 billion or the equivalent of £20 per head of the UK population (Stephens 1996: 253–5).

Black Wednesday was to be the defining moment of the Major government, and the new leader of the Labour Party, John Smith, captured its impact on Major: 'he is the devalued Prime Minister of a devalued Government' (HC Debates, Vol. 212, Col. 22, 24 September 1992). Faith that the Conservatives were competent plummeted in the opinion polls as Labour became viewed as the party best equipped to manage the economy (Denver 1998: 19). The image of policy failure and incompetence created by the ERM disaster would remain for the rest of the Parliament (Norton 1998: 80).

Having stated during the election campaign that ERM membership was the central tenet of their economic policy strategy and their means of countering inflation, the Major government was now operating in a policy vacuum. Kenneth Clarke, who at the time was Home Secretary, but would soon move to the Treasury, admitted that 'I reflected on that day that I'd never been in a government that didn't have an economic policy' (Young 1998: 440). They needed to rapidly construct an entirely new counter-inflationary framework. However, the political imperative of tax cuts was not deemed to be viable due to wider economic constraints. Economic policy formulation was in a structural bind due to the fragility of the economy and the recession and the need to control public expenditure limited the choices available. Stringent corrective action was required. Lamont set about implementing a punitive package of tax increases, which included higher national insurance contributions for employees; freezing of personal tax allowances; a reduction in tax allowances for married couples and mortgage holders; and the initiation of a straightforward tax increase through the extension of value added tax to domestic fuel and power (Denver 1998: 22).

The reaction within the PCP was devastating. Many feared that one of their main electoral assets, their reputation as the party of lower taxation was being blunted (Gove 1995: 238–9). Initially Major stuck by Lamont and withstood the temptation to dismiss him after Black Wednesday. He waited until after the implementation of the unpopular package of taxation increases upon which they had agreed. The rationale for his delayed removal was that Lamont's position had become untenable as he had lost the confidence of industry, of the City and of some of his Cabinet colleagues (Major 1999: 679). Lamont felt that the same could easily be said of Major. A vocal enemy had been created (Seldon 1997: 376). The new chancellor, the pro-European Clarke maintained a tight fiscal squeeze. In the November 1993 Budget, Clarke continued the strategy of reducing the deficit by reducing public expenditure and increasing taxation. Measures implemented included a freeze on income tax allowance; increases in excise duties; reductions in the value of mortgage tax relief; restrictions on married couples allowance; the introduction of new taxes on insurance premiums; punitive taxes on motorists and smokers and the implementation of a public sector pay freeze, which would contribute a 1.3 per cent cut in public expenditure, and reductions in spending on defence, education and transport (Thompson 1996: 180).

Their ejection from the ERM and the need to raise taxation were not the only indications of governing incompetence. The Major administration was damaged by its handling of the pit closure programme in the autumn of 1992 (Negrine 1995: 45–61). Over 20,000 letters of protest were sent to Downing Street. Protesters took to the streets with placards stating 'Sack Major, NOT 30,000 Miners' (Routledge 1994: 232–4). Slowly the crisis was defused and the sense of outrage would dissipate. However, this was only after Major had been forced to back away from the original proposal, which resulted in a review of their energy policy and a reappraisal of the viability of 21 of the pits earmarked for closure (Crick 1997: 393). The cumulative effect of these disasters undermined Conservative electoral strategy. Thatcherite strategy had rested on shaping electoral attitudes around the Conservatives as competent, in order to negate the Labour attack that they were cruel or harsh (Hogg and Hill 1995: 125). Black Wednesday and the pit-closure fiasco suggested the Major administration was cruel but incompetent (Bale 2010: 42).

It was against this backdrop of governing incompetence that party divisions intensified. Black Wednesday unleashed latent Euroscepticism. Thatcher herself exploited this by encouraging Eurosceptic rebels to believe that her removal had been part of a Europhile plot (Gill 2003: 123). Preventing the parliamentary ratification of the Maastricht negotiations, for which Major was immensely protective but had delayed pushing through before the election, was to be the battleground. Major would gain the parliamentary approval that he needed, but at a considerable price. It would be completed after 18 months of debilitating and divisive parliamentary trench warfare. With a small majority the Whips' Office would impose some of the most brutal and controversial whipping in parliamentary history (Baker et al. 1993: 158). As the rebellions continued, the passage of the legislation was only secured by a vote of confidence. Major was thus creating a mutually assured destruction strategy for himself and the rebels given the position of the party in the opinion polls at the time. This was Major's 'take me to Maastricht or I will kill us all' option (Baker et al. 1994: 44). All but one did and Major had secured his objective. Thatcher intervened to stress that she still felt that Major was being duped into a federalist strategy and that Maastricht was a staging post to the single currency (Seldon 1997: 251–3, 328).

On the evening of securing ratification Major's frustrations in dealing with the legacy of Thatcherism were exposed during his accidently recorded post interview comments to ITN (in July 1993):

> Just think it through from my perspective. You are the Prime Minister, with a majority of eighteen, a party that is still harking back to the golden age that was and is now reinvented. You have three right wing members of the Cabinet who actually resign. What happens in the parliamentary party? I could bring in other people. But where do you think most of this poison is coming from? From the dispossessed and the never possessed. You can think of ex-ministers who are going around causing all sorts of trouble. We don't want another three more of the bastards out there. (Major 1999: 343)

A year later, in autumn 1994, when eight Conservatives abstained on a parliamentary division relating to increases to Britain's budgetary contribution to the EU, (which was a confidence motion) Major removed the Conservative whip from them. This was the toughest disciplinary sanction that had ever been imposed in the history of the party. However, the decision to remove the Conservative whip from the eight abstainers inflicted greater damage upon the credibility of Major than it did upon the eight non-complying Conservative parliamentarians. Their readmission 6 months later constituted an ignominious surrender. Without any apparent commitment being made by them to be loyal in future, it left Major looking inept (Alderman 1996a: 19).

The Eurosceptic rebels were still vexed about the fallout from Black Wednesday. The resultant need to increase taxation had stimulated electoral concerns about whether the Conservatives could be trusted. That decline in trust within the electorate was intensified by the 'sleaze' allegations that would engulf the Major administration (Worcester and Mortimer 1999: 71). Numerous Conservatives were involved in sex scandals. Sexual impropriety was then compounded by allegations of wider financial corruption. Two Conservative parliamentarians, Graham Riddick and David Tredinnick, were exposed as being willing to accept cash in return for asking parliamentary questions and three Conservative parliamentarians, Jonathan Aitken, Neil Hamilton and Tim Smith were exposed as being willing to accept hospitality from Mohamed Al-Fayed, the owner of Harrods (See 2013: 114–16). As a response, Major set up the Commission on Standards in Public Life under Lord Nolan, which led, in 1995, to the creation of a new Commons Standards and Privileges Committee (Butler and Kavanagh 1997: 16).

Sleaze began to develop in the aftermath of Major's 'Back to Basics' speech to the 1993 Annual Conference. Given the above governing difficulties, Major was sensitive to the jibe that his administration was losing dominance of elite debate. The demand to define and thereby renew Conservatism led Major to launch his 'Back to Basics' campaign. It was meant to challenge fashionable theories on health, education and crime and in doing so address concerns associated with traditional middle England. However, social conservatives were keen to use the language of Back to Basics to launch a war on permissiveness and portray Labour as a party of the 1960s – a party representing drugs, pornography and family breakdown. Those Conservatives motivated by traditional morality implied that the traditional family was the essential building block of society and that single parenthood was symbolic of social disintegration and a bloated welfare state (Baston 2000: 156–8). Social conservative parliamentarians began to use it as a vehicle to attack single mothers and preach sexual fidelity. They felt justified in doing so as 'rolling back the permissive society' was the underdeveloped aspect of the Thatcher revolution (Fry 1998: 145).

The print media believed it was a moral crusade, meaning that any Conservative not living up to the distorted premise of Back to Basics needed to be exposed (Bale 2010: 46). This justified the lurid tabloid headlines that emerged post 1993, which would destroy Back to Basics as a viable political theme for the Conservatives. It was abandoned, although an increasingly hostile print media and the Labour opposition continued to use it as a means of highlighting the hypocrisy of the Conservatives (Baston 2000: 161).

The Conservatives were displaying the classic symptoms of a degenerating and long-serving administration. Could their decline be arrested or was it irreversible? Was there anything that could be done to undo the damage of the preceding 3 years? Could the Conservatives recast themselves and reclaim their mantle as the natural party of government? They had after all reversed their decline in the mid-point of the previous Parliament. While the actual symptoms of decline remained, a mirage of renewal while in government was created by the removal of Thatcher and the emergence of Major (Bale 2010: 48). A precedent now existed. Would the removal of Major midterm enable the Conservatives to reclaim the party of government characteristics, which had been lost over the preceding 3 years?

Speculation about the probability of a challenge to Major in the autumn of 1995 was more intense than in the three previous years. Rather than wait for his critics to find a candidate to challenge him in the autumn, Major chose to resign in June 1995 to seek a new mandate to lead the Conservatives into the next general election. In announcing his dramatic plan for self-preservation, Major concluded:

> The Conservative Party must make its choice. Every leader is leader only with the support of his party. That is true of me as well. That is why I am not prepared to tolerate the present situation. In short, it is time to put up or shut up. (Seldon 1997: 571)

Major hoped that his critics would show themselves to be cowards. If he was re-elected unopposed it would also make it far harder for his backbench critics to continue to destabilize him. It soon became clear that Major would not secure this best case scenario of an unopposed re-election. Speculation initially focused on Lamont. However, the critics of Major feared that Lamont may not inflict enough damage to Major in the first ballot to force his resignation (Denham and O'Hara 2008: 28). There was an acceptance that the preferred candidate of the right, Michael Portillo, would not be willing to challenge Major outright. Portillo was willing to stand when the leadership was vacant – that is, as Major had done in 1990, but he was not willing to suffer the fate of Heseltine in 1990 of standing to win, but losing and being accused of disloyalty. Similar concerns explain why Heseltine and Clarke did not stand (Heppell 2008b: 100–2).

However, John Redwood resigned from the Cabinet in order to dispute the leadership with Major. The problem for Redwood was the feeling that he could not defeat Major outright. Many Conservatives came to the conclusion that a vacancy being created by Major deciding to resign due to a substantial protest vote going to Redwood would lead to further prolonged conflict. A bitter conflict between candidates from the Europhile left (Clarke and/or Heseltine) and the Eurosceptic right (Portillo and/or Redwood) would leave the eventual victor with an ungovernable party (Alderman 1996b: 323). The Major campaign managed to pull many Conservative parliamentarians back to Major by the fear of something worse (i.e. other options would intensify factional strife) rather than the hope of something better (Heppell 2008b: 105).

Major won by 218 votes to 89 for Redwood and 22 abstentions and he overcame his self-imposed hurdle of 215 votes, which was what he felt he needed to justify continuing (Major 1999: 620). In retirement, Major was clear about the significance of the exercise to the party:

> My re-election as leader postponed – and, I hope, saved the party from an irrevocable split over European policy. It was very likely it would have haemorrhaged if a leader had been chosen who gave unconditional backing to one side or the other in an argument so fundamental to the protagonists that none was prepared to concede. (Major 1999: 647)

The put-up or shut-up strategy ensured that Major was secure until the general election. However, his continuation through a process that highlighted his weaknesses and the endemic divisions within the Conservative Party, worked to the long-term electoral advantage of New Labour. (Foley 2002: 197–8). Significantly, it did not stem the flow of criticism of Major from Thatcherite critics on the backbenchers or within the press (Fowler 2008: 70–2). They felt that the Major era amounted to a betrayal of the Thatcherite policy agenda (Dorey 1999: 225). It is true that shifts in policy prioritization and direction were evident with regard to the poll tax, the commitment to membership of the ERM, the rhetoric of constructive engagement with Europe which explained the commitment to the Treaty of European Union, the attitude towards the public services and the approach to the conflict within Northern Ireland. However, despite this academics have argued that the Major era amounted to a broad adherence to the Thatcherite policy agenda and as such the betrayal thesis lacks conviction (Bale 2010: 61). There was evidence of minimal deviation and a clear adaptation in terms of style and rhetoric but there was no real evidence of retreat and betrayal. It may not have amounted to a zealous continuation but it did constitute steady consolidation or as Evans defines it 'Thatcherism on autopilot' (Evans 1999: 175).

What probably caused their criticism was the inability of the Conservatives to overcome the flat-lining in the opinion polls, which had remained since Black Wednesday. Of real concern was the fear of a vote-less recovery. As the parliament entered its final stages, it was clear that improvements in economic performance were not translating into perceptions of economic and governing competence vis-à-vis the Conservatives (Denver 1998: 34–45). Despite the fact that there was a gradual improvement in key economic indicators, (which suggested that the corrective measures implemented were having the intended impact), negative perceptions of the Conservatives vis-à-vis economic management remained. The electorate simply refused to give the Major administration any credit for the improving economic position in the latter part of the parliament

(Dorey et al. 2011: 18). Given the following indicators this was immensely frustrating for Major:

1 Unemployment was as high as 3 million during the recession in 1992 (or 9.8 per cent) of the working populous but had fallen and was still falling at 1.75 million (7.5 per cent) by 1997.

2 The inflation rate had been as high as 9.7 per cent at the time of the downfall of Thatcher, yet for the duration of the second Major Government, it oscillated between a low of 1.6 and a high of 4.1, which constituted the longest period of low inflation for half a century.

3 Interest rates were reduced following ejection from the Exchange Rate Mechanism and stabilized around 5–6 per cent for the final 4 years of the Major Government.

4 Finally, although the economy was contracting by 1.5 per cent in 1991, the rate of growth had advanced to 3 per cent in 1993 and 4 per cent in 1994 (Heppell 2006: 160).

Major claimed that his administration had left a 'benevolent legacy' and they had eradicated the inflationary cycle (Major 1999: 688–99). However, reductions in the standard rate of taxation in the 1995 budget and then again in 1996 (down to 23p) could not remove the memory of broken promises on taxation in the earlier part of the Parliament, and Black Wednesday had established the image of governing incompetence and disunity (Hayton 2012a: 23–5).

Having refused to adhere to demands for a referendum on the Treaty of European Union, Major attempted to craft a semblance of unity through a 'negotiate and decide' policy stance on Economic and Monetary Union, which would be confirmed via a referendum (Bale 2010: 59). The rationale for holding a referendum on Economic and Monetary Union (agreed to in April 1996) was designed for internal party reasons rather than national interest. The ambivalent Major believed that this should be acceptable to Europhiles, (as the single currency had not been ruled out in perpetuity), and Eurosceptics, (many of whom had long argued for a referendum on the issue).

However, the civil war over the single European currency dominated the prolonged general election campaign of 1997. Major had hoped that his agnostic stance would be sufficient to bridge the divide between Europhile and Eurosceptic alike, thus allowing the Conservatives to provide a façade of unity when campaigning. However, it was increasingly clear that many candidates were openly defying the 'negotiate and decide' formula (Bale 2010: 63). In a futile attempt to stem the tide of dissidence, Major decided to abandon a planned Party Election broadcast on unemployment figures, (which were favourable to the Conservatives), and speak directly to the camera for a full 4 minutes about Europe. However, he appeared to be speaking to his internal party critics rather than the wider electorate when he said 'whether you agree with me or disagree with me, like me or loathe me, don't bind my hands when I am negotiating on behalf of the British people' (Butler and Kavanagh 1997: 106).

Major argued that, first, joining, (or not joining), the single European currency was the most important issue facing Britain for a generation; second, that the electorate should vote for the party that he leads despite their divisions on this seminal dilemma; and third, despite the importance of the decision, he was not going to explain what he would do if re-elected. Major believed that he would enhance his chances of re-election by publicly demonstrating how deep the divisions were within his party, and how he was simply unable to deal with them. Blair countered with a brilliantly succinct sound bite: 'there are two Conservative parties fighting this election. . . . John Major is in charge of neither of them' (Seldon 1997: 723).

While New Labour and Blair had a clearly defined strategy on how they sought to portray the Conservatives, the same could not be said of how the Conservatives sought to portray New Labour. Was their best line of attack to portray Blair as a 'socialist wolf, red in tooth and claw but dressed in Bambi designer-chic' or should they say Blair was 'an opportunistic closet Tory who was stealing Tory policies' (Williams 1998: 69)? Regardless, the improving economic environment in the latter part of the Parliament and reductions in the basic rate of income tax had failed to resonate with the electorate. The Conservatives were thereby trapped in a bind: because the electorate remembered their indirect tax increases at the beginning of the Parliament, and disregarded the reductions in direct taxation at the end of the Parliament, so a 1992 style tax bombshell attack on New Labour would not work. New Labour had the whip hand on the tax issue:

> New Labour countered the attack with two different tactics. Firstly, it made very limited tax commitments, and one of these, a windfall tax on the profits of privatized utilities, was popular amongst voters because of public concerns about profiteering in these industries. Secondly, Labour frontbenchers repeatedly claimed that there had been twenty-two tax rises since 1992, and that these were the equivalent to 7p in the pound in the basic rate of income tax. (Whiteley 1997: 550)

Moreover, New Labour constantly reminded the electorate of sleaze (e.g. cash for questions); the perception of the Conservatives as apologists for greed and selfishness (e.g. boardroom greed and the revolving door ushering Conservative ministers into lucrative jobs in the private sector); and value added tax on fuel (i.e. the impact of which was greatest on the elderly and economically disadvantaged). By doing so, they aimed to show that the Conservatives were uncaring. Standing opposite to the incompetent and uncaring Conservatives was *New* Labour. It retained its traditional reputation for being caring but they had managed to recast themselves as a party of economic trustworthiness. By framing themselves as competent *and* caring, they defined the political terrain (Hilton 1997: 48).

Before the general election campaign began, Major realized that the Conservatives were destined to lose. He had hoped to restrict the New Labour majority to around 20–30 seats. This would have ensured that there was a solid Conservative parliamentary base, and thus a return to government after one-term in opposition was a realistic possibility. This scenario required a parliamentary presence of around 260–280 seats and a 35 per cent vote share. In the final days Conservative expectations were adjusted downwards to 240 seats and a Labour majority of around 80 (Seldon 1997: 713, 734). Just before the polls closed on the day of the election, however, Major was informed that

> exit polls suggested that the revised prediction of the Tory party winning 240 seats had been a grave over-estimation. It was suggested that the result would be much worse than he had ever dared to imagine. Major, went very, very quiet. (Seldon 1997: 734)

From compassionate Conservatism to the core vote strategy 1997–2005

The scale of their electoral rejection was so pronounced that the likelihood of the Conservatives reclaiming power inside 5 years looked extremely remote (Redwood 2004: 141). Their share of the vote at 30.7 per cent was their lowest since the coming of mass democracy and represented an 11.2 per cent reduction from 1992 and their lowest post-war return beating their previous worst of 35.8 per cent in October 1974. Their representation in Parliament was halved with 165 members considerably lower than their previous worst at 213 members in 1945. Labour had won with the biggest parliamentary majority of the post-war era (179) on the back of a 10 per cent swing from Conservative to Labour. The Conservatives were officially the one-nation party as they had no representation at all in Scotland and Wales (Butler and Kavanagh 1997: 244).

They were ill prepared for the demands of opposition. In terms of resources, they were limited both in terms of personnel and finances. They had a remarkably small parliamentary representation from which to construct a shadow ministerial team. Few had been in opposition before and many experienced figures of the Thatcher/Major era retreated to the backbenchers. Financially the party was in a very weak position. They were close to bankruptcy and the election campaign had left the party £8 million in the red (Snowdon 2010: 46–7).

They were immediately thrown into a leadership election as Major resigned. A large field of candidates subsequently emerged. But the most well-known candidates were not available. Health fears prevented Heseltine from standing as a candidate for the Europhile left, and Portillo, the preferred candidate of the Eurosceptic right had lost his parliamentary seat. Three of the candidates were strongly associated with the Eurosceptic right – that is Redwood, Michael Howard and Peter Lilley. The most popular candidate with the electorate was Clarke whose pro-Europeanism would mean he would ultimately lose out to the youngest candidate, William Hague, who was regarded as a Eurosceptic, but whose association with that faction was less pronounced then Redwood, Howard and Lilley (Heppell 2008b: 125).

The first ballot eliminated Lilley (24 votes) and Howard (23 votes) and left Clarke leading Hague by 49 to 41 votes, with Redwood third with 27 votes. The second ballot eliminated Redwood (on 38 votes) and Clarke remained in the lead over Hague by 64 to 62 votes. Somewhat surprisingly the defeated Redwood chose to back Clarke claiming that they were in broad agreement on domestic policy, and that a free vote could be granted on European policy, including members of the shadow Cabinet (Denham and O'Hara 2008: 34). The Hague camp then 'benefitted' from the intervention of Thatcher. The prospect of Clarke winning the leadership forced her to end her position of neutrality, whereupon she provided 'open and active support' in preparation for the final ballot (Alderman 1998: 11–12). Redwood failed to bring enough of his supporters across to Clarke and Hague was elected by 92 to 70 votes, with two abstentions. However, Hague entered the leadership with two constraints that undermined his authority: first, the best Thatcherite candidate was not available (Portillo); and second, he was seen as the ABC candidate – anyone but Clarke (Heppell and Hill 2008: 63–91).

Hague had campaigned for the party leadership on the optimistic slogan of a Fresh Start leading to a Fresh Future. He believed that the re-branding of the party would involve organizational reform and then policy reappraisal. Organizational reform would be geared towards three objectives: first, the creation of a modern integrated party to aid electioneering; second, increasing activist involvement; and third, addressing the ageing and shrinking membership of the party (Norton 2001: 73–4).

Before attempting to proceed with this, Hague sought an endorsement of his party leadership election victory from the party membership and the agenda on which he campaigned that is, unity, decentralization, democracy, integrity and openness. He reinforced these principles for a comprehensive review of the organizational structures of the party in a document entitled *Our Party: Blueprint for Change*. Party members were then balloted to secure their endorsement of Hague as party leader and his change agenda. The 1997 Annual Conference provided Hague with the reinforcing mandate that he needed to proceed. When balloted 142, 299 (81 per cent) of the party members said yes and 34,092 (19 per cent) said no (Norton 2001: 74). Once approved, those proposals were instituted in 1998 under the title *The Fresh Future* (Collings and Seldon 2001: 626).

The organizational reforms set out in *The Fresh Future* brought the three formerly separate elements of the Conservative Party – the parliamentary, voluntary and professional wings – together as a single entity with a constitution, rules and a national membership (Peele 1998: 141–7). A new party board was set up as the supreme decision-making body. It was set up to meet monthly and would comprise seventeen members, five of whom, including the Party Chairman, would be appointed by the leader; five would be activists from the newly formed National Convention, and the remaining four members were to come from Scotland, Wales, the Association of Conservative Councillors and the 1922 Committee. In addition, a National Convention was set up to replace the Central Council. Like the Central Council it would meet twice yearly and would comprise national, regional and area officials, officers of constituency associations and members of other affiliated bodies, such as women's and youth groups. The National Convention would keep the party leadership informed of grass-roots views and would advise the Board on all aspects of extra-parliamentary organization (Kelly 1999: 28).

The six senior officers of the National Convention then formed the National Convention Executive, which was to have day-to-day responsibility for the voluntary section of the Conservative Party, with the Executive being responsible to the Board. Ordinary members were encouraged to contribute their views on policy through the Conservative Policy Forum. Under this system discussion papers were to be sent out to constituencies, with activist feedback forwarded to the shadow Cabinet for consideration (Kelly 2001a: 332). Finally, a centrally administered membership list would be established for the first time. This shift to a national party was significant – previously supporters did not join the national party; there was no national party, but simply a collective of constituency parties (Norton 2001: 74). The existence of national party membership list enabled the party to communicate directly with all party members but it was also necessary to enable the party to complete the one-member one-vote stage of future party leadership elections (Lees-Marshment and Quayle 2001: 204).

The new party leadership election procedures removed the obligation for the incumbent leader to submit themselves to an annual re-election and the requirement that a challenge be instituted by an individual Conservative parliamentarian. Instead, a vote of confidence could be held at any time if proposed by at least 15 per cent of the PCP, and a full-scale party leadership election would be initiated if the incumbent failed to win this initial vote. If the no-confidence vote failed, then another confidence motion would not be permitted during the next 12 months. If a no-confidence motion was carried, the incumbent party leader would be forced to resign and would be barred from standing in the ensuing vacant party leadership election. If there were only two candidates, their names would be submitted to a ballot of all party members, who had been members for at least 6 months prior to the no-confidence motion, on the basis of one member, one vote. If there were more than two candidates, then a series of eliminative primary ballots would be held within the PCP, until only two candidates were left (Kelly 1999: 29).

Organizational reform was necessary, but was not enough; the party needed a coherent strategy to demonstrate change (Bale 2010: 82–6). Initially there was an apologetic tone. Hague acknowledged that the Conservatives had made mistakes in government, such as entry into the ERM (Holmes 1998: 136). Hague believed that the party needed to accept culpability, then draw a line on it and move on politically. He accepted that the PCP had become viewed as conceited, selfish and factional and had a tendency towards moral preaching. Hague was keen to end the association of the Conservatives with intolerance, traditionalism and stuffiness. To create a new image of modern, inclusive Conservatism that was outward reaching, tolerant and pluralistic, Hague instructed Conservatives to break free from old structures (the justification for internal organizational reform) and old habits and modes of thought, which implied that the party needed a fundamental reappraisal of its policies and identity (Norton 2001: 73).

Policy development, however, lacked coherence. By the time of the 2001 general election, two types of Conservatism had been advanced. Hague mark 1 or *Fresh Conservatism* accepted the need to move beyond Thatcherism. It recognized that continued adherence to traditional moral values led to accusations of being out of touch and that voters could not relate to them. For Hague, a pragmatic acceptance of social liberalism and reconfigured attitudes towards single mothers, homosexuals and ethnic minorities would enable the Conservatives to be viewed as compassionate and inclusive (Kelly 2001b: 198). However, this tentative attempt to challenge the right of New Labour to colonize the centre ground of British politics failed to make any discernable impact upon the opinion polls, and thus it would be abandoned in 1999 (Collings and Seldon 2001: 628).

The trigger for abandonment was a speech delivered by Lilley who was now the Deputy Leader of the Conservative Party. Lilley confirmed that the Conservatives needed to broaden their electoral appeal by shifting their focus away from solely economic concerns. His emphasis on the importance of education and health and his desire to reconfigure perceptions of Conservatism around the public services was seen by many on the right as a repudiation of Thatcherism. Rather than stimulating an intellectual debate on the meaning of Conservatism, it provoked emotional and elemental passions about the legacy of Thatcherism. The chaos that ensued demonstrated that attempting to challenge Thatcherism and change the party was too dangerous (Taylor 2005a: 146). Hague initially tried to weather the political storm, but the scale of discontent among the shadow Cabinet, the PCP and the activist base, overwhelmed him. To shore up his position, Hague dismissed Lilley, and thereafter abandoned the attempt to formulate a more inclusive narrative of Conservatism (Walters 2001: 118). To radically alter the attitudes of the party requires evidence that there are electoral rewards in doing so. In this sense, *Fresh Conservatism* was flawed by two fundamental political failings – first, the electorate were not responding positively to it and second, because of this and many of their own prejudices, Conservative parliamentarians and the wider party membership did not like it (Taylor 2005a: 146–8).

Hague Mark II emerged throughout 1999 through the language of the *Common Sense Revolution* which then informed the draft manifesto *Believing in Britain* in 2000. This would then underpin the core vote strategy in the general election campaign of 2001. Hague moved to a populist socially authoritarian agenda as he pandered to the Eurosceptic and socially conservative sentiment within the PCP and the wider party membership. The emphasis was now on anti-Europeanism, attacking bogus asylum seekers, law and order, cutting taxation and bureaucracy and promoting marriage and the family (Taylor 2005a: 148–9). Hague also began berating the opinions of what he called the supposedly trendy liberal elite. Such was its reactive and opportunistic approach that Hague was dubbed 'Billy Bandwagon' and was accused of chasing panaceas (Walters 2001: 105–15). Hague had jumped on a bandwagon to nowhere. This demonstrated an absence of a coherent and settled political and electoral strategy, with its inconsistencies being seen to be a by-product of their internal divisions.

The economic ideological divide had largely been resolved (Garnett 2003: 157). The Thatcherite economic dries were now clearly in the ascendant and the interventionist wets were clearly marginalized (Heppell and Hill 2008: 63–91). Most of those who were interventionist wets were also Europhiles, and it was on this ideological divide that they vented their dissatisfaction with the internal party management of Hague. Given the increasing growth of Euroscepticism and his view of how ambivalence had scarred his predecessor, Hague abandoned the compromise stance, of 'negotiate and decide', that Major had adopted on the vexed question of the single European currency. He ruled out British membership of the single European currency in the next Parliament irrespective of a referendum. This shift to a more sceptical position would culminate in presenting Conservatism as the defender of the national currency. It created policy distinction and would allow the Conservatives to establish clear blue water between themselves and the government (Kelly 2001b: 201). There was a contradiction surrounding the policy. Hague had commented that the single currency exists for all time and that should Britain enter, then it 'could find itself trapped in a burning building with no exits'. The logical concomitant to this argument, which would be intellectually coherent, would be to rule out membership in principle, not for the lifetime of the next Parliament (Holmes 1998: 138).

However, the shift to a more sceptical stance did not end the factional infighting. By moving away from the option of entry, he lost from his shadow Cabinet pro-Europeans such as David Curry, Ian Taylor and later Stephen Dorrell (Bale 2010: 79). Given the refusal of the two leading pro-Europeans, Clarke and Heseltine, to serve in his shadow Cabinet, this meant that pro-European representation was absent from the elite level of the party. While Major had sought an inclusive strategy or incorporating both ideological perspectives in the Cabinet and then sought to unify via discussion and compromise, Hague adopted an exclusive strategy, in which a Europhilic perspective was now absent. His attempt to unify by marginalization largely failed; dissent would remain. For example, Heseltine and Clarke publicly endorsed the Europhile position of Blair, by sharing a platform with him as he began his 'Britain in Europe' campaign (Kelly 2001b: 201–2).

Their fratricidal ideological struggles extended beyond Europe. Just as the economic ideological divide had been superseded by the European ideological divide in the late-Thatcherite era, the European ideological divide became increasingly overshadowed by the ideological conflict between socially inclusive liberals and socially authoritarian conservatives. This ideological divide became tangled up in debates on strategy and electoral recovery. Inclusive social liberals, increasingly coalescing around the revisionist Portillo (re-elected into Parliament in 1999) were also viewed as party modernizers. They argued that modern Conservatism needed to be inclusive and reach out to minority groups within society and display greater understanding and acceptance of alternative lifestyles (Garnett 2003: 117). The tension between the modernizing socially liberal and the socially conservative wings of the party came to match the European policy divide in terms of the difficulties that it was presenting for Hague (Collings and Seldon 2001: 628–9).

In addition to the continuing image of disunity was the problematic image of Hague as a potential prime minister in waiting. Although he was an effective parliamentarian, he lacked popular appeal and he undermined his reputation by his inability to adhere to a settled political strategy. Conservatives were left bemused by the contradictory agenda of their party leader and the impression left was that he focused too much on short-term tactics and not enough on long-term strategy (Bale 2010: 67–133). Furthermore, his style of party leadership was perceived as weak. Despite being a gifted public orator and a devastatingly effective parliamentarian, he was deemed to be inferior in the modern stylistics of politics, at which Blair excelled (Nadler 2000: 209–11). Hague was not user friendly and the party could not utilize his political image for electoral benefit (Broughton 2003: 203–4). The Conservatives compounded these limitations of image by the manner in which they sought to present Hague to the electorate. His appearance at the Notting Hill Carnival and his wearing of a baseball cap embossed with *HAGUE* were public relations disasters of the highest order, and served to establish and then reinforce an image of him as a political lightweight (Snowdon 2010: 62).

The Conservatives hurtled head long into what was generally regarded as a misguided general election campaign. Based around the core-vote strategy, it attempted to ensure that the known 30 per cent plus of Conservatives felt mobilized to vote (Butler and Kavanagh 2001: 54). It was based obsessively around right-wing themes, tax, asylum, and most significantly around Europe and the single European currency, which was encapsulated around the campaign slogan 'save the pound' (Collings and Seldon 2001: 630). This was despite the fact that these issues were of low importance to the electorate when compared to pensions, health and education. Collings and Seldon have eloquently identified the insularity of the approach adopted:

> the hard core of increasingly elderly committed Tory voters no doubt felt their spines tingle as they marched to the polling booths, honoured to play their part in the epic struggle for the pound's survival. But back in the real world, the critical mass of moderate voters . . . saw William Hague and . . . voted Labour. (Collings and Seldon 2001: 630)

The outcome was catastrophic. A sense of déjà vu characterized the outcome. Indeed it appeared to be a mere punctuation mark in the continuing narrative of New Labour hegemony. The parliamentary majority for New Labour was reduced from 179 to 167 and thus fell a long way short of single figures. Conservative representation increased from 165 to 166 parliamentarians. Their share of the popular vote had increased by only 1 percentage point from 30.7 per cent to 31.7 per cent. In a low turnout (only 59 per cent of the electorate voted) the Conservative vote had shrunk by another 1.2 million votes. It was now down to 8.3 million votes. They were 6 million short of the 14 million plus votes that they had secured to secure their fourth successive term just 9 years earlier. That vote base was the smallest Conservative return since 1929 when there was a smaller electorate (Butler and Kavanagh 2001: 251).

Hague had set himself a target of 240 to 260 seats to justify remaining as leader or a Labour majority of around 50 (Bale 2010: 135). His immediate resignation put to the test the new procedures relating to the extension of the franchise to the mass membership. This meant that if more than two candidates emerged, then the PCP would conduct a series of ballots until only two candidates remained, whereupon those two candidates would be presented to the party membership who, on the basis of one member, one vote, would determine the succession (Denham and O'Hara 2008: 53–8).

Five candidates emerged. Three were assumed to be peripheral and relatively lightweight candidates. First, there was former junior minister and current Party Chairman, Michael Ancram. Although he was a moderate sceptic, he hoped that his consensual style would appeal to party loyalists, who would gravitate to him as the candidate best equipped to unify the party. However, he was seen as a 'stop-gap' option (Bale 2010: 135). Second, there was another former junior minister, David Davis. The fact that he had opted out of frontbench responsibilities during the Hague era meant that he could be seen as being disassociated with the errors made during the previous parliament. Third, there was Iain Duncan Smith, who had no ministerial experience as his political reputation had been shaped by his status as a critic of the Maastricht Treaty during the Major era. Europhiles were particularly concerned about his Euroscepticism; while social liberals worried about by his reputation for authoritarian social conservatism. Over and beyond these limitations were concerns about his public image (Carter and Alderman 2002: 573).

It was assumed that Ancram, Davis and Duncan Smith would be eliminated and that the two heavyweight candidates – Clarke and Portillo – would be those who would be presented to the mass membership. Clarke, the Butler of his generation, stood again for the party leadership. The strengths and weaknesses of the Clarke candidature were exactly the same as 4 years earlier. He could offer experience, competence and electoral appeal. His committed Europhilia remained an obstacle. Could he secure enough votes from an overwhelmingly Eurosceptic PCP to ensure that he was one of the two candidates presented to the mass membership? Portillo offered Cabinet experience, and he possessed a high public profile and personal charisma. He was also the candidate who had engaged in the deepest examination of the complex difficulties facing contemporary Conservatism and a willingness to modernize in search of electoral recovery. However, his search for modernization through social liberalism had mobilized a growing army of critics from his former constituency of Thatcherites. Many of them were now implacably against him (Carter and Alderman 2002: 570–8).

The first parliamentary ballot ended with Portillo winning but with Davis and Ancram tying for the last place. Both should have withdrawn but insisted on a re-run. Again Portillo was the victor leading on 50 votes to Duncan Smith on 42 and Clarke on 39. With Ancram and Davis losing support from the first ballot, they both withdrew. The PCP now had to decide which two from Clarke, Portillo and Duncan Smith should be presented to the mass membership. Despite having won both the initial ballots it was Portillo who was eliminated in the final ballot. The party membership would have to select either Clarke, a popular, well-liked, experienced moderate, or Duncan Smith, an unknown, inexperienced ideologue. However, Norton argues that the screening process had produced the worst possible option for the party. He suggests that:

Had the choice been between Portillo and Clarke, then whichever of the two men won, would have resulted in the election of a charismatic political heavyweight with high public visibility. To some extent, it would have been a "win/lose" contest, a Portillo victory having the potential to widen popular support for the party, a Clarke victory having similar potential, but with the prospect of a potentially disastrous party split. In the event party members were offered what appeared to be a "lose/lose" contest. (Norton 2005: 39)

Clarke and Duncan Smith campaigned for 2 months to secure the endorsement of the mass membership. The level of acrimony in the campaign was unprecedented. The Duncan Smith camp attempted to smear Clarke over his business dealings. The Clarke camp derided Duncan Smith as an extremist and implied that his agenda would attract racists to the party. (Carter and Alderman 2002: 584). Once again, Clarke was rejected for an inferior candidate, as Duncan Smith secured 155,933 votes (60.7 per cent) to Clarke on 100,864 votes (39.3 per cent). Clarke could barely conceal his disappointment at losing, nor could his supporters. When the first Duncan Smith shadow ministerial team was declared, a known Clarke supporter commented: 'the lunatics have taken over the asylum' (Garnett and Lynch 2002: 29).

Duncan Smith wanted to decommission the European issue. He felt that the party had become seen to be obsessed by Europe *and* divided over it but their obsession over Europe was not shared by the electorate. He also feared that they were perceived to be narrow, selfish and elitist party. They had a reputation of governing in the interests of the rich rather than in the interests of ordinary people (Hayton and Heppell 2010: 429). This interpretation was to be famously addressed by the then Party Chair, Theresa May, who informed the annual conference of 2002, that the Conservatives were seen as the 'nasty' party (Bale 2010: 162–5).

Duncan Smith made policy renewal and strategic reorientation his main priority. He addressed the first dilemma, that of Europe, in a manner that was largely misconstrued. He believed that the Hague policy was intellectually incoherent. To base the campaign around saving the pound did not make sense when the policy was to rule out the single European currency for a specified period of time. More intellectually coherent was to rule it out indefinitely, which is what Duncan Smith did. It was construed as a clear indication of his profound Euroscepticism, which in many ways it was. But it was not just a matter of principle. It was also a matter of sensible politics for him. To say no meant that the issue was closed. The harder but quieter position would ensure that it would not pollute strategic planning for the next general election campaign (Hayton 2012a: 68–9).

Outside of the European debate, much of the policy review concentrated on the area of public services, an area in which the party felt New Labour had vulnerabilities (Hayton and Heppell 2010: 430). The Conservatives developed a threefold response to the government's handling of the public services. First, the party argued that New Labour's obsession with targets led to huge unproductive bureaucracies leading to a command state. Second, the party talked about devolving control of hospitals and schools down to institutional level. Third, the Conservatives sought to introduce a choice agenda to empower consumers and force schools and hospitals to improve their services (Dorey 2004: 374).

This response was published in 2002 as *Leadership with a Purpose: A Better Society*. Here Duncan Smith identified what he called the five giants that would be policy priorities of an incoming Conservative government. First, there was the problem of failing schools. Second, they identified new thinking on law and order and crime prevention. Third, they expressed concern surrounding substandard health care provision. Fourth, they wanted to address the damaging consequences of child poverty. Finally, they highlighted the problem of insecurity in old age. Reforming the public services was to be the core belief and the new narrative for post-Thatcherite Conservatism (Taylor 2005a: 149–51). This would enable the Conservatives to position themselves as a party wishing to help the most vulnerable in society – a party that was to pursue social justice (Seldon and Snowdon 2005a: 260). The process of policy reappraisal and strategic reorientation would climax in a new policy document, presented in early 2003. Entitled *A Fair Deal for Everyone*, it demonstrated how Duncan Smith wanted to reconfigure perceptions of contemporary Conservatism away from the core vote strategy that Hague had pursued at the tail end of the previous Parliament. It was a strategy that consciously and deliberately moved away from the signature themes of that campaign – tax, crime, Europe and asylum and immigration. The shift reflected the realization that these issues were not the most salient electoral variables. The Fair Deal agenda would then focus on the most salient areas of public concern – pensions, health, education, social services and inner city deprivation (Bale 2010: 179).

Even though he had stuck to his Eurosceptic reputation, Duncan Smith was, in the economic and social sphere, surprising both his colleagues within the party and his critics outside it. He was attempting to craft a strategy that would redefine perceptions of Conservatism. He wanted to extend electoral perceptions of the party beyond economics and the pursuit of the market, and beyond Euroscepticism and issues relating to national identity. It was designed to erode perceptions of the party as selfish, greedy and nasty and to demonstrate their softer and more compassionate side. The use of terms such as compassionate Conservatism and the rhetoric about changing perceptions of the party drew comparisons with the early stages of the Hague tenure. This comparison does have some justification because both identified the importance of modernizing the party, as a means of stimulating political renewal.

However, his approach was largely misunderstood and ignored. Political commentators had pigeonholed Duncan Smith. His emphasis on the public services did not adhere to their stereotyping of him and therefore they did not offer it, or him, a sympathetic interpretation. In addition, Duncan Smith was grappling with the need to construct a new narrative that would unite the PCP and the mass membership. The attempt to configure the Conservatives around public services failed to convince fellow Conservatives. Moderate economic damps and social liberals remained unconvinced about the depth of Duncan Smith's commitment. The emphasis on issues of morality were insufficiently articulated for them to believe that he had changed his views. Meanwhile, Thatcherite economic dries and traditionalist social conservatives had reservations about the rapprochement with the Tory left, having just annexed the leadership on behalf of the Thatcherite right. Beyond that internal dimension of uniting the party, Duncan Smith needed to provide an external dimension: would his new narrative appeal to the wider electorate, especially floating voters with centrist instincts?

Duncan Smith was unable to persuade a sceptical electorate that he had found a new narrative that amounted to a coherent agenda, worthy of government. Although he had identified public services as a core concern of the electorate, and an area on which New Labour might be increasingly vulnerable, the quandary remained. The electorate wanted high-quality public services without increasing taxation. Duncan Smith wanted and needed to retain a view that the Conservatives were the party of lower taxation. He wanted to demonstrate that the Conservatives were more credible than Labour on public services, but that they could keep taxes lower than Labour. How could this be achieved? Claiming to improve public services while keeping taxes lower than New Labour did not seem credible. To escape this bind, the Duncan Smith view that public services could be funded not just from state funding, but from a coalition of charities, churches and the private sector, simply did not resonate with the electorate (Taylor 2005a: 149–51).

If Duncan Smith had survived and contested the 2005 general election, would he have adhered to the Fair Deal strategy and an inclusive approach designed to reach out to non-core voters? We will never know. What we can say is that as the approach failed to mobilize support, and the internal party criticism of Duncan Smith escalated, he did show signs of engaging in a 'lurch to the right' (Taylor 2005a: 151). In the final months Duncan Smith reverted to type. By the time of his final conference speech in October 2003, the focus on inclusiveness and social justice was downplayed, and the emphasis on low taxation and anti-Europeanism resurfaced (Taylor 2005a: 151).

Unity had remained elusive during the Duncan Smith era, although the intensity of the European ideological schism was beginning to erode. The party, however, managed to remain divided over the meaning of the modernizing agenda, between modernizing social liberals, who thought Duncan Smith did not share their views, and traditionalist social conservatives, who were fearful that Duncan Smith might abandon them. The Hague era had witnessed the gradual embedding of a divide over social-, sexual- and morality-based policy. Duncan Smith was tested when he was faced by a parliamentary division on the adoption of children by homosexual unmarried couples. This was the litmus test for the modernizers vis-à-vis his socially liberal credentials. An astute political operator would have recognized that this amounted to an issue of conscience. Traditionally, such issues are free votes, that is, the party leadership imposes no instructions on how to vote. Adhering to this tradition, New Labour imposed no whip. Defying such tradition and logic, Duncan Smith imposed a three-line whip and adopted a strong socially conservative position – Conservative parliamentarians were instructed to vote against (Crick 2005: 413). A total of eight Conservative parliamentarians voted against, with a further 35 not voting, and therefore assumed to be proactively abstaining (Cowley and Stuart 2004: 357). Through sheer political ineptitude Duncan Smith had drawn attention to the ideological fissures that existed within the PCP on social-, sexual- and morality-based matters. Had he offered the traditional free vote he would have limited the scale of division and disloyalty that was reported (Cowley and Stuart 2004: 357). Duncan Smith then compounded his original action of demanding unity over a conscience issue by a disproportionate reaction to the rebellion. He called a press conference, in which he inferred the rebellion was designed to destabilize him and challenge his mandate to lead. He announced that:

> for a few, last night's vote was not about adoption but an attempt to challenge my mandate to lead the party . . . the party, had to "unite or die." (Norton 2005: 39)

Tactical miscalculations had created this crisis and highlighted the splits on social, sexual and moral matters. Meanwhile, on the approach to Iraq, Duncan Smith managed to divide his party, while deriving no political benefits to the Conservatives as Labour pursued an unpopular war on a disputed legal basis (Cowley and Stuart 2004: 359). A more ambivalent initial position would have offered options for the Conservatives over the longer term. A long-drawn out military adventure could impact upon the popularity of the New Labour administration, whereupon ambivalence could have switched to principled opposition as events unfolded. Unconditional support left the Conservatives without a political outlet and meant no long-term political (i.e. electoral) gain was derived from this stance, as the Liberal Democrats became the main beneficiaries of anti-war and anti-Government sentiment (Seldon and Snowdon 2005b: 727).

Duncan Smith suffered from the fact that few believed that he was a prime minister in waiting. He also found it immensely difficult to secure the loyalty and deference of his parliamentary colleagues (Seldon and Snowdon 2005a: 259). The negative media portrayals of the party under his leadership contributed to a decline in party membership. Whereas donations to the Liberal Democrats were increasing, contributions to the Conservative remained at relatively low levels (Fisher 2004: 407). Due to concerns about the leadership capability of Duncan Smith, one benefactor, the millionaire spread betting tycoon, Stuart Wheeler, announced that he would be withholding financial support until the Conservatives changed their leader (Fisher 2004: 406). A link between Duncan Smith as leader and a decline in donations and their electoral prospects now existed and this would be critical in causing his eventual removal from office (Heppell 2008b: 164).

Most significantly, however, Duncan Smith lacked political stature. Whereas Blair was still viewed as an effective presenter of the New Labour brand, Duncan Smith was clearly viewed as an inferior political communicator. His parliamentary performances were weak and his public speeches and television interviews were at times inept, and the 'Quiet Man' image (whose determination should never be underestimated) completely failed to resonate with the electorate (Denham and O'Hara 2008: 72). The weakness of his public profile gave political ammunition to New Labour. They were able to present a particularly negative image of him as an ideological extremist, devoid of personal charisma, lacking in electoral appeal, and as an incompetent figure. New Labour did not need to actively pursue this line too vigorously as his leadership limitations seemed all too evident. One line of sustained attack that New Labour could and would exploit was his record as a parliamentary rebel when the Conservatives were last in government. Many Conservatives agreed with the New Labour argument that Duncan Smith could not demand loyalty and unity from his fellow Conservative parliamentarians, when he himself had been disloyal earlier in his own parliamentary career (Seldon and Snowdon 2005b: 726).

A third successive landslide electoral defeat was imminent. The increasing popularity of the Liberal Democrats had the potential to reduce Conservative representation even further. Of the 166 Conservative-held constituencies, the Liberal Democrats were in second place in 58 of them. If the opinion polls of mid-2003 were to be reflected in a general election, then a further 15 Liberal Democrats seats would be gained at the expense of the Conservatives. Pessimistic Conservatives feared being relegated to third-party status (Kelly 2004: 400).

The limitations of Duncan Smith became an increasing concern of Conservative parliamentarians. By the autumn of 2003 the requisite number of 25 Conservative parliamentarians requested a confidence motion. Duncan Smith added an additional 21 votes to the number he had polled in the final ballot of the parliamentary party 2 years earlier, but he was short of the requisite number of 83 that would have constituted a technical mandate for his continuance. He secured the endorsement of 75 Conservative parliamentarians or 45.5 per cent of the vote, but 90, or 54.5 per cent of his Conservative colleagues did not have confidence in his leadership (Denham and O'Hara 2008: 92–100).

If Conservative parliamentarians could agree upon one candidate, then they could circumnavigate the procedural requirement for party membership participation. A modernized version of the magic circle, in which the new party leader was ritually acclaimed, would make the party look unified (Norton 2005: 40). Conservative parliamentarians began to coalesce around Howard, who had performed well as shadow Chancellor, with such alacrity that it placed potential candidates in a difficult position. How would the likes of Portillo, Clarke or Davis react given that the momentum behind Howard was so pronounced that they could not prevent him from securing a massive lead among parliamentary colleagues (Crick 2005: 433)? For Portillo, Clarke or Davis the other calculation was that even if they could finish second among parliamentarians, and then win among the activists, this would leave him in the same position as Duncan Smith had been, that is, they would have a weak mandate, and they would be devoid of the necessary authority that he would need to lead effectively.

The deadline for nominations passed with Howard as the only candidate; no parliamentary ballots or no mass membership ballots were required. Howard succeeded Duncan Smith within 2 weeks of the confidence motion. For Howard it amounted to a remarkable political comeback, but an outcome that New Labour was comfortable with as they felt Howard would retreat back to the 'Tories right wing comfort zone' (Mandelson 2010: 381). Howard began his leadership with advantages that went beyond the undisputed mandate and his status as an experienced political insider. Unlike Hague and Duncan Smith, who acquired the leadership in the aftermath of Labour landslides, Howard was facing Blair when the gloss was coming off the New Labour brand. The government was increasingly divided over education and health policy. The war in Iraq had fractured unity further, as well as creating massive public opposition to Blair personally. The aura of impregnability that had characterized Blair during their elongated honeymoon period, was giving way to an aura of vulnerability. While the inter-party environment seemed more conducive to Conservative advancement, the manner of Howard's emergence would aid him in improving intra-party relations. The strength of his mandate and the unifying message that it offered, would make Conservative parliamentarians less inclined to be disloyal and rebellious. It also provided him with scope (should he wish to utilize it) to transcend Thatcherism. It was argued that the fact that he was a gold-plated Thatcherite, but crucially a loyal and senior one, could allow him to convincingly argue the case for defining a narrative of Conservatism that transcended Thatcherism, without provoking the levels of dissent and disagreement that overwhelmed Hague and Duncan Smith. That optimism suggested that great things were expected of him (Seldon and Snowdon 2005a: 264).

Howard made a positive initial impact. This was evident from the opinion polling data. Within 2 months of acquiring the leadership the Conservatives had reason to believe that the age of flat-lining might be at an end. They led Labour and had secured a projected vote share above the critical 40 per cent but it was not to be sustained (Broughton 2004: 352–3). Howard was unable to exploit the greatest vulnerability of Blair surrounding Iraq. The inability of the government to contribute to securing a swift resolution to the conflict, the apparent absence of a post-invasion strategy and exit route, and the questioning of the intelligence gathering and decision-making that justified war were dominating political debate. Howard expected the Hutton Inquiry, which was set up to investigate the reasons for the suicide of the Government scientist, Dr David Kelly, to implicate Blair. When the subsequent report exonerated Blair it left Howard looking opportunistic. He had ratcheted things up too much, perhaps hoping that Blair's integrity would be questioned, knowing that this would have the capacity to humiliate New Labour and thus aid the Conservatives (Crick 2005: 445). Moreover, the position that Howard adopted on Iraq, of being in favour of the war but questioning the rationale for war (i.e. the retrospective realization that there were not weapons of mass destruction) lacked credibility (Wheatcroft 2005: 268).

In broader terms the policy-renewal process that had characterized the Duncan Smith era remained incomplete. A viable and utilizable narrative of post-Thatcherite Conservatism that could unify the party internally and appeal to the electorate externally remained elusive. A sense of incoherence remained. Howard needed to articulate an answer to the dilemmas, what is Conservatism and what is the purpose of the Conservative Party? In an attempt to begin the process of explaining his philosophy to a sceptical electorate, Howard launched a personal manifesto, entitled *I Believe*. This was launched in January 2004, and it contained an overview of 16 core beliefs that informed his political approach. The new rhetoric and old record of Howard created contradictory messages. His new rhetoric suggested he was repenting on matters such as his socially conservative instincts (Crick 2005: 440). He appeared to recognize that an image of social intolerance was an electoral impediment and therefore he initially claimed that he wanted the Conservatives to be inclusive. However, the desire to be inclusive did not extend to his core beliefs. There was no mention in his *I Believe* manifesto of homosexual rights or ethnic minorities, which Portillo, for example, would have highlighted (Garnett 2004: 368). His new rhetoric, however, contradicted his ministerial record and this undermined him and the party. Lesbian and homosexual groups remained deeply hostile to him due to section 28. New Labour ridiculed the attempted imagery of a caring and compassionate Howard by frequently referring to the high levels of unemployment during his tenure as Employment Secretary. What was even more problematic was the fact that, first, his socially conservative and traditionalist instincts had remained in opposition; and, second, some modernizers were sceptical about the extent of his conversion (Crick 2005: 440).

What was increasingly problematic was what modernization meant. It appeared to mean different things to different Conservatives at different times. Some Conservatives appeared to spout the mantra of modernization in an unthinking manner on the basis that their current approach was unappealing and therefore needed changing. For Hague, modernization appeared to carry two elements: first, organizational reform to improve the structures of the party to aid voter mobilization; and second, to alter the negative images of the party as being intolerant. For Duncan Smith, modernization did not embrace the first Hague element of organizational reform. The second element of changing the image of the party was less about intolerance and the treatment of minority groups within society. It was more about aiding the status of the most vulnerable within society and addressing concerns about the quality of, and means of delivery within, the public services. For Portillo, the dominant aspect of modernization was the need to broaden the appeal of the party by ending their demonizing of homosexuals, ethnic minorities and public sector workers.

The Howard configuration of modernization appeared to embrace the Duncan Smith emphasis on the issue of the public services, more than it did the Portillo emphasis on inclusivity. The thinking that informed his *I Believe* statements reaffirmed Thatcherite ideological thought. The claim that they would also address the public services conundrum seemed implausible, and reflected the confusion in their strategic thinking. In *I Believe*, Howard demonstrated that, regardless of his rhetoric of inclusivity and modernization, he had no intention of slaying the ghost of Thatcherism (Garnett 2004: 371).

Given the ambiguities that were evident in the Howard manifesto, the intriguing dilemma was how modernizers and traditionalists could both remain satisfied with Howard as leader. In the early stages of the Howard tenure, Garnett speculated that the split between social liberals and social conservatives had not been healed by Howard acquiring the leadership. Rather, both factions had manufactured a temporary cessation of hostilities, given the air of optimism that had permeated the Conservatives when Howard succeeded Duncan Smith. Garnett implied that given the socially conservative instincts of Howard, it would be interesting to see how long he could sustain the rhetoric of inclusiveness. If there was no electoral benefit, would he revert to type? (Garnett 2004: 368).

That initial upsurge in Conservative support, which saw them hit 40 per cent and lead Labour in January 2004, was not sustained. A series of morale-sapping election results followed. The European elections of June 2004 proved to be disappointing. The Conservatives led the poll, but their share of the vote at 27 per cent, was 9 per cent down on the share secured 5 years earlier (Seldon and Snowdon 2005b: 730). Worryingly for the Conservatives, UKIP proved to be an attractive option to disaffected Europhobes and their vote share increased from 7 per cent to 16 per cent (Kavanagh and Butler 2005: 39). Their inability to expand their projected vote share in the opinion polling data, and the small vote share in the European elections, pushed Howard onto the political back foot. Symptoms of a Hague, or to a lesser extent, Duncan Smith, lurch to shore up the core vote become evident. In an attempt to energize Conservatives, Howard switched his emphasis to crime, tax and immigration (Seldon and Snowdon 2005a: 266). As the inevitability of another electoral reversal became apparent, Conservatives and political commentators focused their attention on what the future would hold for a post-Howard Conservative Party. Increasingly, political elites, if not the mass electorate, were focusing their attention on the next generation of modernizers. Most notable among this tendency were David Cameron and George Osborne, who became viewed as Conservative versions of Blair and Gordon Brown. Unless Howard could prove the pundits wrong, then this so-called Notting Hill set of post-Portillo modernizers would have designs on the leadership (Seldon and Snowdon 2005a: 268–9).

A third successive electoral reverse followed. New Labour secured a parliamentary majority of 66, despite the fact that their share of the vote slipped as low as 35.2 per cent, which was down from 40.7 per cent in 2001, and 43.2 per cent in 1997. The Conservative share of the vote increased from 31.7 per cent in 2001 to 32.3 per cent, meaning that in 8 years they had increased their share by only 1.7 per cent from the 30.7 per cent of 1997. The beneficiaries of hostility towards New Labour were the Liberal Democrats who increased their vote share from 18.3 per cent to 22.1 per cent. Despite this, Howard claimed that by increasing their parliamentary representation (from 166 to 198), and by reducing the percentage vote share difference between themselves and Labour from 9 percentage points to 2.9 percentage points, that a Conservative recovery had commenced (Seldon and Snowdon 2005b: 736–7).

Howard had failed to provide a springboard for electoral success at the next election; at this rate, it would take more than one more heave to propel them into office. Two schools of thought emerged on their predicament. The nature of their arguments largely mirrored those expressed in the aftermath of their initial removal from office. Thesis one argued that there was nothing fundamentally wrong with contemporary Conservatism. All that was required was a clear Thatcherite message of a small state, low taxation, Euroscepticism and social conservatism. The failure to be sufficiently Thatcherite explained their respective electoral reversals. Thesis two constituted the modernizers case which suggested that fundamental reform, and the adoption of a new narrative based around compassionate and inclusive conservatism, was essential to securing their electoral recovery.

The collapse of post-Thatcherite statecraft

Their record as a party of government between 1992 and 1997 embedded in the eyes of parts of the electorate that the Conservatives were incompetent, divided, sleazy and poorly led (Taylor 2005a: 145). The planks of the Thatcherite statecraft strategy had dissolved. The Conservatives had traditionally been seen to provide political stability and economic security for much of the middle and professional classes (Dorey 2003: 142). However, the transformation of the economy, that the Thatcher and Major era had stimulated, had actually undermined the Conservatives. The pursuit of neoliberalism had weakened communities and social bonds, and therefore it had become a self-limiting project (Gray 1997: 1–10). Thus, through the rapid processes of economic and social change that had been initiated, old loyalties became questioned and the middle class and professional coalition that had been the base of Conservative support fragmented (Lynch and Garnett 2003: 255). In the short term this social transformation had worked to the advantage of the Conservatives, as disaffected and socially mobile Labour voters defected to the Conservatives. However, over the longer term it 'corroded Tory support in the middle classes', thereby 'hollowing out' Tory England, because the 'economic constituency that gained most from early Thatcherism had been savaged by its longer term effects' (Gray 1994: 47; 1997: 3; 1998: 32).

The loss of a viable electoral strategy was clearly aligned to their inability to demonstrate governing competence in the Major era. Despite the economic improvements of the latter stages of their fourth term in office, the electorate punished them for the mismanagement associated with the ERM debacle. The defeats that followed in opposition demonstrated Labour's dominance in the sphere of economic competence (Dorey 2003). With continuous economic growth being recorded between 1997 and 2005, and low inflation and high employment, New Labour had demonstrated their ability to govern effectively and provide economic stability. In doing so they also denied the Conservatives a trigger that could initiate a political recovery. The proceeds of economic growth, (i.e. the additional tax revenues that growth created), enabled New Labour to invest further within the public services. Thus New Labour was able to frame political competition as a clear choice – growth and investment under New Labour or cuts under the Conservatives. The 'cuts versus spending' strategy was a central explanation for their election victories in 2001 and 2005 (Kavanagh and Cowley 2010: 64).

Conversely, the Conservative pledge to cut taxation *and* invest in public services seemed disingenuous, and undermined their attempts to appear like a potential party of government (Seldon and Snowdon 2005b: 731). The dilemma remained how to improve public service delivery while retaining a small state and thereby low taxation. The problem for the Conservatives was one of credibility on tax and believability on the public services. Conservative electoral success during the Thatcherite hegemony had been predicated on perceptions of superior economic management and their claim to be the party of low taxation. Central to their capacity to argue this were two factors. First, they could portray Labour as economically incompetent, by reminding voters of the financial crises of 1967 or 1976 and the winter of discontent in 1978–79. Second, the continued utility of the taxation claim was dependent on Labour campaigning on a platform of increasing taxation. Labour had negated the tax advantage that the Conservatives had by shedding their image as a tax and spend party, through the symbolic gesture of abandoning their commitment to public ownership. Furthermore, the passage of time, aligned to the rebranding of Labour as New Labour enabled them to disassociate themselves from their own past. Conversely, it was the Conservatives who were unable to wriggle themselves free of their own legacy of economic incompetence. Their reputation for economic competence had been shattered by the ERM disaster. Their reputation as a party of lower taxation had been tarnished by the taxation increases that flowed from the aforementioned debacle. The era of opinion polling flat-lining had commenced at that juncture, back in 1992. Howard, like Major, Hague and Duncan Smith, was unable to reverse the electoral perception that Labour, and not them, was the best-equipped party to manage the economy. Positive electoral perceptions on economic management are the keys to the door of voter popularity. The keys were now owned by New Labour who were dominant in terms of elite debate, as Blair and New Labour appeared to have

> tapped into the widespread belief amongst the British that there need not be – indeed should not be – a trade off between social justice and economic growth, between fairness and efficiency, between quality public provision and higher net disposable incomes. At the same time it also managed to persuade people that a trade off does exist between lower taxes and investment in the NHS and state education, which, along with economic well being remain at the top of voters' list of things that governments are supposed to deliver. (Bale 2010: 5)

The Conservatives had lost political argument hegemony as New Labour crafted an electoral strategy predicated on the importance of the individual and individual achievement on the one hand, and a traditional Labour emphasis on the community and the public services on the other. New Labour derided post-Thatcherism for the economic instability and insecurity that it had created, but the Conservatives could no longer articulate their message around the fears engendered by the thought of Labour in office (McAnulla 1999: 195). The traditional dynamics of party competition had changed. This was partly due to the failings of the Conservatives, but it was also caused by the repositioning and subsequent effectiveness of New Labour under Blair. Not only were they economically competent but they were also more united than Labour had historically been (Cowley and Stuart 2003: 317). Moreover in Blair they had a highly effective leader. In an age of valance, rather than positional politics, where election campaigning has become so focused around the character and competence of political leaders, Blair had come to personify New Labour. Their strategy was shaped by inspiring in the electorate trust in his abilities (Finlayson 2002: 586–99).

Thatcher had apparently claimed that the creation of New Labour was among her 'greatest achievements' (Dorey et al. 2011: 12). If so, it was an achievement with questionable benefits for the Conservatives. By making a pragmatic accommodation with elements of the Thatcherite policy legacy (Hay 1999), the Conservatives were pushed towards either a battle of competence and image with New Labour (where Blair would excel in an era of economic prosperity between 1997 and 2005), or they could reaffirm their commitment to the now outdated politics of Thatcherism (Dorey et al. 2011: 13). It was in the words of Lord Parkinson who Hague brought back as Party Chair between 1997 and 1999 a 'no win situation' (Hayton 2012a: 20). The notion that continued adherence to Thatcherism could rediscover for them their lost claims to political argument hegemony lacked credibility in the eyes of modernizers. This created a tragic irony. Thatcherism had forced the Labour Party to modernize, but now the Thatcherites own dogmatism would impede their own attempt to modernize themselves. They were 'paralysed' while their opponents were 'galvanised' (Hayton 2012a: 27, 36). Post 1997 the ongoing 'fixation' with Thatcherism would undermine attempts to 'reinvigorate' Conservatism and apply it to the new terrain being advanced by New Labour. On this dilemma Portillo concluded [in 2006] that

> they had frozen Thatcherism in time, forgetting that one of the key ingredients of Thatcherism was that it was cutting edge, it was new. Thatcherism now of course is retro, it is twenty years past its sell by date . . . so these rather bone headed old Thatcherites occupy a lot of the positions in the party [in opposition] and that has stopped the party changing. (Hayton 2012a: 26–7)

Thatcherism required 'others' and fears around others to sustain its claim to political argument hegemony. Without excessive trade union power and the ability to plausibly argue that Labour was economically illiterate they appeared to lack 'bearing and purpose' (Gould 1999: xii). Hayton concludes that the Conservative Party 'was a victim' of the 'success' of Thatcherism, as by 'helping to forge' a new post-Thatcherite consensus (as New Labour accepted the market), so 'it robbed itself of its primary purpose and electoral appeal: its opposition to socialism' (Hayton 2012a: 27). Thatcherite statecraft had been shown to be time specific – in the short term it was effective, over the long-term self-defeating. The method by which to transcend Thatcherism and reconstruct Conservatism remained unresolved.

5

From crisis to coalition: Transcending Thatcherism 2005–the present day

After three successive electoral reversals was it possible that the Conservatives might be willing and able to realize that Thatcherism was no longer a viable strategy? (Bale 2010: 253) Their commitment to the Thatcherite rhetoric of taxation, law and order, immigration and Euroscepticism, and the establishing of 'clear blue water' between themselves and New Labour to 'shore up' their traditional base, had failed in spectacular fashion in 2001. The reaction of the Conservatives to the failure of William Hague, a moderate Thatcherite to reconstruct Conservatism and re-establish their electoral appeal, was to replace him with a supposedly more committed Thatcherite in the shape of Iain Duncan Smith. Both of these Thatcherites had then surprisingly attempted to initiate forms of change, but their attempts to 'reach out' to floating centrist voters, so that the Conservatives could transcend Thatcherism, were unsustainable. Their failure to change and modernize was partly due to the lack of evidence that change would improve the position of the party in the polls (given the governing success of New Labour), but it was also due to the fact that neither leader was truly convinced of their own new narrative. Critically both came to fear that they may be removed from the leadership if they sustained their commitment to change. Hague survived a full parliamentary term but Duncan Smith did not, creating the interim leadership tenure of Michael Howard.

Assessing whether the Conservatives were willing to change would be the key aspect of the inevitable leadership election that would take place after Howard resigned in May 2005. Although a Thatcherite himself, Howard was convinced that their third successive reversal had demonstrated that they had 'tested the Thatcherite strategy to destruction' (Bale and Webb 2011: 39). Howard wanted to assist the new younger modernizing generation of Conservatives. To aid the prospects of either David Cameron or George Osborne emerging as his successor Howard decided to announce his 'intention' to resign in May 2005, but that his resignation would only be activated after the Conservatives had an opportunity to reassess their leadership selection rules. The delayed resignation tactic created a protracted succession contest characterized by two stages – the phoney war between May and September, and the real contest between September and December once the rules were agreed upon (Denham and O'Hara 2008: 105–72).

Most parliamentarians wanted to switch back to a system of parliamentary ballots. For many, the outcome of the 2001 succession contest, and the subsequent need to evict Duncan Smith after 2 years had 'discredited the selection system' (Quinn 2012: 107). A consultation paper was put forward outlining the failings of the Hague rules: expensive, time consuming and confusing, most notably with regard to the fact that the membership had the final say in selection (after parliamentary screening), but only the parliamentarians could initiate a removal (Denham and O'Hara 2008: 117). Eventually new proposals were put forward to a constitutional college, comprising of Conservative MPs, MEPs and peers and senior figures from the voluntary wing of the party. The new proposals retained an element of party membership involvement through a National Conservative Convention. Parliamentarians would nominate candidates. If one candidate had over half of the PCP, they were automatically elected. If not then only candidates who had the backing of 10 per cent of the PCP would be allowed to proceed to eliminative contests. Those passing that threshold would then be subject to two parallel procedures. There would be the aforementioned eliminative ballots in which only Conservative parliamentarians could participate. However, alongside the candidate who was ranked highest by members of the National Conservative Convention, made up from the voluntary wing of the party, would be guaranteed a place in the final parliamentary ballot, thus meaning they could 'pass to the eliminative ballots'. Of course in the final eliminative ballot the PCP could choose an alternative candidate to the one who was selected first by the National Conservative Convention. At best they could send a signal, but their signal was non-binding (Denham and O'Hara 2008: 118). In order to replace the existing Hague rules they needed the backing of two thirds of the constitutional college, but the mandate for change was not forthcoming. Only 61 per cent endorsed the proposals, meaning the existing Hague rules, widely felt to be dysfunctional among Conservative parliamentarians, would remain in place (Bale 2010: 267).

With the phoney war now complete and the rules of the game understood, this allowed the candidates to parade themselves at the 'beauty contest' that was their Annual Conference. The succession contest was seen as a 'tale of two primaries' – David Davis versus Liam Fox for the Thatcherite primary, and Kenneth Clarke versus Cameron for the non-Thatcherite primary. In reality, it became a tale of two speeches – one candidate-making one by Cameron, and one candidate-breaking one by Davis (Denham and Dorey 2006: 35–41).

It is valid to describe Davis and Fox as both being candidates of the Thatcherite right and advocates of tax cuts, Euroscepticism and social conservatism (Quinn 2012: 108–9). However, although Clarke and Cameron were less well associated with Thatcherism their positioning was more complex than simply being characterized as the primary of the left. Cameron tilted towards Thatcherite orthodoxy on the economy and Europe, albeit that he may be best described as dry and soft in his Euroscepticism. He deviated from Thatcherism on social, moral and sexual matters. Meanwhile, Clarke was more clearly associated with the old style Conservative left with his economic dampness, his moderation on social matters and his Europhilia. What fuelled the right and left wing primary argument was where the respective candidates were drawing their support from. The majority Thatcherite bloc within the PCP was expected to fracture between Davis and Fox, and the minority non-Thatcherite grouping to split their support between Clarke and Cameron (Heppell 2008b: 180).

The central conundrum for the modernizing Cameron was whether the Conservatives were ready to change. Cameron was convinced of the need to modernize in order to distinguish the Conservatives from their recent failed past, and in order to do so he was keen to prioritize pragmatism over ideology. Although respectful of the politics of Thatcherism, he understood the realities of the focus group findings and opinion polling evidence. Preaching the Thatcherite gospel to the Tory faithful did not convert floating voters into new Conservative voters. For Cameron decontamination of the Conservative brand was required. In this context the findings of Michael Ashcroft, a Conservative donor, in his post-election analysis *Smell the Coffee*, justified the need for modernization both symbolic and substantive. Not only were the Conservatives trailing New Labour by 40 points in terms of governing competence, but they were seen to be 'stuck in the past', 'uncaring' and that they 'had not learnt the mistakes of the past' (Ashcroft 2005: 49–52, 94–7). Cameron would thus be an unashamed modernizing and change candidate.

What of the tale of two speeches argument? The speeches of Clarke and Fox generated little excitement. Clarke was to be undermined by the performance of Cameron. As the least experienced candidate Cameron used his speech to enhance his profile and his credibility and to showcase his impressive communication skills. Reaction within the conference hall was 'enthusiastic, even electric', and the print media coverage was 'equally positive'. Not only did Cameron look 'fresh faced' and 'highly personable' but he showcased that he was 'media-savvy' by inviting his young wife onto the stage after the speech and then gently tapping her pregnancy bump (Bale and Webb 2011: 42). He was also optimistic, as without notes, he informed conference that he understood the problem, could identify the solution, and that New Labour was beatable. He brought the hall to their feet as he promised to deliver 'a modern, compassionate Conservatism, that is right for our times, right for this generation, right for our party, and right for our country' (Bale 2010: 275).

The response changed the dynamics of the contest. But Cameron did not create that change alone. The change was in part a by-product of how Davis performed. Not only was his speech negative and defensive, but it was badly presented. The end of his speech was so anti-climactic that his audience did not realize he was ending and he had to beckon them to stand and applaud (Quinn 2012: 110). Worryingly this conjured up memories of 'the communication and presentational difficulties that had characterised the Duncan Smith tenure' (Heppell 2008b: 182).

Although Davis claimed to have 66 public endorsements within the PCP, only 62 backed him in the first eliminative parliamentary ballot, but he led Fox (on 42) in the right wing primary. Cameron led Clarke in the non-Thatcherite primary by 56 to 38, meaning that Clarke was eliminated, and the vast bulk of his supporters gravitated to Cameron who defeated Davis by 90 to 57 in the second eliminative ballot, with Fox trailing in third on 51. As Davis and Fox were splitting the Thatcherite voting bloc, it was inevitable that whichever of them led would nonetheless be a long way behind Cameron (Quinn 2012: 111). By the time the contest reached the membership stage Cameron had developed real momentum. He had strong backing from within the press with *The Sun* (still nominally New Labour); *The Daily Mail*, *The Times* and eventually *The Daily Telegraph* all endorsing him. Cameron also benefitted from polling data showing he had leads among both known Conservative voters but also swing voters (Denham and O'Hara 2008: 166–7). Eight years earlier they had rejected similar data that should have instructed them to endorse Clarke over Hague, but now the Conservatives were sufficiently desperate to back a candidate whose ideological identity may not be entirely to their liking, but who might win. Cameron secured 134,446 votes (or 67.6 per cent) to Davis on 64,398 (32.4 per cent) and thus he had a clear mandate to modernize (Elliott and Hanning 2009: 256–90). The significance of this was that they had selected a lesser Thatcherite candidate for the first time in the whole of the post-Thatcherite period.

Reconstructing Conservatism: The politics of modernization 2005–2010

Cameron entered the leadership with a clear strategy which was essentially driven by the stylistics of change. This meant acknowledging that the Conservatives were perceived to be 'nasty' (and incompetent) and that they would need to engage in 'brand decontamination' by changing their image, altering their rhetoric and adopting a more socially inclusive approach. Cameron felt that the Conservatives could only 'secure permission to be heard' (Bale 2010: 285) if they could change their image to overcome the negativity that informed attitudes towards them in the period between 1992 and 2005.

This would require a dual approach. First, the Conservatives would deliberately move away from prioritizing the issues associated with Thatcherism – that is, taxation, immigration and Euroscepticism. They would then deliberately move onto the political terrain that New Labour could claim ownership over (McAnulla 2010: 295). Increasingly public pronouncements would focus on discussing work/life balance, maternity leave, childcare provision and the need to address the gender pay gap, as part of his feminization agenda. Ensuing rhetoric on the environment, on supporting state schools, defending professional autonomy in the public sector, attacking 'fat cat' salaries and emphasizing the importance of international aid were all designed as 'reach out' strategies that symbolized how the Conservatives were transcending Thatcherism (Dorey 2007; Carter 2009; Childs and Webb 2012; Heppell and Lightfoot 2012). Although the modernizing wing was convinced that the embracing of social liberalism was necessary, the traditional right felt that this smacked of abandoning their past (Evans 2008: 291–314). They were voluntarily walking away from their known strengths and downplaying the issues on which they were seen to be superior to New Labour, notably immigration and crime (Green 2010: 69).

Cameron himself would 'do everything he could to personally embody change' (Bale and Webb 2011: 44). This was central to the 'project', as the electorate was being 'invited' to believe that the Conservatives 'are no longer nasty because he [Cameron] is likeable' (Elliott and Hanning 2009: 291). The Conservatives initiated a 'shock and awe' campaign in the opening months of his leadership tenure, so as to 'get disillusioned voters to take another look at the Tories' (Bale 2012b: 224). In a sympathetic assessment of his performance as leader of the opposition Bale notes that Cameron knew that a 'picture is worth a thousand words', and as a consequence a steady diet of new images of Cameron emerged. He was shown doing the washing up with his wife and children around him or going shopping with them, and riding his mountain bike (Bale 2012b: 224). More often than not and somewhat surprisingly given his elitist background, he succeeded at appearing authentic. He used interviews to demonstrate normality such as acknowledging that the electorate were 'pissed off' with the political class, or when he dismissed UKIP as a 'bunch of fruitcakes and loonies and closet racists' (Bale 2012b: 225).

Cameron was seeking to detach the extremist label from the Conservative brand. He wanted to move beyond the fact that it was understood in terms of what it was against (immigrants, homosexuals and the European Union), rather than what it stood for (Norton 2009: 39). Accepting where the Conservatives had been both negative and wrong, and them moving on became part of the Cameron strategy. Apologies were made to distinguish his new Conservatism from that of the past, such as section 28 of the 1988 Local Government Act. On this piece of Thatcherite legislation that had made it illegal for local authorities to be seen to 'promote' homosexuality, Cameron informed Gay Pride: 'I am sorry for section 28. We got it wrong. I hope that you can forgive us' (Bale and Webb 2011: 46). A similar apology was made to the people of Scotland for the 'cultural insensitivity' shown by the Thatcher administration which had treated them like 'guinea pigs' by their 'clumsy and unjust' implementation of the poll tax there one year before rolling it out across England and Wales (Dorey et al. 2011: 63).

Cameron wanted to emphasize what the Conservatives were for. One important example for him was the NHS. As he had a disabled son (Ivan who died in 2009), his family was reliant on the NHS and this meant that Cameron seemed more authentic on health care than other Conservatives. Another example was the family. He was pro-family, but not in an old-fashioned Conservative sense of being for only certain types of family units. He was pro-equality when it came to homosexual rights, and this more enlightened position was more in tune with popular opinion (especially among younger voters) (Norton 2009: 40). Cameron was thus seeking to triangulate contemporary Conservatism to reflect the altered terrain created by changes in society and the impact of New Labour in office. Thus Cameron's objective was to make the Conservatives appear more centrist and position them closer to the location of the median voter in order to negate New Labour dominance on key electoral variables (Taylor 2010: 490).

The modernization strategy was more values driven than policy driven. They avoided making too many specific policy commitments (Norton 2009: 40). The early years would showcase how values would come to *inform* policy as they constructed a revamped statement. Entitled *Built to Last*, it emphasized the following values as the key determinants of modern Conservatism: eliminating poverty through raising quality of life for all; fighting social injustice; tackling environmental threats; improving the quality of public services; bolstering internal security; human rights; and enabling communities (Kerr 2007: 50–1). The initiation of a wide-ranging policy-review process by necessity took time to make recommendations. This had the 'added benefit of delaying the need to announce detailed policy proposals' (Hayton 2012a: 128). Even the construction of the policy-review process itself was designed to imply change. Only two of the groupings – National Security and Economic Competitiveness – were 'typically regarded as Thatcherite priorities', whereas the others 'were all designed to reinforce the message that the party was changing' – Social Justice; Globalization and Global Poverty; Public Services; and Quality of Life (Hayton 2012a: 128).

The six policy-review groups would publish interim reports by late 2006 leading to final reports by mid-2007. These final reports would then be considered by the shadow Cabinet and would help in the construction of more detailed policies for the forthcoming manifesto. However, the recommendations of the various groups were not binding on the leadership, allowing Cameron to select which ideas he and the shadow Cabinet wanted to advance further. However, all the groups were making their recommendations within the context of a thriving economy. Thus, while the intention might have been based on long-term planning and the rolling out of carefully thought-through policies, the reality would be that policy formulation would have to become reactive and reflective of the altered circumstances post 2008 (Dorey et al. 2011: 96).

In the short term – between 2005 and mid-2007 – the opinion polling appeared to justify modernization. By the time Gordon Brown was selected to replace Tony Blair, the projected Conservative share was 40 per cent, and they possessed a lead over Labour which stretched into double figures. Such leads indicated that the Conservatives could secure victory at the next general election, and that they could secure an overall majority, albeit a relatively small one (Bale 2010: 329). The high point for the Conservatives would be the summer of 2008. Between June and August the Conservatives were leading Labour by 45 to 26; the net satisfaction rating of Cameron was +22 and Brown was −51, and the Conservatives had a lead of 38 to 23 on the question of which party was most competent economically (Curtice 2009: 175, 180, 182).

Modernization had been predicated on an acceptance of the success of New Labour and the need to neutralize their advantages. The Conservatives had been successful between 1979 and 1992 because they had been able to persuade enough voters that Labour would increase taxes to fund their ambitious public expenditure plans. This worked then. But the climate of opinion had changed. The defeats of 1997–2005 showcased how New Labour had initiated or exploited a change in the climate of opinion. In an environment of continued economic growth they had reframed the choice as investment in public services under New Labour (funded from the proceeds of growth rather than increased tax), or cuts in public services under the uncaring and incompetent Conservatives (Bale and Webb 2011: 45). The modernizers had thus decided to neutralize this issue as it was central to the electoral strategy of New Labour. The approach rested on a clear assumption. The economy had been characterized by growth in the New Labour era, and growth helped to reinforce New Labour as the party of economic competence. Therefore, for the opposition Conservatives, no political opportunities existed from challenging New Labour on their economic record (Lee 2009a: 58). Negating the Labour investment versus Tory cuts choice was thus the objective. This was evident from the following speech by Cameron:

> Creating wealth cannot be the only objective of Conservative economic policy . . . we must share the proceeds of economic growth between tax reduction and public sector investment . . . we must make the creation of wealth *and* the elimination of poverty the central objectives of Conservative economic strategy. (Kerr 2007: 50)

Cameron aimed to compete with New Labour on public expenditure and negate the investment versus cuts choice that had fuelled New Labour electoral strategy. He pledged to increase public expenditure, especially on health and education, to break that association with Thatcherism.

Thus, by transferring their attack from the economic towards social issues, they could showcase how the Conservatives were genuine in their desire to 'tackle social fragmentation and inequality' and thereby mend what they now defined as 'broken Britain' (Dorey 2009: 260).

This was a phrase that was developed by the Centre for Social Justice (CSJ) which was created by Duncan Smith in 2004. The CSJ sought to identify the causes of social breakdown and advance policy solutions that would address poverty and social exclusion. Their means, outlined in *Breakthrough Britain* published in July 2007, proposed the revival of civic institutions as the primary means by which to address social difficulties. Their rhetorical emphasis on social justice tied in with Cameron's instinct to triangulate. Social justice was an issue assumed to be owned by the centre left, but here the Conservatives were implying that New Labour's state-first, target driven and top down solutions had not worked. In response to New Labour's failure to solve these embedded social problems the Conservatives also acknowledged that markets alone were not enough. Thus it sought a third way between the market and the state, which acknowledged that there was such a thing as society; it just was not the same as the state. (Dorey and Garnett 2012: 390, 398).

This had been gradually acknowledged in the opposition era (Streeter 2002) and it is from these intellectual roots that the Big Society narrative was to evolve. This was a process that was in part shaped by two parliamentarians other than Duncan Smith who would serve as ministers in Cameron's administration after May 2010: David Willetts and Oliver Letwin. Willetts had been a long-term advocate of civic Conservatism (Willetts 1992, 1994). He had argued that there was a need to mould together economic liberalism with increasing awareness of social issues. During the course of the long post-Thatcherite malaise he had attempted to educate the party on the importance of communities but also stressed that 'collective action does not necessarily mean state action' (Willetts 1994: 23). There was clear intellectual overlap between Willetts' and Letwin's communitarian Conservatism. Letwin similarly condemned the top-down state-driven strategies of New Labour that had 'emasculated' communities and had failed to address social problems, which he felt could be addressed more effectively via bottom-up responses which would empower individuals and communities (Letwin 2003: 41). He thereby concluded that social problems could only be addressed by 'setting people – neighbourhoods, schools, hospitals, professionals, patients, pupils, teachers, everyone everywhere in this country – free to act, together or individually', but 'with a helping hand from the State' rather than with 'the dead hand of bureaucracy upon them' (Letwin 2003: 46). Letwin would later argue that empowering communities and localism required a 'gentle push' to move society 'in a direction of greater responsibility, or greater coherence, or kindliness' (Letwin 2009: 76).

At this juncture Letwin appeared to be buying into the concept of nudge economics and the ideas of Thaler and Sunstein (2008). This provided an alternative explanation regarding behaviour to that of neoliberals who argued that actors would make rational self-maximizing choices. Rather they argued that individuals could be steered towards socially responsible choices and that the top down methods associated with New Labour were neither desirable nor necessary. Their advocacy of libertarian paternalism would thereby nudge individuals towards good behaviour while preserving liberty (Thaler and Sunstein 2008: 3–5). McAnulla noted that Cameron and Osborne were attracted to this as it appeared to offer a 'way of avoiding moral indifference towards people's behaviour, yet also eschewing the kind of heavy-handed moralism that arguably was a feature of Thatcherism' (McAnulla 2012: 170).

Comparable to the communitarian Conservatism that Letwin was advancing was the Red Toryism associated with the work of Philip Blond, first for the think-tank Demos and then for his own think tank *Res Publica* formed in 2009. Blond argued that just as 1979 had witnessed a paradigm shift that signalled the exhaustion of the Keynesian welfare model, so there was now a similar paradigm shift which would prompt the end of the Thatcherite neo-liberal market state model. The objective for Cameron and the Conservatives was to promote a new model – the civic state (Blond 2009: 1). Blond identified that Thatcherism and both Old and New Labour were all culpable for their excesses of statism and individualism, which collectively had undermined social responsibility and cohesion but also civic institutions (Dorey and Garnett 2012: 400).

The modernizing project embraced much of this thinking and as such did appear to offer a critique of Thatcherism. Equally Margaret Thatcher would probably view Cameron as a pragmatic one-nation Conservative, seeking to construct a new middle way between Thatcherite Conservatism and New Labour (Beech 2009: 22). However, irrespective of the arguments made above, the reality is that there are clear continuities with Thatcherism as Cameronism amounts to an amalgam of social and economic liberalism blended with soft Euroscepticism. As such, it neither fully endorses Thatcherism nor does it fully repudiate it. If Thatcherism constituted economic liberty, national independence and moral order, then Cameron is a 'textbook' Thatcherite in terms of his neoliberalism and Euroscepticism, but he challenges the Thatcherite social conservative orthodoxy in the social and moral sphere (Beech 2009: 29).

There is a tendency to restrict the interpretation of how Cameron deviates from Thatcherism to just the moral sphere. However, that deviation is actually broader than that. McAnulla argues Cameron appears to have challenged Thatcherism in two other key ways: first in terms of attitudes towards poverty; and, second in terms of centralization (McAnulla 2012: 168). On poverty Cameron accepted that Thatcherism had been incorrect when it had rejected the concept of 'relative poverty', and that they needed to think of it in 'relative' terms (Hickson 2009: 358). In doing so, he noted that while Thatcherism had been successful in aspects of its economic record, it had been lacking in terms of social reform (McAnulla 2012: 168). However, Cameron endorsed the Blond emphasis that poverty was a social problem that could only be addressed through collective action, and not solely through the apparatus of the state. He argued in 2008 that:

> for Labour there is only the state and the individual, nothing in between. No family to rely on, no friend to depend on, no community to call on. No neighbourhood to grow in, no faith to share in, no charities to work in. No-one but the Minister, nowhere but Whitehall, no such thing as society – just them, and their laws, and their rules, and their arrogance. . . . You cannot run our country like this. (Hickson 2009: 358)

This is tied into the second Cameron critique of Thatcherism – its central-izing tendencies. Thatcherism may well have attempted to roll back the frontiers of the state in the economic sphere, but had constructed a centralized and strong state to facilitate this process. Thatcherites would retrospectively claim that these 'authoritarian steps' had been necessary to free people from municipal socialism and to then foster 'greater individual freedom through the spread of the market' (McAnulla 2012: 169). However, Cameron felt that these processes had contributed to social disconnection and isolation, meaning that power had been removed from the local institutions that created positive social bonds (Kruger 2007: 2). It was from this that the decentralizing and localism emphasis of the modernization project was justified, and began the process of aligning the Conservatives more closely with the Liberal Democrats (Dorey and Garnett 2012: 404).

The cumulative effect of the ideological repositioning of the Conservatives under Cameron was critical to their capacity to form a coalition with the Liberal Democrats in 2010. Cameron made it clear that the Conservatives were ideologically converging with the Liberal Democrats, who themselves were increasingly recasting themselves through the emergence of the orange book tendency (Evans 2012: 481). Cameron identified this convergence as early as 2007 when he argued that there was a liberal influence in the renewal of Conservatism. He argued the case for Liberal Conservatism by stating that 'we need a new liberal consensus in our country. Without the Conservative stress on communal obligations and institutions, liberalism can become hollow individualism. . . . And without the liberal stress on individual freedom, Conservatism can become hollow individualism' (McAnulla 2012: 171).

Such rhetoric irritated traditional Thatcherites. Indeed, throughout the modernizing era of 2005–10, Cameron had to contend with murmurings of discontent. Norman Tebbit complained (in 2006) that Cameron was 'purging the name and memory of Thatcherism' (Dorey et al. 2011: 82). The most visceral critics of Cameron were located in the Cornerstone Group, a 30–40 strong grouping of Conservative parliamentarians. They argued that adherence to pure undiluted Thatcherism was necessary and that meant a stronger and more authoritarian core vote approach, with a rhetorical emphasis on immigration and tax cuts, to prevent disaffected right-wingers defecting to UKIP or even the BNP. One prominent Cornerstone member, Edward Leigh, was reportedly head of the queue of Conservative right-wingers who wanted to see Cameron so that he could tell him to his face that he thought he was the 'anti-Christ' (Dorey et al. 2011: 81).

This claim was made before the economic crisis and then crash of 2008 forced Cameron to rethink his whole approach towards downgrading the economic sphere. The Conservatives needed to construct a response to the part nationalization of some of the leading banks, notably RBS and Lloyds; the bailing out of the financial sector; the creation of both a deep recession and unprecedented levels of public debt (Heffernan 2011: 167). However, the Cameron strategy appeared to 'assume, indeed necessitate', continued economic growth (Dorey 2009: 261). The response of the Conservatives to the ensuing economic crisis was thus not entirely convincing. Indeed it was 'almost as embarrassing for the Conservatives as it was for the Labour government' as the financial services sector had been deregulated in the era of Thatcherism (McAnulla 2010: 291). The Conservatives could only escape culpability through an 'extraordinary act of political and historical amnesia' (Lee 2009b: 74). Thereafter policy was constructed more through pragmatism and expediency than anything else (Lee 2011a: 61). The immediate and expedient option as a party of opposition was to a build a critique of Labour for 'allowing' the crisis to happen. The language was explicit – the Brown government were accused of a 'borrowing binge' and having 'maxed out our nation's credit card' (Lee 2009b: 68–71).

Thus, by the mid to latter part of the Parliament, the modernizers had been forced to reassess and abandon their strategy of matching the spending commitments of Labour. By 2009 the rhetoric had shifted to reducing debt and borrowing to rebalance the economy through an age of austerity (Lee 2009a: 46; 2009b: 77) By the time of the general election of 2010 the divergence between the parties was one of speed: Labour planned £24 billion of tax increases and £47 billion of spending cuts, whereas the Conservatives planned £14 billion of tax increases and £57 billion in spending cuts. While the Conservatives planned immediate cuts, Labour wanted to delay fiscal tightening until 2011–12 (Pirie 2012: 356). Ultimately, the turbulence of the 2008–09 period destabilized the predetermined strategy that the modernizers had carefully crafted in the 2005–07 period. That shift from convergence to critique to divergence made them look reactive (Lee 2009a: 59). This may well explain why 'there was not a simple translation of concerns' from Labour and the economic downturn 'towards trust in a Conservative government to solve [such] economic problems' (Green 2010: 680).

As an opposition party facing an unpopular prime minister, who was leading a discredited administration that had presided over a seismic economic collapse and had created a massive fiscal deficit, this should have translated into support for the Conservatives. This argument carries even greater validity when we note that the Conservatives had reclaimed a majority of the support of the press, and the fact that they were in a far stronger financial position than their rivals. By the time of the 2010 general election, Labour had lost the support of all but *The Mirror*. *The Sun* returned to the Conservatives, while *The Guardian* endorsed the Liberal Democrats. The Conservatives commanded 74 per cent support from the total daily circulation of papers, and significantly the swing from Labour to Conservative among *Sun* readers was 13.5 per cent, as compared to the national 5 per cent swing (Wring and Deacon 2010: 451). Furthermore, without the press backing of the previous three elections, Labour also had to contend with financial and organizational constraints which greatly undermined them during the lead up to the 2010 general election. Whereas Labour received donations of £3,754,985 in the first quarter of 2010 (down nearly 5 million from the first quarter of 2005), and a further £5,283,198 during the 30 days of the election campaign, the Conservatives received £10,659,521 in the 3-month lead-in period, and £7,317,601 during the campaign itself (Dorey 2010: 411, 429). The Conservatives thus had the advantage of being able to spend up to the campaign limit of £18.9 whereas Labour could not (Fisher 2010: 778–93).

Despite all of these advantages, however, the reality was that the Conservatives faced a 'formidable challenge' in securing an overall majority (Curtice 2009: 182). They needed to gain an additional 120 plus seats simply to secure a majority of one. This required that the Conservatives had to make their largest number of gains since 1931. The necessary swing was 6.9 per cent, which was greater than the swings that had propelled the last three Conservative oppositions back into office (Stuart 2011: 39). The positive spin on the Conservative performance in 2010 is to compare the condition of the Conservatives in 2005 (198 MPs) to that of Labour in 1983 (209 MPs). Noting this, alongside the aforementioned size of the challenge facing the Conservatives to win outright, Bale argues that Cameron did 'pretty well' by ensuring that he became prime minister for 'he had to do in just four or five years what it had taken three Labour leaders some thirteen years to accomplish' (Bale 2012b: 236). However, critics of the modernization process blamed Cameron when the Conservatives fell short of 326 seats needed for outright victory (Conservatives 307; Labour 259; Liberal Democrat 59; others 29) (Kavanagh and Cowley 2010: 351).

Four issues can be discussed concerning the Conservative campaign: first, the impact of the leadership debates; second, the failure of the Big Society narrative; third, the increased competition that existed on the right through the rise of UKIP; and fourth, residual doubts about the Conservatives regarding their likeability and the extent to which they had changed (Dorey 2010: 429–32).

For nearly five decades it had been impossible to secure an agreement between the parties (and broadcasters) to enable formal leadership debates to become part of the electioneering process. Conservative strategists were now keen to participate. They thought the ill-humoured and socially gauche

Brown would compare badly with the relaxed and self-assured Cameron (Dorey et al. 2011: 164). Leadership debates would allow Cameron to frame the election as a referendum on the performance of Labour in office and the need for change. Most significantly, pre-debate polling reinforced these perceptions. They showed that the electorate expected Cameron to outperform Brown (Allen et al. 2011: 185). However, given their poll lead throughout the 2 years leading into the campaign, entering the leadership debates was a 'high risk strategy' (Seawright 2012: 37). They had not considered the scenarios that could emerge from participating and critically there was 'little discussion about how to deal with a strong performance from the Liberal democrat leader' (Snowdon 2010: 401).

The problem for the Conservatives was the weaker-than-expected performance of Cameron and the stronger-than-expected performance by Nick Clegg. Cameron suffered from the weight of expectation and his performance was overladen with prepared anecdotes which left him open to ridicule (Allen et al. 2011: 188). His most significant failing, however, was that he addressed the audience in the television studio, rather than talking to the camera and the voters watching on television (Seawright 2012: 34–6). The less well known Clegg did so, which helped contribute to the immediate polling that stated that he was felt to have won the debate (ICM Guardian poll had Clegg on 51 per cent to Cameron on 20 and Brown on 19 per cent). Cameron would improve his performance in the second and third debates, running Clegg closer in the second (Clegg 33 per cent, Cameron and Brown both 29 per cent) and winning the third (Cameron 35 per cent, Brown 29 per cent and Clegg 27 per cent). However, the impact of the first debate had altered the dynamics of the campaigning period (Kavanagh and Cowley 2010: 247). It prompted a significant surge in projected support for the Liberal Democrats as they increased their projected vote share by nearly 10 points. This surge was at the expense of both the main parties, and Clegg challenged Cameron as the so-called agent of change (Seawright 2012: 35). For the remainder of the campaign the Liberal Democrats battled with Labour for second place in the polls, as the rise of a genuine three-party system seemed imminent (Allen et al. 2011: 190–1). Given this it was inevitable that Cameron would come in for internal criticism. To some Conservatives this was part of the explanation as to why they failed to secure an outright majority (Dorey 2010: 420).

The other critique of Cameron would relate to their supposedly unifying narrative – the 'Big Society'. It was meant to provide coherence to their agenda of decentralization and involvement of the voluntary sector in addressing the problems of 'broken Britain' (Green 2010: 683). However, as a slogan 'Big Society, not Big Government' completely failed to capture the imagination of a sceptical electorate (Seawright 2012: 39). They either did not understand what it meant, or if they did they were doubtful about it as it looked like an attempt to shrink the welfare state. Part of the difficulty with the Big Society as a core narrative to underpin an election campaign was that the Conservatives had only started to use the term in late 2009 (Snowdon 2010: 399). As a consequence many Conservative parliamentarians had reservations about its usefulness as a way of garnering support for the party. Such Conservatives had been Cameron critics all along. Their argument was that the Big Society was 'woolly and lacking in clarity' (Seawright 2012: 39), and that victory would have been possible if they advanced a 'potent, readily understandable message'. This argument implies that a greater focus on their Euroscepticism and more emphasis on tax and immigration (in the style of the core vote strategies of 2001 and 2005) would have worked in 2010. This is an argument that cannot be proven or disproven but was held by many Conservatives in part due to the impact of UKIP (Dorey and Garnett 2012: 406)

Those Thatcherite Eurosceptic Conservatives felt that the rise of UKIP had been a consequence of Cameron moving the Conservatives closer to the centre and creating the political space for UKIP to thrive. They argued that the UKIP rhetoric was broader than its anti-Europeanism and its emphasis on immigration. They noted that UKIP offered an essential Thatcherite economic platform alongside a healthy dose of social conservatism, which had cost the Conservatives votes in marginal constituencies. The UKIP vote share was only 3.1 nationally, but it was calculated that the presence of a UKIP candidate may have cost the Conservatives the opportunity to annex 21 additional marginal target seats and thereby a majority. This calculation was based on identifying the gap between the incumbency vote and the Conservative candidate in second place, and then adding the UKIP vote to see if the joint Conservative-UKIP vote would have been greater than the incumbent vote. Although this association cannot be proven, it is reasonable to assume that a significant proportion of the UKIP vote came from disaffected Conservatives who are sceptical about the downplaying of Euroscepticism and immigration that had characterized the Cameron era (Dorey 2010: 432; Dorey et al. 2011: 182).

The final explanation as to why the Conservatives could not secure for themselves an overall majority relates to residual issues to do with party image. Despite the modernization process Labour still retained a lead in terms of the party best equipped to deal with issues such as health (33 to 24 percent) and unemployment (30–24). Despite the scale of the economic meltdown in 2008 the Conservative lead in terms of economic competence was very narrow (29–26) (Green 2010: 412). The electorate did not fully believe that the Conservatives had changed, indicating that Cameron had only 'partially succeeded in throwing off old reputations' (Bale and Webb 2011: 56). They were not sure what the Conservatives stood for and they did not fully trust them on their values, with many fearing that they still put the better off first (Kavanagh and Cowley 2010: 64). As Green concludes, 'by the time of the 2010 campaign many voters wanted change, but could not yet put their faith in a government run by the Conservatives' (Green 2010: 668). Thus it was an election campaign characterized by a credibility gap for both parties on the critical issue of economic management. Whatever reservations they may have had about the performance of Labour was almost equalled by the level of concern about the consequences of electing the Conservatives – that is, the choking of the fragile recovery by cutting the deficit too speedily, and then creating a double dip recession (Dorey 2010: 429).

The transition to coalition government: The necessity of austerity 2010–

The Conservatives had made only limited preparations for the eventuality of a hung Parliament (Kavanagh and Cowley 2010: 206). Nonetheless Cameron was 'impressively adroit' over the crucial 5 days that followed, especially 'given the stakes he was playing for, (and) the fatigue he must have been suffering' (Dorey et al. 2011: 184). Three realistic options in terms of government formation existed. First, there was the nightmare scenario of a Labour-Liberal Democrat or rainbow coalition. Should this scenario emerge, not only would the Conservatives be resigned to another period of opposition, but there could be longer-term implications. The real fear was that the Liberal Democrats would instinctively prefer to align themselves with Labour. Centre-left progressives had long harboured a wish for greater cooperation between the parties, with a possible arrangement over voting reform and AV, which could 'mobilise the supposedly natural anti-Tory majority in the electorate to lock the Conservatives out of power, possibly forever' (Bale and Sanderson-Nash 2011: 249). This fear had led to the hastily arranged Hung Parliament party election broadcast that the Conservatives used in the latter stages of the campaign, a move that now, given the parliamentary arithmetic, seemed rather ironic (Evans 2011: 58–9).

The second option was to establish a minority Conservative administration. However, there were doubts as to whether they would be able to pass an emergency budget (Bale 2011: 247). There were also other strategic issues to take into account even if an emergency budget could be passed. Given the economic environment they would be forced into policy choices that might reduce their support in the short term. This concern was hugely important. This was because their minority status would make them vulnerable to defeat if a vote of confidence was called. The combined impact could be that they would be forced into an election before the year was out with huge doubts as to whether they could hold onto their 307 seats or sustain their 36.1 vote share (Evans 2012: 480). For Cameron a minority administration meant instability and the fear of removal from office and a temporary tenure as prime minister (Quinn et al. 2011: 297–300).

While the merits of the second option (i.e. a minority administration) would be debated within the party, the need to avoid a Labour-Liberal

Democrat coalition being formed was paramount. To undermine the prospect of this Cameron made a dramatic move in order to 'set the agenda' to the period of the coalition negotiations (Quinn et al. 2011: 301). In doing so, he was to show 'remarkable tactical guile' (Russell 2010: 511). Cameron informed the Liberal Democrats that he wanted to make a 'big, open and comprehensive offer' of a full coalition, and invited them to work with the Conservatives to provide economic and political stability (Quinn et al. 2011: 301). That the Conservatives were 'open minded and flexible about the contours of a coalition' was leadership driven, and by pushing for this it 'deflected' attention away from the argument that their campaign had been poor and the result a disappointment (Stuart 2011: 48–9). Cameron instructed his party to concede political ground to enable a coalition with the Liberal Democrats to be entered into. This would be not only 'in the national interest' and in the interests 'of forging an open and trusting relationship' with the Liberal Democrats (Fox 2010: 611).

Cameron was thus crucial to the chances of the negotiations being successful. His reputation and methods mattered to the Liberal Democrats. Cameron was seen to be a pragmatist who 'recognised the value of an alliance as part of the new politics' (Norton 2011a: 255–6). The emotional literacy of Cameron was critical to persuading the orange book Liberal, Clegg, as an economic liberal, that a coalition was viable. Cameron and Clegg were clearly different to their predecessors. Just as Cameron was a modernizer as opposed to his three Thatcherite predecessors, Clegg had three predecessors who were not orange book liberals – Paddy Ashdown, Charles Kennedy and Menzies Campbell. All three of them tilted to Labour out of instinct, not just because they were to the left of the Liberal Democrat spectrum, but because Hague, Duncan Smith and Howard were to the right of the Conservative spectrum. However, it was not just an issue of positioning within their respective parties. Personality would matter too. The two young leaders (Cameron was 44 and Clegg was 43) were said to have a 'good personal chemistry' and came from similar backgrounds (Cameron went to Eton and Clegg to Westminster), and it was felt that they would be able to work together (Stuart 2011: 49). Personality and working relationships were also factors in terms of a possible Labour-Liberal Democrat coalition. Clegg was concerned about his ability to construct a viable working relationship with Brown, who he found to be 'lecturing, hectoring and bullying' (Mandelson 2010: 550).

However, the fact that the Liberal Democrats had decided to hold parallel negotiations with Labour was hugely distressing to Cameron (Kavanagh and Cowley 2010: 213). The 'sticking point' was electoral reform (Laws 2010: 104). Labour were willing to offer a referendum on AV and Clegg was asking Cameron to match this. It was at this critical juncture that Cameron held two meetings, one with his shadow Cabinet and one with the PCP. The shadow Cabinet accepted Cameron's argument that they must offer the Liberal Democrats a referendum on AV to ensure that the coalition agreement could proceed (Qvortrup 2012: 109). Cameron informed the PCP that he *believed* that Labour would be offering the Liberal Democrats AV *without* a referendum (Wilson 2010: 206). If Labour were actually offering the Liberal Democrats the prospect of AV without a referendum, then the PCP would be willing to accept the 'still distasteful' option of AV with a referendum (Wilson 2010: 179). Cameron had ensured that for the Conservatives the coalition process had been:

> a top-down one, driven by a handful of Cameron's close confidants, and involving the Shadow cabinet and Parliamentary Party only sporadically, and only when the leadership needed it. On Tuesday night when Prime Minister Cameron went before Conservative MPs, it was essentially a *fait accompli*. It was difficult for Conservative MPs who harboured doubts about the coalition deal to air them openly in an atmosphere where the new Prime Minister was being paraded triumphantly in front of them. Nor were they shown a copy of the coalition agreement which had been drawn up between the two parties. (Kavanagh and Cowley 2010: 221)

It may have been 5 days later than hoped, but Cameron had achieved his objective. He had taken his party from crisis and back into government, albeit only coalition. Of his 'transformative impact', Gamble compares him, not with Thatcher, but with Blair. Although it was not his intention, Cameron had used the circumstances that he faced opportunistically, and had achieved what Blair:

> had failed to achieve, a realignment of British politics, a big tent involving the full participation of two of the three national parties. . . . The realignment of the centre left which had been the aspiration of so many progressives had been transformed by Cameron into a realignment on the centre right. (Gamble 2010: 644)

What of the coalition agreement? How favourable was this to the Conservatives? Bale argues that the Conservatives did remarkably well, to such an extent that it shows 'what happens when vegetarians negotiate with carnivores' (Bale 2012c: 328). We can assess how the rewards of office were distributed by two means: personnel and policy.

In terms of personnel the coalition agreement established that ministerial posts would be allocated 'in proportion to the parliamentary representation of the two coalition parties', and yet the Liberal Democrats secured 19.3 per cent of all frontbench portfolios despite holding only 15.7 per cent of all coalition representation in the House of Commons (Matthews 2011: 499). This intensified irritation in the Conservative ranks. After all, 95 Conservative MPs who were holding shadow ministerial positions prior to the election were expecting office under a majority Conservative administration. Granting 24 ministerial positions to the Liberal Democrats created 24 bruised egos on the Conservative backbenchers, as well as other new ministers who were offered lower ranking posts than they had hoped for (Jones 2010: 620). (Simultaneous to this Cameron made a misguided attempt to ensure that Conservative ministers should not only attend 1922 Backbench Committee meetings, but that they should attend as voting members and not just as observers, as was tradition. His backing down from this and the subsequent election of the right-wing Graham Brady to the 1922 chair made him look weak – Dorey et al. 2011: 189).

However, while the Liberal Democrats came out of the forming of the coalition in a numerically strong ministerial position, they did not secure through ministerial appointments a strong capacity to influence the policy agenda. Cameron outmanoeuvred Clegg on the prestige aspect of portfolio allocation (Evans 2011: 55). Whereas 14 Conservatives entered Cabinet positions that mirrored their shadow Cabinet portfolios when they had been in opposition, none of the Liberal Democrats did so (Russell 2010: 519). The significant offices of state were saved for Conservatives – Foreign Office (Hague), Treasury (Osborne) and the Home Office (Theresa May). The Conservatives retained control of ministries to which they did not want to allow the Liberal Democrats to take ownership. For example, retaining the Department for International Development under the leadership of Andrew Mitchell was central. Having ring fenced spending cuts in this department, claiming ownership of this policy arena was significant. It was an illustration of their awareness of global poverty and social injustice, and would help to overcome the nasty imagery which Cameron felt had undermined their electoral appeal (Heppell and Lightfoot 2012: 130–8). The Liberal Democrats were not permitted to lead any of the big spending departments – Work and Pensions, Health and Education were all Conservative led (by Duncan Smith, Andrew Lansley and Michael Gove respectively), with the appointment of Duncan Smith central to placating the right of the PCP (Debus 2011: 300).

Of the five Cabinet posts secured by the Liberal Democrats, none of those were in departments' central to the Conservatives identity (Lees 2011: 284). Their allocation tied in with the Conservative need to bind, marginalize or undermine. In terms of binding, offering the Liberal Democrats a Cabinet post within the Treasury, which was subordinate to Osborne, ensured that they had shared responsibility for the austerity measures that were to be pursued. By positioning first David Laws, and then Danny Alexander in this post, it allowed the Conservatives to articulate their agenda as being in the national interest, with greater conviction (Laws 2010: 200). The need to marginalize explained the offer of the Scottish Office, which in the post-devolutionary era is a relatively 'unsubstantial' office, and one which the Liberal Democrats had previously advocated abolishing (Bennister and Heffernan 2012: 781). The more important marginalization was that of Clegg himself. Clegg was left co-ordinating what might be portrayed as self-interested, and low salient issues for many voters (electoral and House of Lords reform), from the Office of Deputy Prime Minister, where he was 'overworked and understaffed'

(Bale 2012c: 329). Offering the Liberal Democrats the Departments of Energy and Climate Change and Business, Innovation and Skills fulfilled the Conservative need to undermine. At Energy Chris Huhne was compelled to announce the development of eight new nuclear power stations (in August 2010) which contravened their manifesto commitment which stated their objection to further nuclear power stations (Russell 2010: 516). However, the most humiliating experience for the Liberal Democrats was the sight of Vince Cable piloting through Parliament the imposition of increased tuition fees, which directly contradicted the position that they had campaigned for during the general election (Evans 2011: 57). This reflects the success that Cameron secured when combining the debate on personnel and policy. When placing this in its wider comparative context, Bale concludes that it was

> difficult to conceive that a continental European party in the same position as the Liberal Democrats would have negotiated a deal which left all of the high offices of state in their partners' hands, left that partner in full control of fiscal and economic policy, made it chiefly responsible for devising and implementing a policy (university tuition fees) that made a mockery of its prior commitments, and offered it so few tangible policy wins on which to fight the next election. (Bale 2011: 248)

This assertion reflects the view that in policy terms the Conservatives did reasonably well out of the coalition agreement. Other than on political and electoral reform, the Liberal Democrats could also claim to have secured significant concessions and gained policy ground in terms of public services. However, the coalition agreement recognized that the trajectory of social policy would be subordinated to deficit reduction (Quinn et al. 2011: 302–5). Although the Liberal Democrats secured a concession of a tax cut for the lowest paid, the Conservatives prevailed in terms of deficit reduction and the retrenching of the state. The Conservatives prevailed in terms of security matters embracing national security, crime and policing, immigration, justice and defence. The Conservatives also prevailed on the European Union. Ensuring that the deficit reduction took precedence over others, however, constituted a clause that 'trumped all others'. Therefore, the coalition deal was 'a decisive victory for the Conservatives' (Norton 2011a: 256; Dorey et al. 2011: 191).

The Conservatives faced two dominant issues upon entering government – one short term relating to electoral reform and the AV referendum; and one longer term relating to the deficit reduction strategy and economic recovery. These issues would determine the future of the party. They needed to win the AV referendum for clear partisan reasons – it was a potential 'game changer' that could harm their electoral competitiveness in the future (Lees 2011: 180). Simulations on the 2010 general election were conducted to see how AV would have altered the levels of parliamentary representation.

The Conservatives would have had 284 seats (down 22); Labour 248 (down 10) and the Liberal Democrats 89 (up 32 from 57) and this could have created a hypothetical Labour-Liberal Democrat coalition with a majority of 11 (337 seats) (Sanders et al. 2011: 5–23).

Cameron secured a considerable success for the Conservatives when the AV referendum produced a clear result in May 2011. Circumstances conspired against reform for a variety of reasons. The Liberal Democrats were left asking the electorate to endorse a process of change that they themselves did not fully want. AV was not their preferred option, (indeed Clegg had previously described it as a miserable little compromise), but nonetheless it was an advance on FPTP and a staging post towards PR (Russell 2010: 515). The Conservatives were also able to imply that during times of austerity electoral reform should be a low priority and the desire for reform reflected the self-interest of the Liberal Democrats. This insinuation reflected public opinion which showed that AV was a reform with limited appeal (Pinto-Duschinsky et al. 2011: 16–17). If the Liberal Democrats were compromised by advancing a reform that they did not truly believe in, then the problem for Labour was that they were fundamentally divided on the issue. Ed Miliband campaigned for a 'yes' vote, (but refused to share a platform with Clegg). However, his own frontbench was not in full agreement with him. The 'No' campaign was also boosted by heavyweight Labour figures from the Blair era, notably John Reid and Margaret Beckett. The Conservatives were completely unified throughout as AV was comfortably defeated by 68 to 32 per cent, thus removing electoral reform from the political agenda for a generation or more. Such was the strength of opposition to changing to AV it was argued that it would be 'unlikely' to be on the 'agenda in coalition negotiations' if a future general election produces another inconclusive outcome (Whiteley et al. 2012: 319).

However, electoral reform was only one aspect of the 'new politics' that was being advanced partly through the Liberal Democrat influence within the coalition. In securing dominance in the economic sphere, the Conservatives appeared to have conceded ground in terms of political reform, only for their AV referendum result to stall the Liberal Democrat advance (Fox 2010: 34). Three other aspects warrant assessment: first, the establishment of fixed term Parliaments; second, proposals for House of Lords reform; and third, constituency equalization. Had the Conservatives formed a majority administration, the first two aspects outlined above would not have been pursued (Norton 2011b: 158). First, the Fixed Term Parliaments Act was designed to ensure the dissolutions were no longer at the discretion of the incumbent prime minister (Bogdanor 2011: 109). It should ensure that parliamentary elections will occur on the first Thursday in May in the fifth year after the last general election, although Bogdanor suggests that the act is 'misnamed' and it merely makes dissolutions 'more difficult' (Bogdanor 2011: 107–9). The motivation for both as new coalition partners in a time of economic difficulties was clear. The act formed a way of embedding their new partnership and providing them with the time to allow their austerity measures (tax increases and expenditure cuts) to be implemented and the economy to recover before they then both had to face the electorate again in May 2015 (Evans 2012: 480).

This attempt at mutually assured protection was not feasible when it came to House of Lords reform and constituency equalization. The Conservatives were keen to push constituency equalization. An examination of the 2005 general election highlighted the Conservative view that variations in the sizes of constituencies contributed to a bias in favour of Labour. Blair's final election victory had been secured on the back of a 36.1 per cent vote share which created for them 56.5 per cent of the parliamentary seats. However, the Conservatives secured 32.3 per cent of the vote but only 31.5 of the parliamentary seats and the Liberal Democrats secured 9.9 per cent of the parliamentary seats as a reward for 22.6 per cent of the vote (Borisyuk et al. 2010: 4). The changes that Cameron hoped to advance involved reducing parliamentary representation from 650 to 600 and in the process achieve greater equalization in terms of constituency sizes. The aim for Cameron had been to obtain parliamentary approval leading to proposed reductions and then implement equalization so that each constituency was within 5 per cent of the average size (76,641) – that is, between 72,010 and 80,473 (Baston 2011). The benefits that could have been created to the Conservatives can be seen from simulations of voting behaviour in the 2010 general election across 600 constituencies rather than 650. It was calculated that equalization and reduction would lead to the loss of 18 Labour seats (around 7 per cent of their 2010 representation), 15 Conservative seats (just under 5 per cent) and 14 Liberal Democrats seats (around 25 per cent). The actual impact would not have enabled the Conservatives to win outright but would have left them at 292 rather than at 307 (short by 9 of the new majority of 301 as opposed to short by 19 of the 326 majority threshold), Labour on 240 rather than on 258 and the Liberal Democrats on 43 rather than on 57, with the others at 23. In reality, the Labour–Liberal Democrat coalition option was short as it amounted to 315, instead of 326; in the Baston simulation, it would have been even further short at 283, instead of 301 (Baston 2011). However, when the Conservatives rebelled in significant numbers on the second reading of the House of Lords Bill (in July 2012), forcing the government to abandon their attempts at reform, the Liberal Democrats responded by abandoning their willingness to back the Conservatives on constituency equalization.

The above debates on new politics showcased the classic gap between political rhetoric and reality. The rhetorical claim was that the political system was broken (a claim which was not really strongly held by the Conservatives), and reforming it would rebuild trust in the political process (Norton 2011b: 157–60). The reality was that the real determinant of success for the Conservatives by 2015 would be in the economic sphere, and not in terms of political reform. The Conservatives have used opposition and then coalition government to try and shape how the post-economic crash period should be interpreted. Their strategy involves *deflection* (i.e. apportioning blame) and then the *reluctant* responsibility of the Conservatives to take remedial action (Lee 2011b: 9–13). Here it has been necessary for the Conservatives to repeatedly emphasize how New Labour had mismanaged the economy (Beech 2011: 271–6). In the context of solidifying the deflection strategy being in coalition has its advantages. During the general election campaign the Liberal Democrats had sided with Labour in terms of the danger of cutting too much and too soon. During the course of the coalition negotiations the Conservatives had ensured that the Liberal Democrats 'succumbed' to their view on deficit reduction (Russell 2010: 515). This ensured 'joint responsibility for tough decisions, not sole blame for the painful cuts to come' (Laws 2010: 51), and gave Cameron greater credibility when he talked about the politics of necessity ('there is no alternative') and the national interest (Kerr et al. 2011: 203). Critically this benefits the Conservatives at the expense of the other two parties. A Conservative administration engaging in a similar political strategy would be seen to be more ideologically motivated. The endorsement of the Liberal Democrats legitimates the strategy and ensures that the so-called progressive alliance is on opposing sides of this debate (Lee 2011b: 10).

The economic strategy of the Conservative-dominated coalition was geared towards cutting the deficit and rebalancing the economy. This was based around a rejection of unsustainable debt and the promotion of a growth model based on more investment, higher exports and increased savings (Lee 2011a: 60). The measures that Osborne introduced involved a fiscal retrenchment of 6.3 per cent of GDP or £113 billion over the course of the Parliament, and 77 percent of rebalancing would be achieved via spending cuts and only 23 per cent through increases in taxation (including increases in VAT from 17.5 to 20 per cent and in capital gains tax from 18 to 28 per cent). With the exception of ring-fenced departments (Health and International Development), there would need to be a 20 per cent reduction in spending (Lee 2011a: 63). In addition there would be a public sector pay freeze, an acceleration of the increase for the state pension age, and a new tax on the banks would be levied. A newly formed Office for Budget Responsibility forecast that the economy would expand by 1.2 per cent in 2010, 2.3 per cent in 2011, 2.8 per cent in 2012, 2.9 per cent in 2013 and 2.7 per cent in 2014 (Ganesh 2012: 257–8). However, very early on these projections were made to look widely optimistic. A beleaguered Osborne was later forced to acknowledge this as the 2.3 per cent growth forecast for 2011 was reduced to 0.9 per cent, and the projected unemployment rate was adjusted to 8.7 per cent instead of 8.3 per cent. More worryingly in political terms Osborne was forced to admit that eliminating the structural deficit would go into the next Parliament, and would not be completed in this one. The plan to present the electorate in 2015 with 'healthy public finances, a buoyant economy and a new tax cutting budget', as a 'reward for their stoic endurance of austerity', was 'gone' (Ganesh 2012: 278). Osborne would now ask the electorate to reward the Conservatives simply for dealing with the deficit inherited from Labour and to ask them to recognize that it would take longer than expected. There could be no acknowledgement that Plan A had failed, and no plan B could be considered. Amending their austerity plans

> would not be seen as pragmatic – it would be portrayed as a U-turn. To back down [would] incur the wrath of the financial markets but it would also carry with it seismic *political* implications. The parliamentary right of the Conservative Party, long suspicious of Cameron, would be apoplectic and in fear of this eventuality they have already begun comparing Cameron to Edward Heath, whose 1970–1974 administration incurred the derision and despair of the right for their economic policy U-turn. Not only would the internal cohesion of the Conservatives be damaged but their external appeal would be undermined as their claim to economic credibility would be questioned. Ed Balls would berate them and assert that the deficit reduction plan had been a "reckless gamble" and they had been forced to back down. Backing down on the speed and scale of the deficit reduction plan would also legitimate Labour as an opposition party by validating the position that Balls has taken. (Heppell and Seawright 2012: 232)

Three years into the Conservative-dominated coalition the picture remains one of economic weakness. There is only limited evidence to suggest that the austerity measures are working (Kirby 2013: 43–62). Given the absence of a sustained economic recovery and diminishing living standards, Labour should have made more progress in opposition. However, opinion polling on economic competence shows only limited movement up to early 2013. At the first year anniversary of the coalition 31 per cent agreed with the economic approach that Cameron and Osborne were pursuing and 48 per cent disagreed. While not necessarily encouraging, these figures were better than those for Miliband and Balls – of their alternative approach 18 per cent agreed and 54 per cent disagreed. By February 2013 those figures had hardly shifted: Cameron and Osborne were now scoring 27 agreed (down 4) and 51 disagreed (up 3), whereas Miliband and Balls were 20 agreed (up 2) and 55 disagreed (up 1). Therefore, although the electorate were displaying doubts about the austerity measures being pursued, they were not ready to trust Labour as an alternative. Indeed while 26 per cent of the electorate regard both New Labour and the coalition as jointly responsible for the economic difficulties (as at February 2013), 27 per cent blame the coalition, but 36 per cent blame the previous Labour administration alone. This possibly explains how more of the electorate appeared to believe that the coalition was cutting out of necessity, rather than for ideologically driven reasons (Curtice 2013: 53–7).

All of these governing difficulties that the Conservatives have experienced, or would claim they inherited, however, have to be placed within the wider context of increasing public dissatisfaction with the political class. The parliamentary expenses scandal of 2009 did not hurt one particular party (although Cameron was seen to have managed the crisis more effectively than Brown), but rather it eroded electoral trust in politicians generally (Kelso 2009: 453). This was relevant when considering the London Riots of 2011. Cameron wanted to attribute this to the legacy of the 'broken society' left by New Labour, within which 'poor parenting' and 'moral decay' had created 'sick communities' (Birch and Allen 2012: 32, 36). Left-wing critiques preferred to attribute the riots to 'prevailing economic conditions' and 'specifically to levels of relative deprivation and rising inequality' all exacerbated by the 'spending cuts initiated under the Coalition government's deficit-reduction programme' (Birch and Allen 2012: 32). However, some drew a link between the riots and 'elite scandals' – that is, of bankers and politicians in the financial and expenses crises of the 2008 and 2009 period. It was alleged that these scandals had appeared to 'condone selfishness', and had created a culture that made some feel it was acceptable to 'take want they wanted, when they wanted it' (Allen and Birch 2012: 32, 36).

This corroding of public life was tied to the phone hacking scandal, which was to cause considerable embarrassment to the Conservatives. During their time in opposition Cameron had appointed Andy Coulson as his Director of Communications and Planning (June 2007). Coulson was deemed to have the following advantage: as the former Editor of the *News of the World,* he was well connected and 'had the ear' of Rupert Murdoch, and Cameron was understandably keen to secure the endorsement of the News International stable of newspapers again. However, Coulson was a risky appointment as he 'carried baggage', after being forced to resign as editor of the *News of the World* in January 2007, after his royal reporter was convicted of illegally hacking the phones of aides to the royal family (Snowdon 2010: 255). Cameron accepted the view that Coulson had no knowledge of this, but the fact that he had to resign should have led Cameron to fear that this story might resurface. Nonetheless, Cameron appointed Coulson as director of communications to the prime minister in May 2010, but Coulson was forced to resign within 8 months due to renewed speculation about his involvement in phone hacking. This led to the closure of the *News of the World* in July 2011, and Coulson was arrested and went on trial for phone hacking and illegal payments to police officers in late 2013. Cameron would admit that he 'regretted hiring' Coulson. He set up the Leveson inquiry to examine the relationship between politics, media and the police, which subsequently and embarrassingly exposed the lengths that Cameron would go to in order to ingratiate himself with Rebekah Brooks, the Chief Executive of News International (Ganesh 2012: 274–5).

The cumulative impact of their economic inheritance and the obstinate refusal of the economy to recover, alongside the inability of his Big Society narrative to gain traction, meant that Cameron could ill afford the distraction of scandal. The transition from opposition to government and from the politics of modernization to the necessity of austerity has not been easy for Cameron and the Conservatives.

Cameronism as statecraft

There has been a tendency to compare the modernization project that Cameron pursued with that of New Labour under Blair post 1994. Bale has argued, however, that the extent to which 'change' had occurred within the Cameron Conservatives was not as advanced as had been the case under Blair and New Labour. The renewal of New Labour involved a 'reengineering' of the party, based on a changed policy/ideological outlook and political approach. The completion of the modernization process of New Labour was Blair challenging them over Clause IV. This was hugely symbolic, but that defining Clause IV moment was lacking for Cameron in opposition. As a consequence, whereas Blair had 'reengineered' his party in creating New Labour, Cameron had merely 'restyled' the Conservatives (Bale 2010).

Hayton argues that by agreeing to join the Conservatives in coalition, it was Clegg who handed Cameron his Clause IV moment. Cameron's desire to form the coalition was, according to Hayton, an astute act of pragmatic (and necessary) statecraft (Hayton 2012b: 60–78). It was a necessary but defensive or protective act – that is, Cameron needed to create a roadblock to prevent a potential centre-left realignment of British politics in which Labour and Liberal Democrats could be allowed to marginalize the Conservatives. Cameron thus not only stalled the assumption that a hung Parliament would facilitate a progressive centre-left alliance, but he manipulated the circumstances that he faced to manufacture it into a potential realignment of the centre-right. It proved his modernizing credentials as he created the type of 'big tent' politics that was assumed to be the objective of Blair and New Labour (Geddes and Tonge 2010: 866–73). Having bound the Liberal Democrats to the Conservatives, Cameron has attempted to use collaboration in the short term as a means to exploit and erode the Liberal Democrats over the longer term.

How the electorate assesses the economic competence of the coalition and cohesion between and within the coalition partners will be critical to the future of the Conservatives as the dominant coalition partner. The Conservative approach has been framed by the Thatcherite rationale of there is no alternative. It has also been influenced by the Thatcherite statecraft objective of de-politization. It can be argued that the Big Society is their tool of de-politization and their weapon through which to seek to gain dominance of political debate. Their capacity to obtain and sustain political argument hegemony is dependent on the ability (or lack of it) of Labour to successfully expose an alternative interpretation of the Big Society narrative.

Labour under Miliband will have to go beyond simply arguing that the Big Society is 'a smokescreen for public service cuts through the promotion of volunteering as a cut-price alternative to state provision', and they will have to outline a more credible alternative (Mycock and Tonge 2011: 56; Curtice 2013: 57). Should the economic strategy be deemed to have been necessary *and* effective then the Big Society narrative might become seen as 'short-hand for a new settlement between British citizens and their state, much as the Welfare state captured the new dispensation after World War Two' (Pattie and Johnston 2011: 404). However, should the economic strategy come to be seen as flawed and a failure (i.e. cutting too much and too quickly and choking the economy) then the Big Society narrative will be exposed and will gradually fade from view (Pattie and Johnston 2011: 405).

Cameron and Osborne have staked their political reputations and the future of the Conservatives on the expectation that the economic and electoral cycles would work in tandem. That is to say that come the time of the 2015 general election the electorate will recognize that the remedial action was necessary, and the Conservatives will retain a lead over Labour as the party best equipped to manage the economy. If by May 2015 the remedial economic shock therapy does start to show belated evidence of working, then the Conservatives will assume the following: they will reap the electoral dividend and not the Liberal Democrats (Russell 2010: 522). Conservative strategists have thus assumed that Cameron's 'embrace of the Liberal Democrats will prove to be fatal for the latter, leaving the country no option, unless it is prepared to give Labour another try, to elect a Conservative majority government next time around' (Bale and Sanderson-Nash 2011: 250).

However, perceptions of economic competence are not the only determinant of how the Conservatives should be viewed in office. Another key statecraft determinant demands that the party is managed effectively. On this criteria Cameron's record is not necessarily that strong if we restrict ourselves to parliamentary rebellions. A post-war record rebellion rate of 44 per cent on all divisions was recorded between 2010 and 2012. The overall rebellion rate is magnified by being in coalition, but nonetheless the Conservative rebellion rate (at 28 per cent) is the highest post-war rate for a Conservative administration. It is notable for being double the 13 per cent rebellion rate in the 1992–97 Parliament (Cowley 1999: 19–20). Two rebellions are of note. Over 90 Conservative MPs rebelled in July 2012 on the Second Reading of the House of Lords Bill, forcing the coalition to drop the legislation, and in October 2011, over 80 rebelled on a motion calling for a referendum on Britain's future membership of the European Union (Cowley and Stuart 2012a; 2012b).

In the early stages of the coalition Cameron managed to avoid the savage criticism that Major endured. This was partly due to the circumstances of being in coalition. For example, had the Conservatives been a majority administration then the media attention would have been solely on them when a small number of Conservatives rebelled over tuition fees. However, it was a far more interesting media story to focus on the 21 Liberal Democrats (and 8 abstainers) who defied Clegg in order to register their disapproval at abandoning their manifesto commitment (Lee 2011b: 15). Moreover, whereas Cameron led a united Conservative Party into the AV referendum in May 2011 (united in fear that is) divisions within Labour over AV generated considerable media attention and widespread criticism of Miliband (Hasan and MacIntyre 2011: 289–90).

However, as political journalists adapted to the new politics of the coalition era, the Conservatives have been subjected to more extensive criticism for their internal divisions, notably over Europe. Since the complete failure of the Save the Pound electioneering rhetoric in 2001, the Conservatives have pursued a 'harder but quieter' approach to the European Union which they hoped might diffuse the issue (Hayton and Heppell 2010: 425–55). However, the 'harder but quieter' approach has proved difficult to sustain when in power and when constrained by being in coalition with the pro-European Liberal Democrats. For Cameron the challenge of managing the European divide is different than it was for Major. Then the party fault-line was between the pro-European and Eurosceptic factions. For Cameron the divide is between soft and hard variants of Euroscepticism. Cameron has attempted to maintain unity around a soft Eurosceptic stance, meaning support for membership of the EU but opposition to further integration such as EMU, and the extension of EU competence in the realms of social policy, justice and home affairs, and foreign and security policy (Lynch 2012: 86). However, the strength of the hard Eurosceptic faction has developed during his leadership tenure, and notably the 2010 intake has a significant hard Eurosceptic element to it (Heppell 2013a). Demands for the repatriation of powers and for a referendum have grown, as have the number of Conservatives who now openly advocate withdrawal. (Lynch and Whittaker 2013a).

Although Cameron was keen to avoid 'both divisions' within his party *and* 'confrontation' within the European Union, circumstances have led to both occurring (Lynch and Whittaker 2013b). At a party management level Cameron's critics have argued that the move to the centre ground, and the associated desire to make the European Union a low salience issue, created the political space for UKIP to emerge. UKIP has thereby been able to develop their narrative as 'authentic' Conservatives through their rhetoric on immigration, crime and taxation. In doing so, they have attempted to delegitimize the soft Euroscepticism of Cameron and create a choice that could appeal to disillusioned Conservatives who are sceptical of modernization – that is, embrace the status quo or withdrawal (Lynch and Whittaker 2013b). The unease that these developments have created within Conservative ranks became clear in October 2011 on the aforementioned motion calling for a referendum (see above), when there the 80 official rebels had the sympathies of many Conservative ministers (Cowley and Stuart 2012a). In total during the course of the 2010–12 parliamentary session (May 2010 to May 2012) a total of 93 Conservatives (or 30 per cent of the PCP) rebelled against the whip on a total of 29 votes on European integration matters (Lynch and Whittaker 2013a).

Critics would say that the need to stem the flow of disaffected Conservative supporters to UKIP and to placate his own backbenchers has pushed Cameron towards provocative actions within the European Union. Two illustrations can be identified. First, in December 2011, Cameron used the British veto to block the fiscal compact that other European leaders wanted to construct to address the Euro-zone crisis (Gamble 2012: 469). Second, his position on the EU budgetary negotiations in February 2013, (where a real terms cut in the European budget was agreed for the first time in its history), was used to demonstrate not only that British taxpayers' money was being protected (echoes of Thatcher), but that the dire warnings about renegotiation within the European Union might be unmerited.

Strategically, the rationale for a commitment to renegotiation and to a subsequent referendum was expected to provide the following political dividends. First, it was hoped that adopting a clear position on how the future relationship between Britain and the EU could evolve, would allow the Conservatives to avoid obsessing around the issue. This was perhaps a naive assumption, which failed to appreciate how obsessed many Conservative parliamentarians can be. Second, it was assumed that this commitment would create political difficulties for Miliband. At the time of Cameron making this commitment, Miliband appeared unwilling to make a similar commitment, and Conservative strategists assumed that they could make political mileage from being decisive, leaving Miliband as being obstructive and elitist, or (if he were to match the commitment) a follower rather than a leader on the issue. Third, the commitment was seen as a mechanism to stall the advance of UKIP, with a referendum commitment theoretically neutralizing the need for voters to embrace a supposedly single-issue party. However, the timing and details surrounding the commitment to renegotiate and seek a mandate for continued membership or withdrawal still troubled many Eurosceptic Conservatives. Is Cameron playing a similar sticking-plaster tactic that Harold Wilson utilized in the 1970s, that is, commit to a referendum and then present to the electorate an essentially cosmetic negotiation that ensures that membership is continued (Bale 2013)? Despite having secured the concession of acceding to their demands, and advocating renegotiation and a referendum, those of a harder Eurosceptic persuasion still remain suspicious of Cameron. Can the threat of UKIP be contained with the delays implicit within this strategy? Would not an in/out referendum before the next general election be a more sensible move?

Bale also notes that 'team Cameron' were shocked how many hard Eurosceptic Conservatives simply 'banked' the concession that they had secured from Cameron, and moved onto their next target – opposing gay marriage (Bale 2013). The coalition promoted legislation allowing for same-sex couples to be married in civil and religious ceremonies. Conservative backbench objections fell into two types: first, that they opposed it in principle; and, second, that this was not a priority and should not distract the government from its focus on economic recovery (Clements 2013). The party management difficulty for Cameron was as follows. As a social liberal and calculating political leader, he understood the need to position the Conservatives on the right side of social attitudes. Public support for same-sex marriage was increasing, and increasing within all age groups. The level of support remained low among the over 65s (increasing from 11.3 to 16.5 per cent between 2008 and 2012), but there were majorities in the younger voters (up from 42.6 to 50.7 per cent in the 30–44 age group; and up 53.8 to 60.6 per cent in the 18–29 age group). Therefore, as a pragmatic act to confirm the detoxification of the nasty party imagery, supporting gay marriage was a rational act for Cameron as a vote-maximizing political leader (Clements 2013). However, social conservatives used Conservative Home to vent their spleen, where membership polls showed that 64 per cent opposed gay marriage, and 78 per cent felt that Cameron had misread the political situation and underestimated their strength of feeling on the issue (Grice 2012). Again UKIP surfaced as a concern. Their opposition to gay marriage (but acceptance of civil partnerships) provided another rationale for disaffected Conservatives, who object to modernization, to abandon the Conservatives for UKIP (Watt and Wintour 2012). Cameron secured parliamentary backing on this conscience issue with strong Labour support, but only 127 backed his socially liberal view, with 136 Conservative parliamentarians opposing and the remainder abstaining (Watt 2013). The cumulative impact of 'hard' Eurosceptic rebellions and following on from this the vocal criticisms of his socially liberal agenda from the moral authoritarian wing, showed that party management was becoming increasingly complicated for Cameron as he entered the second part of the coalition's term.

At the third year anniversary of the coalition it is clear that the statecraft approach that Cameron has utilized is best described as high risk, not just in the economic context of the austerity programme, but through his wider strategic choices of promising referenda – on AV (successfully); on Scottish independence (by the autumn of 2014); and on continuing membership of the European Union (by 2018 if re-elected). Ultimately, however, their electoral prospects will be determined by the performance of the economy. Cameron and Osborne have been reasonably effective at apportioning blame for their inherited difficulties, and residual doubts clearly exist among the electorate with regard to Labour and economic management. However, the process of fiscal consolidation has become more prolonged than Conservative strategists had hoped meaning that the economic and electoral cycles might not be in sync by May 2015. Should this result in electoral defeat it would be only the second post-war Conservative administration to be evicted from office after only one term. Cameron will be desperate to avoid the comparison with Heath and the 1970–74 government.

Conclusion

When political historians used to comment upon the dominance of the Conservatives in the period between the early 1950s and the mid-1990s, the explanations seemed straightforward. The Conservatives had a set of cultural norms that made them well equipped for the demands of government, and well positioned to recover quickly when they faced the inconvenience of opposition. They were a party characterized by first, unity and loyalty; second, they were a pragmatic party that avoided ideology, and third, they were the natural party of government, a claim which reflected their superior governing competence (Ramsden 1999).

However, the explanatory label of an 'appetite for power' that underpins these assumptions is too straightforward. To understand political success requires a deeper understanding of failure. Post-war Conservatism is not simply a case of stating that the Conservatives have shown a remarkable capacity for adaptation. Rather it involves explaining why processes of adaptation have worked – that is, when they have provided the route map from opposition and into long-term periods of government (e.g. post 1945 and post 1975). It also involves analysing why some processes of adaptation partially worked – that is, electoral recovery but not governing competence (e.g. post 1965 and the failure of the Heath administration and perhaps the Cameron era). It demands that we evaluate why the process of adaptation post 1997 was so problematic. Thus the chapters within this book examined the processes of adaptation in terms of success, partial success and failure.

This book has charted the journey for the Conservatives across five periods of time which are seen to represent the different strategic approaches – or statecraft methods – that the party has used. These five periods are loosely defined as One Nation (1945–65); Heathite Modernization (1965–75); Thatcherite (1975–92); Post-Thatcherite (1992–2005); and Cameronite Modernization (2005 –). In each period considered, the leadership has sought to, or struggled to, gain acceptance within the party for a particular narrative of Conservatism. Constructing that narrative, and gaining acceptance for it, then determines the viability of the statecraft strategy – will it be accepted internally by the party and provide the basis for unity? Will it provide a basis for being dominant or competitive in political debate? Will it provide a means for effective voter mobilization? And once elected, will it provide a means for effective governance?

Statecraft allows us to examine elite strategy and explore the elements that were successful and why, and the elements that were not and why not.

Statecraft shows an awareness of the prevailing economic climate, the evolving patterns of party positioning and competition, and the changing interests and preferences of the electorate. It is sensitive to structural constraints (and opportunities), but it also provides a clear means by which respective leadership cliques confronted, and tried to resolve, political dilemmas in a way that promoted their governing competence and protected their electoral appeal (Buller and James 2012: 534).

The conclusion reconsiders the dimensions of statecraft and relates them to the traditional assumptions that have characterized much of the scholarship on the Conservatives. The unity and loyalty assumption is tied to the party management dimension of statecraft; the pragmatism and non-ideological assumption is tied to the political argument hegemony dimension of statecraft; and the natural party of government assumption is tied to the governing competence dimension of statecraft. The conclusion will examine these one by one, before examining the final statecraft dimension, (electoral strategy), against a key underdeveloped aspect of traditional historical work on the Conservatives – that is, the need for more awareness of Labour.

The 'Statecraft' party management dimension: The unity and loyalty myth

Statecraft places an emphasis on the politics of support. It involves externally voter mobilization, but internally it requires the support of the party for the approach adopted. As the analysis below demonstrates, notions of 'unity' and 'loyalty' are questionable when we examine Conservative developments since 1945.

The unity myth: Increasing parliamentary rebellions

Parliamentary cohesion was the norm within the PCP of the 1950s (Beer 1969: 377). Conservative rebellion rates in the first five parliaments after 1945 were 1945–50 (2.1 per cent); 1950–51 (0.8 per cent); 1951–55 (1.4 per cent); 1955–59 (1.4 per cent), and then 11.8 per cent in the 1959–64 Parliament as the third-term administration degenerated (Norton 1978: 208). The primary explanation for this was the effectiveness of the Whips' Office in terms of their liaison role, that is, making compromises or retreats to limit rebellions and defeats (Searing 1994: 240–80). It is not to say that disputes did not exist within the PCP (for example, Suez), but Berrington argues that they were 'temporary' and over 'solitary and specific issues' (Berrington 1961: 368). The era in which 'cohesion was strained but never broken' (Berrington 1961: 362) has not really been seen since. There was a significant upsurge in parliamentary dissent during the 1970–74 government that had a 18.5 per cent rebellion rate overall, which was partly due to the inflexible leadership methods of Edward Heath (Norton 1978: 208). Margaret Thatcher found parliamentary party management less problematic than Heath, primarily due to her large majorities. Rebellion rates actually remained similar to the Heath era but seemed to matter less. The 1970–74 Parliament witnessed 204 incidences of Conservative rebellion, and the four terms between 1979 and 1997 provoked similar levels: 1979–83 (159); 1983–87 (203); 1987–92 (198) and 1992–97 (174) (Cowley and Stuart 2003: 315–31).

Before the 1983 general election, Francis Pym expressed concerns about securing an excessively large majority as it could embed patterns of rebellion that might prove difficult to stop later on (Pym 1985: 78). This fear became reality by the 1992 Parliament, where John Major suffered from the difficulties (and resentments) created by occupying power for so long. The list of those who have been 'dispossessed' (former ministers) and 'never possessed' (those backbenchers for whom ministerial office has not been forthcoming) grew (Seldon and Sanklecha 2004: 61–2). Moreover, the rebellion rate in the 1992–97 Parliament would have been considerably higher but for his willingness to compromise and make concessions in order to avoid a continuation of the parliamentary guerrilla warfare that characterized the passage of the Maastricht Treaty in 1992–93 (Heppell 2006: 81–115).

The above analysis demonstrates the increasing difficulty of maintaining legislative unity among Conservative parliamentarians. However, rebellions only matter in the sense of how they are interpreted by the political media and thereby understood by the electorate. The Major administration actually became rather adept at limiting formal parliamentary dissent. However, despite this formal legislative cohesion the electorate thought that they were divided due to their behaviour outside of Parliament. Conservative critics of the leadership appeared to be 'afflicted with the College Green mentality', where between 1992 and 1997 the 'electronic media were in almost permanent session, offering a camera to any Conservative parliamentarians willing to criticise Major'. Behavioural dissent did destabilize the Major administration, but the 'willingness' of backbenchers to 'advertise' their attitudinal differences 'was far more politically debilitating' (Heppell 2006: 115). Furthermore, the Thatcher/Major era saw the embedding of labelling with the PCP. This categorizing of Conservatives as being either wet or dry, or Europhile or Eurosceptic undermined their electoral appeal (Foley 2002: 27–30).

A litany of non-parliamentary symbols of division contributed to their defeat in 1997. Major constantly reminded his own party of the need for unity and loyalty, and the damage that division and disloyalty would do to their electoral appeal. However, Major also contributed to the impression of division. He played the victim as he talked about the difficulty of dealing with the 'bastards' within his own Cabinet in 1993, by resigning the leadership in his infamous 'put up or shut up' speech in 1995, and his pleading of 'don't bind my hands' during the 1997 election campaign. An indelible image of weakness was added to the impression of division (Foley 2002: 201).

The loyalty myth: The insecurity
of Conservative leaders

When parties select their leaders statecraft considerations should be paramount, that is, which candidate offers electability (the politics of support), but also competence (the politics of power) (Stark 1996). Thereafter, the primary requirement of the leader is to ensure that the Conservatives are well placed to do well at the next election, with the relationship between the leader and the followership being dependent on whether s/he looks likely to succeed in that objective (Bale 2010: 17). As a hierarchical organization, the Conservatives have historically placed an emphasis on strong leadership, as 'the leader is expected to lead, to impart a sense of direction . . . if things go well, the leader is praised, if things go badly, the leader is blamed' (Norton 1998: 77). The contingent nature of that relationship is best described as 'autocracy tempered by assassination' (Bale 2010: 17).

After 1965 the evolution of the rules governing how the Conservatives select their leaders began to undermine the security of tenure of incumbents. The loyalty to the leader assumption has to be questioned by considering the events of 1975, 1989, 1990, 1995 and 2003. In the autumn of 1974 the Conservatives amended their leadership procedures to ensure that Heath could be challenged, whereupon Thatcher challenged him. Thatcher would be the victim of two annual challenges, one unsuccessful in 1989 and one indirectly successful in 1990. Both acts of disloyalty were initiated with minimal difficulty, requiring only a challenger backed by a proposer and seconder. John Redwood showed no loyalty to Major when 'challenging' in 1995, and the credibility of the loyalty claim was undermined further by the speed with which Iain Duncan Smith was removed in 2003 (Quinn 2012: 31–55, 97–129).

However, the removal of Duncan Smith should not detract from the fact that the existing leadership selection/ejection procedures have left David Cameron in a stronger position than Thatcher or Major. First of all, Cameron is not subject to the annual re-election procedures that led to Thatcher being challenged in 1989 and 1990, and contributed to Major being undermined by speculation about possible challengers. Nor does Cameron have to fear an actual direct named challenger. To remove Cameron the PCP now have to secure the backing of 15 per cent of fellow Conservative parliamentarians for a confidence motion to take place. To remove Cameron in that confidence motion they need a majority of Conservative parliamentarians to state that they have no confidence in Cameron. However, this process is fraught with more risks than the procedures that unseated Thatcher, and 'the constraints of government make the successful activating of the confidence motion less likely than in opposition' (Heppell 2013b: 145). This is because removing Cameron via a confidence motion would only create a vacancy, which would be filled via first, the eliminative parliamentary ballots to screen out the least attractive candidates; and then second, the decisive membership ballot.

Unless the Conservatives 'can agree on only one candidate standing, the costs associated with this – time; financial; and disunity – make this procedure ill suited to government' (Heppell 2013b: 145).

Alongside the fact that Cameron is more secure through the confidence motion, he has also been fortunate that being in coalition initially masked the extent of the divisions within his own party. In the first year of coalition political journalists appeared to be more interested in divisions within the coalition – for example, over tuition fees and AV – than the divisions within the Conservatives as the dominant coalition partner. They have continued to show an interest in coalition fissures as the Parliament progressed – for example, over House of Lords reform and constituency equalization. Like Major before him the European issue has become the dominant concern in terms of party management. As identified in the latter stages of the last chapter, the rebellion rate within the PCP is the highest in post-war Conservative history. However, this can be attributed to the necessity of compromise that comes with coalition, a defence case that was not available for Major. It is also possible that the reduced number of ministerial posts on offer, and the reduced prospect of ministerial reshuffles that flow from being in coalition, have meant that the power of patronage is not as powerful a weapon of party management under Cameron as for previous Conservative leaders.

Party management is thus a hugely challenging area for Conservative leaders. Notions of unity and loyalty as secret weapons lack conviction. Political scientists can obsess about parliamentary rebellion rates, and they can also create semantic debates between behavioural and attitudinal divisions or whether the Conservatives are a party of tendencies or a party of factions (Cowley and Norton 1999, 2002; Heppell 2002). However, these ivory tower debates are not that important; what is important is the electoral perception of division. Those perceptions are shaped by political journalists. And here lies a type of new challenge that earlier leaders could not have imagined: Conservative Home. Described as a 'party within a party', Conservative Home acts as a forum for discussion for the 'remote' and 'voiceless' membership, allowing them to bypass the centralized mentality of the party, and get straight to the heart of Westminster debate. Its founder and editor, Tim Montgomerie, has been described as the 'high priest of Conservatism' and one of the 'most influential' Conservatives, despite being unelected and holding no formal position within the official structures of the party. His relentless criticisms of Cameron – a 'disappointing leader', presiding over 'error upon error', and his 'talking up' of Boris Johnson, explain why Montgomerie is regarded as a 'problem' for Cameron (Helm 2012; Beckett 2012). The existence of this forum to mobilize dissent and coordinate criticism of the leadership presents a new party management dilemma.

Presenting the electorate with an image of a unified party is central to successful electioneering. This is why effective party management is a key requirement for successful Conservative leaders, and why it is a key component of successful statecraft. The previous five chapters have demonstrated that far from being straightforward, party management is a complex and evolving challenge. Two notable academics – John Barnes and Arthur Aughey – have questioned the oversimplified notions of unity and loyalty and the assumption that the party is made up of tendencies, rather than factions (Barnes 1994: 342–3; Aughey 1996: 85). However, they have been in the minority. After reading the last five chapters hopefully the reader will appreciate the scale of the party management difficulties since 1945, which (prior to 1997) 'makes the party's historic achievement of containing the effects of division (electoral defeat)', and their periods of 'electoral success that much more striking' (Aughey 1996: 85).

The 'Statecraft' party political argument hegemony dimension: Pragmatic or ideological responses to quandaries?

Political argument hegemony is the second statecraft dimension. It refers to the need to ensure that the party is competitive or dominant when it comes to shaping the political agenda. Bale describes this as the 'struggle to establish a particular version of commonsense', so that they are perceived to be the more plausible party in terms of policy solutions (Bale 1999: 14). In the fight to establish a particular version of common sense, the most important issue is what is seen as the dominant concern, even though this changes over time. Responding to those prevailing social concerns constitutes the 'quandary' around which the core beliefs or narrative of Conservative statecraft is understood (Taylor 2005a: 134).

The 1945–1970s quandary: The full employment expectation

Between 1945 and 1975 the quandary was how to address electoral expectations of full employment. The Conservatives responded to the negativity surrounding their record in the 1930s during the depression and the era of mass unemployment. Their positional changes in the immediate post-war era constituted their mechanism for renewal and enabled the one-nation narrative to humanize and legitimize Conservatism. Harold Macmillan in particular was wedded to the pursuit of a mixed economy and welfare spending as the narrative of Conservatism, as this addressed the quandary of maintaining full employment (Evans and Taylor 1996: 84).

Even during the retrospectively viewed era of affluence there was a fear that inflationary pressures were threatening 'Conservative statecraft by stoking up resentment within the Party, and threatened a clash with the unions' (Taylor 2005a: 138). Macmillan's unwillingness to agree with Peter

Thorneycroft's view that they should permit a small rise in unemployment to discipline bargainers, led to Thorneycroft resigning alongside Nigel Birch and Enoch Powell in 1958 (Green 2000: 409–30). The period between 1961 and 1964 saw attempts to adhere to the existing strategy of maintaining the post-war settlement, and involved attempts to modernize (and thereby preserve) it. In the late Macmillan era this would result in the Keynesian plus package, based around first, the establishment of the National Economic Development Council to advance economic growth; second, the National Incomes Commission was formed with the objective of reigning in inflationary pressures by controlling wage increases; and finally, entry into the EEC which was the final piece of Macmillan's 'grand design' for modernization (Hennessy 2000: 257).

The process of policy renewal undertaken under Heath in opposition culminated in the Selsdon Agenda and the Quiet Revolution which appeared to challenge post-war Conservative strategy. The implementation of the Selsdon agenda created such an increase in unemployment that Heath feared that re-election would not be possible, whereupon either a pragmatic adjustment in policy (or a U-turn) was undertaken. The quandary of full employment had been threatened by the dual threat of trade union power and inflationary pressures to such an extent that a new quandary existed – the stagflation of rising unemployment and inflation. Conservative statecraft had 'collapsed' (Taylor 2005a: 140).

The 1970–1980s quandary: The trade union problem and inflation

Advocates of the one-nation tradition and defenders of the Conservative approach post 1945 attempted to attribute their strategic positioning of the party to their pragmatism. Take for example the view of Conservatism of Iain Gilmour and Francis Pym. Gilmour argued that Conservatism is 'not an ideology or a doctrine', it is 'not an -ism' and 'cannot be aggregated into a creed' (Gilmour 1977: 121), while Pym concluded that 'the main strength of Conservatism is adaptability' and 'its main enemy is ideology' (Pym 1985: 172). The likes of Gilmour and Pym would come to question the new narrative of Conservatism from 1975 (their criticisms being more vocal as ex-ministers after 1981 and 1983 respectively). The intellectual influence for the Thatcherite solution to the quandary of trade union power and the inflationary spiral was Powell, and his advocacy of deregulation, denationalization and control of the money supply as the means for controlling inflation (McLean 2001: 128–40).

The strategy was a challenge to traditional Conservative orthodoxies. It was to allow unemployment to rise. Without permitting this there would be no incentive for greater discipline within the public sector or from the trade unions. The threat of redundancy would intensify if the intervening instincts of the post-war era were abandoned. Wets felt the approach was 'extreme' (Prior 1986: 119) and feared 'electoral catastrophe' (Evans 2013: 49). However, not only did inflation fall but the electoral consequences of increased unemployment did not prevent Thatcher from securing two re-elections, thus undermining the wets. The narrative of Thatcherism achieved dominance by the 1980s as their solution to the stagflation quandary sought to establish that there was no alternative to a smaller state, lower direct taxes, restrictions on trade union power and the eradication of socialism (Taylor 2005a: 143).

By the late 1980s Thatcher was assumed to have won the 'battle of ideas'. Labour had been defeated three successive times; the threat of the SDP breaking the mould of British politics had not occurred; the trade union movement had been neutered and within her own party her wet critics had been marginalized. However, Thatcherism led to the creation of New Labour, and

> if the battle of ideas at elite level is so complete that the main opposition party capitulates on the main points and continues to quibble over only the details of policy, the electoral advantage can be nullified or even turned against the "winning side," which can be vulnerable to a public demand for fresh faces if all other considerations are roughly equal. (Dorey et al. 2011: 13)

The 1990–2000s quandary: High-quality public services

Once New Labour set about courting middle England by making an accommodation with Thatcherism in key areas of economic policy, social policy, privatization and trade union reform, this placed the Conservatives in a strategic bind (Hay 1999: 77–103). If New Labour had expropriated much of the thinking of Conservatism – market economics, privatization, property ownership, and tough law and order policies – this left the Conservatives with limited grounds for critiquing them, and 'left Conservatism bereft of a mobilising statecraft' (Taylor 2005a: 152). The Conservatives faced an 'invidious choice' as they 'could either shift their policy stance to the right – thus threatening their own political argument hegemony by appearing more extreme than Thatcher herself', or they could 'claim that Tony Blair was much more left wing than his programme implied' (Dorey et al. 2011: 13)

This is a legitimate argument but it is only part of the equation. New Labour was more than simply an accommodation with Thatcherism. The New Labour pursuit of the Third Way combined an acceptance of the market *with* the notion of an active and enabling state. The Third Way moved beyond the old politics of state intervention from the old left and the *laissez-faire* mentality of the new right, and claimed that traditional 'opposites' could be combined into a coherent discourse. This allowed New Labour 'to position themselves against an outmoded Conservative obsession with the free market' that had 'blunted their ability to address problems with the social fabric' and thus portray the Conservatives 'as socially regressive and lacking in compassion, particularly with respect to the excluded'. (Buckler and Dolowitz 2009: 24).

The Conservatives were to lose dominance of elite political debate in the post-Thatcherite era because the nature of the quandary had evolved. The quandary was public service delivery and issues relating to quality of life, in which Labour were dominant (Seldon and Snowdon 2005a: 253). The electorate had switched their policy prioritizations and attitudes away from the primacy of tax reductions and privatization, the very policy domains that had acted as the pillars of Conservative political argument hegemony in the age of Thatcherism. It was actually Duncan Smith who made the greatest strides in attempting to persuade the Conservatives to re-orientate their efforts towards addressing this, rather than fighting the battles of the Thatcherite era. To educate the party Duncan Smith attempted to draw comparisons with the 1970s, as he argued that then: 'we were faced with the task of turning Britain around' and 'the challenges were mainly economic'. However, he warned his party that although 'we tamed the power of the unions and unleashed the latest spirit of enterprise within our nation' we must recognize that 'time has moved on' (Taylor 2005a: 150). He instructed the Conservatives to compete with New Labour over the central quandary of the quality of public services, and in doing so his solutions would help form the basis of the Big Society narrative that Cameron would embrace.

After 1945 the Conservatives overcame two quandaries – to the post-war settlement after 1945 to address the quandary of full employment; and in the late 1970s to markets in order to address the quandary of the inflationary spiral stimulated by excessive trade union power and governmental overload. These constituted successful adaptations in terms of ensuring that the Conservatives were deemed to be competitive or dominant in terms of political debate. The process of adaptation that would lead to being competitive once more in terms of political debate took far longer to achieve after 1997. When faced with the new quandary of public service delivery, New Labour possessed political argument hegemony. Part of the reason why the Conservatives were slow to adapt to this was a consequence of the previous quandary. The Thatcherite solution had changed the culture and norms of the party. Not only were the claims to unity and loyalty finally shattered by the politics of Thatcherism, but their claim to pragmatism and rejection of ideology was also exposed. For much of the New Labour era the Conservatives remained dogmatically attached to Thatcherism, and were resistant to attempts to transcend it. That Thatcherism had successfully rooted out socialism, and that New Labour was more moderate was an additional part of their strategic problem (Taylor 2005a: 133, 152).

Writing in 2005 Taylor suggested that because the Conservatives could not offer a convincing narrative for financing and delivering public services – the prevailing quandary – they were 'locked into a systemic crisis' (Taylor 2005a: 152–3). Their recovery and return to power, albeit through coalition could be partly attributed to the modernizing impact of Cameron, but it was also due to the discrediting of New Labour due to the economic crash (Heffernan 2011: 167). This created a new quandary of how to rebalance the economy creating space for the Conservatives. It undermined New Labour's political argument hegemomy based around the choice of investment versus cuts. As Peter Mandelson admitted, it left Labour open to the accusation that 'we would simply keep on spending, borrowing and taking on debt' (Mandelson 2010: 477). The post-crash quandary of how to rebalance the economy switched the debate not to reducing the role of the state, but into a debate about the timing or prioritization of that reduction. The challenge for the Conservatives was to promote a rational and necessary retrenchment of the state pragmatically pursued in the national interest, rather than looking as though they were being driven by ideology.

The 'Statecraft' party governing competence dimension: The natural party of government?

The third dimension of statecraft is whether the party when in government can demonstrate competence through their policy choices (Bale 1999: 14). Demonstrating competence is not solely about the policy choices that are selected (and those rejected) but electoral understanding of their implementation. The Conservatives have often benefitted from the fact that Labour administrations have been more associated with major economic policy failures that can be easily understood by the electorate. Not until Black Wednesday did the Conservatives suffer an economic policy failure that matched the symbolism of failure associated with Labour in 1947, 1967, 1976 or 1979. The two sustained periods of Conservative government in the post-war era (1951–64 and 1979–97) were achieved primarily because the Conservatives were viewed as being more competent than Labour.

The one-nation claim for competence: 'Never had it so Good'

The multi-term Conservative administration after 1951 was able to use the age of affluence to showcase that their politics was that of prosperity. The fears of what an incoming Conservative administration might do proved to be groundless – there would be no rolling back of the Attlee settlement.

As the decade progressed, the Conservatives crafted their appeal around their superior competence relative to Labour and thereby their suitability as the custodians of the enlarged state (Gamble 1988: 64). The consumerism of the 1950s in the 'never had it so good' era provided their claim to governing competence. It was ruthlessly exploited for electoral advantage by the famous 1959 poster campaign: 'Life's Better with the Conservatives' and the warning 'Don't Let Labour Ruin it' (Macmillan 1972: 15). Conservative claims to superior governing competence were threatened by the humiliation of Suez, which was dealt with by apportioning blame to Anthony Eden and replacing him, and then the highly effective leadership of Macmillan between 1957 and 1960.

However, the viability of the one-nation statecraft approach was not sustainable beyond the 1950s. It lacked a sustainable mechanism through which to depoliticize contentious issues (the pre-eminent concern for Conservative governments) and thus put them at one remove from the government. Their embracing of Keynesian demand management techniques was supposed to act as an automatic economic pilot and an instrument of statecraft. It was intended that it would enable the political elite to set the overall framework by oversight through the Treasury, meaning that 'the autonomy shells of both business and unions would not be broken by state action' and thereby 'demand management could be carried on by Governments as a relatively autonomous activity'. Bulpitt suggests that Conservative acceptance of Keynesian techniques and methods reflected the fact that there was

> a very neat fit between Keynes' politics and the Conservative statecraft *for office* . . . both regarded government as the concern of an insulated elite, and both were especially interested in gaining relative autonomy in matters of high politics. It follows that the Keynesian consensus was not so much a policy consensus, but one of statecraft. Therefore, any thesis of a "corporate bias" in this period must be heavily qualified. In so far as corporate practices existed they were the froth on the beer, not the beer itself. Centre autonomy was always the principal rule of Conservative statecraft. (Bulpitt 1986a: 27–8)

The failure to demonstrate competence under Heath: 'Who Governs?'

Adherence to Keynesian demand management provided an appropriate, but time-specific, instrument of statecraft for the Conservatives. However, the degeneration of the Conservative administration of the early 1960s ran concomitant to the need to develop a post-Keynesian strategy for economic management, as the automaticity offered by Keynesian demand management was unable to provide evidence of governing competence when addressing the quandary of inflation or increasing trade union militancy (Evans and Taylor 1996: 225).

The prevailing orthodoxy between 1962 and the mid-1970s became the modernization of the British economy, but in order to stimulate economic growth an even more interventionist stance from government was required. This evolving new orthodoxy carried with it overtly statist connotations creating a gravitational pull towards Labour as the more appropriate conduit for implementing modernization. Through its social contract with the trade unions Labour had a statecraft strategy; furthermore they appeared to have acquired dominance in the quest for political argument hegemony. Meanwhile, the Conservatives were devoid of an instrument of statecraft. Having lost political argument hegemony it possessed no viable strategy to provide potential governing competence, and their internal unity began to unravel in the Heath era. For many Conservatives engagement with modernization, as an instrument of statecraft to demonstrate their competence, was futile and self-defeating (Bulpitt 1986a: 27–8).

The Thatcherite claim to competence: 'There is No Alternative'

For Thatcherites the solution to the quandary of militant trade unionism, the inflationary spiral *and* the route map to demonstrating Conservative competence was a smaller state, free markets, lower direct taxation and the curbing of trade union power (Taylor 2005a: 142–3). Thatcherism made its claim for electoral acceptance as much through necessity as through evidence of its success. This was underpinned by the 'constant repetition' of the claim that 'there is no alternative' (McLean 2001: 226). The phrase was central to the Thatcherite response to critics within (the wets) and outside (Labour and the SDP Liberal Alliance) and became emblematic of her political style (Berlinski 2008).

The claim for competence came through two devices: deflection and depoliticization. Deflection involved persuading the electorate that they were pursuing remedial policy choices that were necessary due to the governing mistakes of the consensus era that had created decline (Stevens 2002: 120). Depoliticization was pursued in different forms. For example, Thatcherites feared that the politicization of wage determination had intensified the conflict between government and trade unions, thus leading to an increasing perception that governments were incompetent. The combined impact of eschewing a formal incomes policy, the reform of the trade unions and their pursuit of privatization was designed to 'take government out of Labour disputes' (McLean 2001: 220). Ultimately, privatization was both an economic *and* political weapon through which they could question the competence and suitability of Labour to the demands of government. Would Labour be able to look credible as a potential party of government while maintaining their commitment to nationalization, and the need to increase taxation to fund multiple re-nationalizations (McLean 2001: 219–20)?

In this context two observations about the 'competence' of Thatcherite Conservatism can be identified. First, it was through time-specific means by which the Conservatives could rhetorically claim to be the party of low taxation, as the sales of nationalized assets provided the revenue stream to allow the tax deductions to seem credible. This process of rolling back the frontiers of state provided considerable opportunities for the Conservatives, but in time there would be less left to realistically roll back. So, for example, the privatizations of the Major era, Coal and Rail were more contentious, and Major actually backed away from attempting to privatize the Post Office (Seldon 1997: 505). Second, the logic of the privatization strategy for funding tax cuts and implying that taxes would have to rise under Labour was dependent upon Labour being bound to Clause IV (see below pp. 176–7).

Committed Thatcherites like to construct an interpretation of history that states that the Thatcher era restored their claim to competence, and the defeat of 1997 was solely due to the weak leadership of Major. It is fair to comment that post-Thatcherite Conservatism was undermined by evidence of policy failure. Within the first 18 months of their fourth term in office two cataclysmic policy failures – ejection from the ERM and the economic mismanagement that necessitated increases in taxation – destroyed their reputation for economic competence (Heppell 2008a: 585–8).

However, Conservative claims to governing competence were threatened in the late-Thatcher years by her unyielding commitment to the poll tax, which they were only able to overcome by removing her from the leadership. The Thatcher years also produced the conundrum of how they can be viewed as competent when unemployment escalated so rapidly. McLean implies that the Thatcherite electoral coalition was sustained by the considerable benefits secured for the south. This was sufficient to secure parliamentary majorities in a distorted first past the post-system especially when the centre/centre left was fractured. This suggests that the hardest hit by the rise in unemployment was predominantly in the industrial cities (and the north) which were Labour heartlands anyway. Those suffering were thus 'politically excluded' anyway and were so concentrated as to prevent Labour mobilizing them as a 'political force' (McLean 2001: 217, 227). However, when economic insecurities hit the Conservative south in the second recession of the late 1980s/early 1990s, this left the Conservatives far more vulnerable. That vulnerability was not exploited by Labour until the mid-1990s as they moved beyond the old politics of state intervention from the old left and the market of the new right to offer a third way alternative. The Third Way triangulated and transcended the old ideological debates by offering a new politics based on economic efficiency and social justice. It created not only a new electoral base for the left (the politics of support), but as the decade after 1997 showed, it also created a new (and competent) policy programme for the left (the politics of power) (McAnulla 2006: 138). The triumph of New Labour appeared to have challenged the assumption that the Conservatives were the natural party of government, and this claim was built around their apparent superiority in the realm of economic management (Beech 2008: 1–3).

The 'Statecraft' party winning election strategy dimension: The Conservatives versus Old and New Labour

This last point demonstrates that Conservative statecraft strategies have to be viewed through the lens of their competition. Thus perceptions that the Conservatives did or did not possess internal unity, did or did not have dominance of elite debate and did or did not offer competence were claims made relative to Labour. Of these, the primary comparative advantage that the Conservatives were able to exploit electorally was the perception that Labour lacked governing credibility due to their 'inability to manage the economy in such a way as to improve the lot and the living standards of the mass of the people' (Mitchell 2000: 178–80).

Conservative exploitation of these perceptions was relentless and shaped the thinking of New Labour by the mid-1990s. New Labour modernizers realized that the Conservatives had crafted a potent narrative of 'Old' Labour which undermined their capacity to appeal to the middle classes. Not only were Labour governments incompetent, but they were a threat to the economic stability and security of the middle classes. Labour governments would increase income tax; they were dominated by the trade unions, and they only represented the interests of the poor (Buckler and Dolowitz 2009: 17).

The rhetorical use of 'Old' and 'New' Labour was central to the renewal of Labour and the unravelling of the Conservatives in the 1990s. The term 'New' helped the modernizers to distance *their* Labour Party from the traditional Conservative narrative of Labour as 'economically inefficient' (Buckler and Dolowitz 2009: 11, 16). Blair and the modernizers set about disassociating themselves from both the negative politics, but also the negative images, of Old Labour. The litmus test of modernization was the reform of clause IV of the Labour Party constitution, which through its commitment to public ownership was a symbol of Old Labour. Its continued existence was anachronistic, (as Labour would not re-nationalize if returned to office), and it provided electoral utility for the Conservatives. It enabled the Conservatives to infer that taxation would have to rise under Labour, (to finance re-nationalizations), and it indicated Labour's misunderstanding of the global economy and the role of markets. Clause IV was successfully challenged and reformed by Blair. Labour had broken with its past and now possessed a new clause, which noted their belief in a dynamic economy, the enterprise of the market and the rigour of competition. By doing so, the electoral strategy of the Conservatives was fatally undermined, as it was predicated on Labour's continued adherence to 'Old' Labour. Conservatives needed the threat of socialism, and the perils of trade union militancy to instil fear into the middle classes. If the trade unions were tamed, then the threat lacked the potency necessary to validate Conservative electioneering (Heppell 2006: 287–8). The mid-1990s 'New Labour, New Danger' electioneering slogan failed to gain traction as not enough of the electorate feared Blair as they had previous Labour leaders.

Once in office New Labour utilized a statecraft strategy that the Conservatives could not penetrate. New Labour had secured dominance in terms of the dimensions of statecraft – that is, party management, political argument hegemony and governing competence. Notably in the period between 1994 until the impact of Iraq, Blair secured a degree of unity that his predecessors could have only envied (Cowley and Stuart 2003: 317).

However, the primary explanation for the success of New Labour in the Blair era was the performance of the economy. With 10 years of continuous quarters of economic growth being recorded between 1997 and 2007, New Labour had a superior economic performance than any previous Labour government (Lee 2008). Moreover, until the onset of the economic crisis of late 2007, Labour could claim to have usurped the Conservatives as the party of governing competence as the economy maintained steady growth and low inflation rates while unemployment was falling (Beech 2008: 2–3). The prudence that they displayed during their first term in office helped to establish credibility with the financial markets. What was really problematic for the Conservatives was the fact that 'New Labour did not make any dramatic mistakes', and 'there was no currency crisis; no flight of capital; no balance of payments crisis; no recession; no failure to control either public spending or inflation' (Sanders et al. 2001: 801). By presiding over such prolonged economic stability they had denied the Conservatives the trigger that could allow them to demonstrate the economic incompetence of Labour. They framed party competition on economic matters as a choice between investment under Labour or cuts under the Conservatives (Rawnsley 2010: 654).

Conservative statecraft dilemmas: Post-Cameron?

The economic crisis of 2008 changed the dynamics of British politics. The prevailing quandary of public service delivery which had provided political argument hegemony for New Labour changed. A new quandary emerged in the shape of deficit reduction and the need to rebalance the economy. The Conservative narrative of moving away from Big Government to allow space for the emergence of the Big Society has not gained the traction within the electorate that Cameron would have hoped for. While there is a reluctant acceptance of the necessity for a retrenchment of the state, gaining dominance on the methods and speed will be central to electoral competition in forthcoming years. Compelling the Liberal Democrats to endorse their economic recovery route map in order to form the coalition gave the Conservative initial benefits. It enabled them to narrate unpopular choices around necessity and national interest, rather than ideology. However, the subsequent economic record of the coalition has magnified electoral concerns about their competence. A positive that the Conservatives can take is that electoral doubts still remain about the credibility of Labour; thus deflection and the appropriating of blame will remain a key ingredient of Conservative electioneering.

With the Big Society narrative unable to provide the basis for dominance in elite debate, and the performance of the economy limiting their claims to competence, it is not surprising that tensions within the PCP have gathered apace. Cameron had initiated a modernization process in opposition that sought adaptation of Conservatism from its Thatcherite legacy. Cameron accepted the Thatcherite legacy in the economic and European spheres and is legitimately labelled as dry and Eurosceptic. His deviation from, and transcending of Thatcherism, was in the social sphere, and has never truly been embraced by a PCP which is predominantly socially conservative (Heppell 2013a). Many social conservatives happen to also be hard Eurosceptics, who fear that Cameron is allowing the Conservatives to be outflanked on the right by UKIP. Due to these concerns, combined with the limits to the use of patronage caused by being in coalition, Cameron has experienced an increase in rebellions (in Parliament), and criticism (through the media) of his strategic approach. This interpretation shows that moving beyond Thatcherism has been hugely problematic for the Conservatives. The Cameronite statecraft strategy is characterized by fragility. Doubts exist about his capacity to keep the Conservatives in office after 2015. Should they enter opposition then a further process of adaptation will occur, re-orientating Conservatism once again.

BIBLIOGRAPHY

Addison, P. (1975), *The Road to 1945: British Politics and the Second World War*, London: Cape.

—(1992), *Churchill on the Home Front*, London: Cape.

Alderman, K. (1992), 'Harold Macmillan's Night of the Long Knives', *Contemporary British History*, 6 (2): 243–65.

—(1996a), 'The Passage of the European Communities (Finance) Act (1995) and its aftermath', *Contemporary British History*, 10 (3): 1–20.

—(1996b), 'The Conservative Party Leadership Election of 1995', *Parliamentary Affairs*, 49 (2): 316–22.

—(1998), 'The Conservative Party Leadership Election of 1997', *Parliamentary Affairs*, 51 (1): 1–16.

Allen, N., Bara, J. and Bartle, J. (2011), 'A Much Debated Campaign', in N. Allen and J. Bartle (eds), *Britain at the Polls 2010*, London: Sage.

Ashcroft, M. (2005), *Smell the Coffee: A Wake up Call for the Conservative Party*, http://www.lordashcroft.com/pdf/GeneralElectionReport.pdf.

Ashford, N. (1980), 'The European Economic Community', in Z. Layton-Henry (ed.), *The Conservative Party Politics*, London: Macmillan.

Aughey, A. (1996), 'Philosophy and Faction', in P. Norton (ed.), *The Conservative Party*, London: Harvester Wheatsheaf.

Baker, D., Gamble, A. and Ludlam, S. (1993), 'Whips or Scorpions? Conservative MPs and the Maastricht Paving Motion Vote', *Parliamentary Affairs*, 46 (2): 151–66.

—(1994), 'The Parliamentary Siege of Maastricht 1993: Conservative Divisions and British Ratification of the Treaty of European Union', *Parliamentary Affairs*, 47 (1): 37–60.

Baker, K. (1993), *The Turbulent Years: My Life in Politics*, London, Faber and Faber.

Bale, T. (1999), *Sacred Cows and Common Sense: The Symbolic Statecraft and Political Culture of the British Labour Party*, Aldershot: Ashgate.

—(2010), *The Conservatives from Thatcher to Cameron*, Cambridge: Polity Press.

—(2011), 'I don't agree with Nick: Retrodicting the Conservative – Liberal Democrat Coalition', *Political Quarterly*, 82 (2): 244–50.

—(2012a), *The Conservative Party since 1945: The Drivers of Party Change*, Oxford: Oxford University Press.

—(2012b), 'David Cameron 2005-2010', in T. Heppell (ed.), *Leaders of the Opposition: From Churchill to Cameron*, Basingstoke: Palgrave.

—(2012c), 'The Black Widow Effect: Why Britain's Conservative-Liberal Democrat Coalition might have an unhappy ending', *Parliamentary Affairs*, 65 (2): 323–37.

—(2013), 'David Cameron's EU referendum pledge may not guarantee a
  Conservative victory in the next UK general election', *European Politics and
  Policy at LSE*, 16 February. http://blogs.lse.ac.uk/europpblog/2013/02/16/
  cameron-referendum/.
Bale, T. and Sanderson-Nash, E. (2011), 'A Leap of Faith and a Leap in the Dark',
  in S. Lee and M. Beech (eds), *The Cameron-Clegg Coalition: Coalition Politics
  in the Age of Austerity*, Basingstoke: Palgrave.
Bale, T. and Webb, P. (2011), 'The Conservative Party', in N. Allen and J. Bartle
  (eds), *Britain at the Polls 2010*, London: Sage.
Ball, Simon (2004), *The Guardsmen*, London: Harper Collins.
Ball, Stuart (1996), 'The Conservative Party and the Heath Government', in
  S. Ball and A. Seldon (eds), *The Heath Government 1970-1974: A Reappraisal*,
  Harlow: Longman.
—(1998), *The Conservative Party since 1945*, Manchester: Manchester University
  Press.
—(2001), 'Churchill and the Conservative Party', *Transactions of the Royal
  Historical Society*, 6th series (11): 307–30.
—(2005), 'Factors in Opposition Performance: The Conservative Experience since
  1867', in S. Ball and A. Seldon (eds), *Recovering Power: The Conservatives in
  Opposition Since 1867*, Basingstoke: Palgrave.
Barnes, J. (1987), 'From Eden to Macmillan 1955-1959', in P. Hennessy and
  A. Seldon (eds), *Ruling Performance: British Governments from Attlee to
  Thatcher*, Oxford: Blackwell.
—(1994), 'Ideology and Faction', in A. Seldon and S. Ball (eds), *Conservative
  Century*, Oxford: Oxford University Press.
Baston, L. (2000), *Sleaze: The State of the Nation*, London: Channel 4.
—(2004), *Reggie: The Life of Reginald Maudling*, Stroud: Sutton.
—(2011), *Summary of Democratic Audit: Boundary Change Simulation*, London:
  Democratic Audit.
Beckett, A. (2012), 'Tim Montgomerie: Pushing for a right-wing party with a heart',
  The Guardian, 23 October.
Beech, M. (2008), 'New Labour and the Politics of Dominance', in S. Lee and
  M. Beech (eds), *Ten Years of New Labour*, Basingstoke: Palgrave.
—(2009), 'Cameron and Conservative Ideology', in S. Lee and M. Beech (eds), *The
  Conservatives under David Cameron: Built to Last?*, Basingstoke: Palgrave.
—(2011), 'A Tale of Two Liberalisms', in S. Lee and M. Beech (eds), *The Cameron-
  Clegg Coalition: Coalition Politics in the Age of Austerity*, Basingstoke:
  Palgrave.
Beer, S. (1969), *Modern British Politics*, London: Faber.
Behrens, R. (1980), *The Conservative Party from Heath to Thatcher*, Farnborough:
  Saxon House.
Bell, P. (2004), *The Labour Party in Opposition 1970-1974*, London: Routledge.
Benn, T. (1987), *Out of the Wilderness*, London: Hutchinson.
Bennister, M. and Heffernan, R. (2012), 'Cameron as Prime Minister: The Intra-
  Executive Politics of Britain's Coalition Government', *Parliamentary Affairs*,
  65 (4): 778–801.
Berlinski, C. (2008), *There is No Alternative: Why Margaret Thatcher Matters*,
  New York: Basic Books.
Berrington, H. (1961), 'The Conservative Party: Revolts and Pressures', *Political
  Quarterly*, 32 (4): 363–73.

Birch, S. and Allen, N. (2012), '"There will be burning and a-looting tonight":
The Social and Political Correlates of Law-breaking', *Political Quarterly*,
83 (1): 33–43.

Birkenhead, Lord (1969), *Walter Monkton: The Life of Viscount Monkton of
Brenchley*, London: Weidenfeld and Nicolson.

Black, L. (2004), 'The Impression of Affluence', in L. Black and H. Pemberton
(eds), *An Affluent Society? Britain's Post War Golden Age Revisited*, London:
Ashgate.

Black, L. and Pemberton, H. (2004), 'Introduction: The Uses (and Abuses) of
Affluence', in L. Black and H. Pemberton (eds), *An Affluent Society? Britain's
Post War Golden Age Revisited*, London: Ashgate.

Blake, R. (1998), *The Conservative Party from Peel to Major*, London: Arrow.

Blond, P. (2009), *The Civic State: Re-moralise the Market, Re-localise the Economy
and Re-capitalise the Poor*, London: ResPublica.

Bogdanor, V. (1994), 'The Selection of the Party Leader', in A. Seldon and S. Ball
(eds), *Conservative Century: The Conservative Party Since 1900*, Oxford:
Oxford University Press.

—(1996), 'The fall of Heath and the End of the Post War Settlement', in S. Ball and
A. Seldon (eds), *The Heath Government 1970-1974: A Reappraisal*, Harlow:
Longman.

—(2011), *The Coalition and the Constitution*, Oxford: Hart.

Borisyuk, G., Johnston, R., Rallings, C. and Thrasher, M. (2010), 'Parliamentary
Constituency Boundary Reviews and Electoral Bias: How Important Are
Variations in Constituency Size', *Parliamentary Affairs*, 63 (1): 4–21.

Bosanquet, N. (1988), 'An Ailing State of National Health', in R. Jowell,
S. Witherspoon and L. Brook (eds), *British Social Attitudes*, Aldershot: Gower.

Brittan, S. (1968), 'Some Thoughts on the Conservative Opposition', *Political
Quarterly*, 39 (2): 145–55.

Broughton, D. (2003), 'The 2001 General Election', in M. Garnett and P. Lynch
(eds), *The Conservatives in Crisis*, Manchester: Manchester University Press.

—(2004), 'Doomed to Defeat? Electoral Support and the Conservative Party',
Political Quarterly, 75 (4): 350–5.

Bruce-Gardyne, J. (1974), *Whatever happened to the Quiet Revolution?*, London:
Charles Knight.

Buckler, S. and Dolowitz, D. (2009), 'Ideology, Party Identity and Renewal', *Journal
of Political Ideologies*, 14 (1): 11–30.

Buller, J. (1999), 'A Critical Appraisal of the Statecraft Interpretation', *Public
Administration*, 77 (4): 691–712.

—(2000), *National Statecraft and European Integration: The Conservative
Government and the European Union 1979-97*, London: Pinter.

Buller, J. and James, T. (2012), 'Statecraft and the Assessment of National Political
Leaders: The Case of New Labour and Tony Blair', *British Journal of Politics
and International Relations*, 14 (4): 534–55.

Bulpitt, J. (1983), *Territory and Power in the United Kingdom*, Manchester:
Manchester University Press.

—(1986a), 'The Discipline of the New Democracy: Mrs Thatcher's Domestic
Statecraft', *Political Studies,* 34 (1): 19–39.

—(1986b), 'Continuity, Autonomy and Peripheralisation: The Anatomy of the
Centre's Race Statecraft in England', in Z. Layton-Henry and P. Rich (eds),
Race, government and Politics in Britain, Basingstoke: Macmillan.

—(1988), 'Rational Politicians and Conservative Statecraft in the Open Polity', in
    P. Byrd (ed.), *British Foreign Policy under Thatcher*, Deddington: Philip Allan.
—(1992), 'Conservative Leaders and the Euro-Ratchet: Five Doses of Scepticism',
    Political Quarterly, 63 (3): 258–75.
Burnham, P. (2001), 'New Labour and the Politics of Depoliticisation', *British
    Journal of Politics and International Relations*, 3 (2): 127–49.
Butler, D. and Kavanagh, D. (1974), *The British General Election of February
    1974*, London: Macmillan.
—(1984), *The British General Election of 1983*, London: Macmillan.
—(1988), *The British General Election of 1987*, London: Macmillan.
—(1997), *The British General Election of 1997*, London: Macmillan.
—(2001), *The British General Election of 2001*, Basingstoke: Palgrave.
Butler, D. and King, A. (1965), *The British General Election of 1964*, London:
    Macmillan.
—(1966), *The British General Election of 1966*, London: Macmillan.
Butler, D. and Pinto-Duschinsky, M. (1971), *The British General Election of 1970*,
    London: Macmillan.
Butler, D. and Rose, R. (1960), *The British General Election of 1959*, London:
    Macmillan.
Butler, D. and Stokes, D. (1969), *Political Change in Britain*, London: Macmillan.
Butler, R. A. (1971), *The Art of the Possible*, London: Hamish Hamilton.
Campbell, J. (1993), *Edward Heath*, London: Jonathan Cape.
—(2000), *Margaret Thatcher. Volume One: The Grocer's Daughter*, London:
    Jonathan Cape.
—(2003), *Margaret Thatcher. Volume Two: The Iron Lady*, London: Jonathan Cape.
Carrington, L. (1988), *Reflect on Things Past: The Memoirs of Lord Carrington*,
    London: Collins.
Carter, N. (2009), 'Vote Blue, Go Green? Cameron's Conservatives and the
    Environment', *Political Quarterly*, 80 (2): 233–42.
Carter, N. and Alderman, K. (2002), 'The Conservative Party Leadership Election
    of 2001', *Parliamentary Affairs*, 55 (3): 569–85.
Castle, B. (1984), *The Castle Diaries 1964-1970*, London: Weidenfeld and Nicolson.
'Cato' (1940), *Guilty Men*, London: Gollancz.
Charmley, J. (1996), *A History of Conservative Politics 1900-96*, Basingstoke:
    Macmillan.
Childs, S. and Webb, P. (2012), *Sex, Gender and the Conservative Party: From Iron
    Lady to Kitten Heels*, Basingstoke: Palgrave.
Clark, A. (1998), *The Tories: Conservatives and the Nation State 1922-1997*,
    London: Weidenfeld and Nicolson.
Clarke, H., Mishler, W. and Whiteley, P. (1990), 'Recapturing the Falklands:
    Models of Conservative Popularity, 1979–83', *British Journal of Political
    Science*, 20 (1): 63–81.
Clarke, H., Sanders, D., Stewart, M. and Whiteley, P. (2004), *Political Choice in
    Britain*, Oxford: Oxford University Press.
Clarke, H., Stewart, M. and Zuk, G. (1986), 'Politics, Economics and Party
    Popularity in Britain 1979-83', *Electoral Studies*, 5 (2): 123–41.
Clements, B. (2013), 'Partisan attachments and attitudes towards same sex marriage
    in Britain', *Parliamentary Affairs*, doi: 10.1093/pa/gstoo3.
Collings, D. and Seldon, A. (2001), 'Conservatives in Opposition', *Parliamentary
    Affairs*, 54 (4): 624–37.

Cosgrave, P. (1972), 'The Winter of their Discontent', *The Spectator*, 2 December.
—(1978), *Margaret Thatcher: A Tory and her Party*, London: Hutchison.
Cowley, P. (1996), 'How did he do that? The Second Round of the 1990 Conservative Leadership Election', in D. Broughton et al. (eds), *British Elections and Parties Yearbook*, London: Frank Cass.
—(1999), 'Chaos or Cohesion: Major and the Parliamentary Conservative Party', in P. Dorey (ed.), *The Major Premiership*, Basingstoke: Palgrave.
Cowley, P. and Bailey, M. (2000), 'Peasant's uprising or Religious War? Re-examining the 1975 Conservative Contest', *British Journal of Political Science*, 30 (4): 599–629.
Cowley, P. and Norton, P. (1999), 'Rebels and Rebellions: Conservative MPs in the 1992 Parliament', *British Journal of Politics and International Relations*, 1 (1): 84–105.
—(2002), 'What a Ridiculous Thing to Say! Which is Why We Didn't Say It: A Response to Timothy Heppell', *British Journal of Politics and International Relations*, 4 (2): 325–9.
Cowley, P. and Stuart, M. (2003), 'In Place of Strife? The PLP in Government, 1997-2001', *Political Studies*, 51 (2): 315–31.
—(2004), 'Still Causing Trouble: The Conservative Parliamentary Party', *Political Quarterly*, 75 (4): 356–61.
—(2012a), 'The Cambusters: The Conservative European Union referendum rebellion of October 2011', *Political Quarterly*, 83 (2): 402–6.
—(2012b), *The Bumper Book of Coalition Rebellions*, http://nottspolitics. org/2012/05/08/the-bumper-book-of-coalition-rebellions/.
Crewe, I. (1988), 'Has the Electorate become Thatcherite', in R. Skidelsky (ed.), *Thatcherism,* Oxford: Blackwell.
—(1992), 'The Thatcher Legacy', in A. King (ed.), *Britain at the Polls 1992*, London: Chatham House.
Crewe, I. and Searing, D. (1988), 'Ideological Change in the British Conservative Party', *American Political Science Review*, 82 (2): 361–84.
Crick, M. (1997), *Michael Heseltine: A Biography*, London: Penguin.
—(2005), *In Search of Michael Howard*, London: Simon and Schuster.
Critchley, J. (1994), *A Bag of Boiled Sweets*, London: Faber and Faber.
Crowcroft, R. (2008), 'The 'High Politics' of Labour Party Factionalism, 1950-5', *Historical Research*, 81 (124): 679–709.
Crowson, N. (2007), *The Conservative Party and European Integration since 1945: At the Heart of Europe?*, London: Routledge.
Curtice, J. (2009), 'Back in Contention: The Conservatives' Electoral Prospects', *Political Quarterly*, 80 (2): 172–83.
—(2013), 'Time for Labour to establish Economic credibility', *Public Policy Research*, 19 (4): 253–7.
Davies, A. (1996), *We the Nation: The Conservative Party and the Pursuit of Power*, London: Abacus.
Debus, M. (2011), 'Portfolio allocation and policy compromises: How and why the Conservatives and Liberal Democrats formed a coalition government', *Political Quarterly*, 82 (2): 293–304.
Denham, A. and Dorey, P. (2006), 'A Tale of Two Speeches: The Conservative Party Leadership Election', *Political Quarterly*, 77 (1): 35–41.
Denham, A. and Garnett, M. (2001), *Keith Joseph*, Chesham: Acumen.
Denham, A. and O'Hara, K. (2007), 'The Three Mantras: Modernisation and the Conservative Party', *British Politics,* 2 (2): 167–90.

—(2008), *Democratising Conservative Leadership Selection: From Grey Suits to Grass Roots*, Manchester: Manchester University Press.

Denver, D. (1998), 'The Government That Could Do No Right', in A. King et al. (eds), *New Labour Triumphs: Britain at the Polls*, London: Chatham House.

Doherty, M. (1988), 'Prime Ministerial Power and Ministerial Responsibility in the Thatcher Era', *Parliamentary Affairs*, 41 (1): 49–67.

Dorey, P. (1995a), *British Politics since 1945*, Oxford: Blackwell.

—(1995b), *The Conservative Party and the Trade Unions*, London: Routledge.

—(1999), 'Despair and Disillusion Abound: The Major Premiership in Perspective', in P. Dorey (ed.), *The Major Premiership*, Basingstoke: Macmillan.

—(2001), '*Wage Politics in Britain: The Rise and Fall of Incomes Policies since 1945*', Brighton: Sussex Academic Press.

—(2003), 'Conservative Policy under Hague', in M. Garnett and P. Lynch (eds), *The Conservatives in Crisis*, Manchester: Manchester University Press.

—(2004), 'Attention to Detail: The Conservative Party Policy Agenda', *Political Quarterly*, 75 (4): 373–7.

—(2007), 'A new direction or another false dawn? David Cameron and the crisis of British Conservatism', *British Politics*, 2 (2): 137–66.

—(2009), 'Sharing the Proceeds of Growth: Conservative Economic Policy under David Cameron', *Political Quarterly*, 80 (2): 259–69.

—(2010), 'Faltering before the Finishing Line: The Conservative Party's Performance in the 2010 General Election', *British Politics*, 5 (4): 402–35.

—(2011), *British Conservatism: The Politics and Philosophy of Inequality*, London: I. B. Tauris.

—(2014), 'Margaret Thatcher', in R. Hayton and A. Crines (eds), *Conservative Orators: From Baldwin to Cameron*, Manchester: Manchester University Press.

Dorey, P. and Garnett, M. (2012), 'No such thing as the 'Big Society'? The Conservative Party's unnecessary search for 'narrative' in the 2010 general election', *British Politics*, 7 (4): 389–417.

Dorey, P., Garnett, M. and Denham, A. (2011), *From Crisis to Coalition: The Conservative Party, 1997-2010*, Basingstoke: Palgrave.

Downs, A. (1957), *An Economic Theory of Democracy*, New York: Harper.

du Cann, E. (1995), *Two Lives: The Political and Business Careers of Edward Du Cann*, Upton upon Seven: Images.

Dunleavy, P. (1993), 'The Political Parties', in P. Dunleavy et al. (eds), *Developments in British Politics 4*, London: Macmillan.

Dutton, D. (1997), *Anthony Eden: Life and Reputation*, London: Hodder Arnold.

Dyson, S. (2009), 'Cognitive Style and Foreign Policy: Margaret Thatcher's Black-and-White Thinking', *International Political Science Review*, 30 (1): 33–49.

Elliott, F. and Hanning, J. (2009), *Cameron: The Rise of the New Conservative*, London: Harper Perennial.

Evans, B. (1999), *Thatcherism and British Politics 1975-1999*, Stroud: Sutton.

Evans, B. and Taylor, A. (1996), *From Salisbury to Major: Continuity and Change in Conservative Politics*, Manchester: Manchester University Press.

Evans, Elizabeth (2011), 'Two heads are better than one? Assessing the implications of the Conservative-Liberal Democrat Coalition for UK politics', *Political Science*, 63 (1): 45–60.

Evans, Eric (2013), *Thatcher and Thatcherism*, London: Routledge.

Evans, S. (1998), 'The Earl of Stockton's Critique of Thatcherism', *Parliamentary Affairs*, 51 (1): 17–35.

—(2008), 'Consigning the Past to History? David Cameron and the Conservative Party', *Parliamentary Affairs*, 61 (2): 291–314.

—(2010), '"A Tiny Little Footnote in History": Conservative Centre Forward', *Parliamentary History*, 29 (2): 208–28.

—(2012), 'Reluctant Coalitionists: The Conservative Party and the Establishment of the Coalition Government in May 2010', *Political Quarterly*, 83 (3): 478–86.

Fielding, S. (2007), 'Rethinking Labour's 1964 Campaign', *Contemporary British History*, 21 (3): 309–24.

Findley, R. (2001), 'The Conservative Party and Defeat: The Significance of Resale Price Maintenance and the General Election of 1964', *Twentieth Century British History*, 12 (3): 327–53.

Finlayson, A. (2002), 'Elements of the Blairite Style of Leadership', *Parliamentary Affairs*, 55 (3): 586–99.

Fisher, J. (2004), 'Money Matters: The Financing of the Conservative Party', *Political Quarterly*, 75 (4): 405–10.

—(2010), 'Party Finance: Normal Service Resumed', *Parliamentary Affairs*, 63 (4): 778–801.

Fisher, N. (1977), *The Tory Leaders: Their Struggle for Power*, London, Weidenfeld and Nicolson.

Flinders, M. and Buller, J. (2006), 'Depoliticisation: Principles, Tactics and Tools', *British Politics*, 1 (1): 293–318.

Foley, M. (2002), *John Major, Tony Blair and the Conflict of Leadership: Collision Course*, Manchester: Manchester University Press.

Fowler, N. (2008), *A Political Suicide: The Conservatives' Voyage into the Wilderness*, London: Politicos.

Fox, R. (2010), 'Five Days in May: A New Political Order Emerges', *Parliamentary Affairs*, 63 (4): 607–22.

Fry, G. (1998), 'Parliament and Morality: Thatcher, Powell and Powellism', *Contemporary British History*, 12 (1): 139–47.

—(2005), *The Politics of Decline: An Interpretation of British Politics from the 1940s to the 1970s*, Basingstoke: Palgrave.

—(2008), *The Politics of the Thatcher Revolution: An Interpretation of British Politics 1979-1990*, Basingstoke: Palgrave.

Gamble, A. (1974), *The Conservative Nation*, London: Routledge and Kegan Paul.

—(1988), *The Free Economy and the Strong State*, London: Macmillan.

—(1996), 'An Ideological Party', in S. Ludlam and M. Smith (eds), *Contemporary British Conservatism*, Basingstoke: Macmillan.

—(2010), 'New Labour and Political Change', *Parliamentary Affairs*, 63 (4): 639–52.

—(2012), 'Better off out? Britain and Europe', *Political Quarterly*, 83 (3): 468–77.

Ganesh, J. (2012), *George Osborne: The Austerity Chancellor*, London: Biteback.

Garnett, M. (2003), 'Win or bust: the leadership gamble of William Hague,' in M. Garnett and P. Lynch (eds), *The Conservatives in Crisis*, Manchester: Manchester University Press.

—(2004), 'The Free Economy and the Schizophrenic State: Ideology and the Conservatives', *Political Quarterly*, 75 (4): 367–72.

—(2005), 'Planning for Power: 1964-1970', in S. Ball and A. Seldon (eds), *Recovering Power: The Conservatives in Opposition since 1867*, Basingstoke: Palgrave.

—(2012), 'Edward Heath', in T. Heppell (ed.), *Leaders of the Opposition: From Churchill to Cameron*, Basingstoke: Palgrave.

Garnett, M. and Aitken, I. (2002), *Splendid, Splendid! The Authorised Biography of William Whitelaw*, London: Jonathan Cape.

Garnett, M. and Lynch, P. (2002), 'Bandwagon Blues: The Tory Fightback Fails', *Political Quarterly*, 73 (1): 29–37.

Geddes, A. (2005), 'Europe', in K. Hickson (ed.), *The Political Thought of the Conservative Party since 1945*, Basingstoke: Palgrave.

Geddes, A. and Tonge, J. (2010), 'An Absorbing Hanging', *Parliamentary Affairs*, 63 (4): 866–73.

George, S. (1990), *An Awkward Partner: Britain in the European Community*, Oxford: Oxford University Press.

Gifford, C. (2008), *The Making of Eurosceptic Britain: Identify and Economy in a Post-Imperial State*, Aldershot: Ashgate.

Gilbert, M. (1988), *Winston Churchill: Never Despair 1945-1965*, London: Houghton Mifflin.

Gill, C. (2003), *Whips' Nightmare. Diary of a Maastricht Rebel*, London: Memoir Club.

Gilmour, I. (1977), *Inside Right: A Study of Conservatism*, London: Hutchison.

—(1992), *Dancing with Dogma: Britain under Thatcherism*, London: Simon and Schuster.

Gilmour, I. and Garnett, M. (1998), *Whatever Happened to the Tories? The Conservatives since 1945*, London: Fourth Estate.

Goodhart, P. (1973), *The 1922*, London: Macmillan.

Gould, P. (1999), *The Unfinished Revolution*, London: Abacus.

Gove, M. (1995), *Michael Portillo: The Future of the Right*, London: Fourth Estate.

Gray, J. (1994), *The Undoing of Conservatism*, London: Social Market Foundation.

—(1997), *Endgames: Questions in Late Modern Political Thought*, Cambridge: Polity.

—(1998), *False Dawn: The Delusions of Global Capitalism*, London: Granta.

Green, E. H. H. (2000), 'The Treasury Resignations of 1958: A Reconsideration', *Twentieth Century British History*, 11 (4): 409–30.

—(2006), *Thatcher*, London: Bloomsbury.

Green, J. (2010), 'Strategic Recovery: The Conservatives under David Cameron', *Parliamentary Affairs*, 63 (4): 667–88.

Grice, A. (2012), 'Tories Warn PM That He's Splitting His Party over Gay Marriage, As Leadership Speculation Mounts', *The Independent*, 27 December.

Hailsham, Lord (1990), *A Sparrow's Flight: Memoirs*, London: Harper Collins.

Harris, K. (1988), *Thatcher*, London: Weidenfeld and Nicolson.

Hasan, M. and MacIntyre, J. (2011), *Ed: Ed Miliband and the Re-making of the Labour Party*, London: Biteback.

Haxby, S. (1939), *Tory MP*, London: Gollancz.

Hay, C. (1999), *The Political Economy of New Labour: Labouring under False Pretences*, Manchester: Manchester University Press.

—(2010), 'Chronicles of a Death Foretold: The Winter of Discontent and Construction of the Crisis of British Keynesianism', *Parliamentary Affairs*, 63 (3): 446–70.

Hay, C. and Farrell, S. (2011), 'Establishing the Ontological Status of Thatcherism by Gauging its Periodisability: Towards a Cascade Theory of Public Policy Radicalism', *British Journal of Politics and International Relations*, 13 (4): 439–58.

Hayton, R. (2012a), *Reconstructing Conservatism: The Conservative Party in Opposition 1997-2010*, Manchester: Manchester University Press.

—(2012b), 'The Conservative Party', in G. Baldini and J. Hopkin (eds), *Cameron's Britain: UK Politics and the 2010 Election*, Manchester: Manchester University Press.

Hayton, R. and Heppell, T. (2010), 'The Quiet Man of British Politics: The Rise, Fall and Significance of Iain Duncan Smith', *Parliamentary Affairs*, 63 (3): 425–45.

Heath, E. (1998), *The Course of My Life: My Autobiography*, London: Hodder and Stoughton.

Heffer, S. (1998), *Like the Roman: The Life of Enoch Powell*, London: Faber and Faber.

Heffernan, R. (2011), 'Labour's New Labour Legacy: Politics after Blair and Brown', *Political Studies Review*, 9 (2): 163–77.

Helm, T. (2012), 'Tim Montgomerie: The Man who takes the Conservative pulse', *The Observer*, 12 February.

Hennessy, P. (1986), *Cabinet*, London: Blackwell.

—(2000), *The Prime Minister: The Office and its Holders since 1945*, London: Penguin.

Heppell, T. (2002), 'The Ideological Composition of the Parliamentary Conservative Party 1992–1997', *British Journal of Politics and International Relations*, 4 (2): 299–324.

—(2006), *The Conservative Party Leadership of John Major 1992-97*, Lewiston: Edwin Mellen.

—(2007), 'A Crisis of Legitimacy: The Conservative Party Leadership of John Major', *Contemporary British History*, 21 (4): 471–90.

—(2008a), 'The Degenerative Tendencies of Long Serving Governments...1963... 1996...2008', *Parliamentary Affairs*, 61 (4): 578–96.

—(2008b), *Choosing the Tory Leader: Conservative Party Leadership Elections from Heath to Cameron*, London: I. B. Tauris.

—(2010), *Choosing the Labour Leader: Labour Party Leadership Elections from Wilson to Brown*, London: I. B. Tauris.

—(2012), 'Hugh Gaitskell', in T. Heppell (ed.), *Leaders of the Opposition: From Churchill to Cameron*, Basingstoke: Palgrave.

—(2013a), Cameron and Liberal Conservatism: Attitudes within the Parliamentary Conservative Party and Conservative Ministers, *British Journal of Politics and International Relations*, 15 (3): 340–61.

—(2013b), 'British Prime Ministers and their Parties', in P. Strangio, P. t'Hart and J. Walter (eds), *Understanding Prime Ministerial Performance: Comparative Perspectives*, Oxford: Oxford University Press.

Heppell, T. and Hill, M. (2008), 'The Conservative Party Leadership Election of 1997: An Analysis of the Voting Motivations of Conservative Parliamentarians', *British Politics*, 3 (1): 63–91.

Heppell, T. and Lightfoot, S. (2012), 'We will not balance the books on the backs of the poorest people in the world': Understanding Conservative Party Strategy on International Aid', *Political Quarterly*, 83 (1): 130–8.

Heppell, T. and Seawright, D. (2012), 'Conclusion', in T. Heppell and D. Seawright (eds), *Cameron and the Conservatives: The Transition to Coalition Government*, Basingstoke: Palgrave.

Heseltine, M. (2000), *Life in the Jungle*, London: Hodder and Stoughton.

Hickson, K. (2005), 'Inequality', in K. Hickson (ed.), *The Political Thought of the Conservative Party since 1945*, Basingstoke: Palgrave.

—(2009), 'Conservatism and the Poor: Conservative Party attitudes to poverty and inequality since the 1970s', *British Politics*, 4 (3): 341–62.

Hilton, S. (1997), 'The Conservative Party's Advertising Strategy', in I. Crewe,
    B. Gosschalk and J. Bartle (eds), *Political Communications: Why Labour Won
    the General Election of 1997*, London: Frank Cass.
Hoffman, J. (1964), *The Conservative Party in Opposition 1945-51*, London:
    MacGibbon and Kee.
Hogg, Q. (1947), *The Case for Conservatism*, Harmondsworth: Penguin.
Hogg, S. and Hill, J. (1995), *Too Close to Call: Power and Politics: John Major
    in 10,* London: Little, Brown and Co.
Holmes, M. (1995), *Political Pressures and Economic Policy: British Government
    1970-74*, London: Butterworth.
—(1998), 'The Conservative Party and Europe: From Major to Hague', *Political
    Quarterly*, 69 (2): 133–40.
Home, A. (1976), *The Way the Wind Blows*, London: Harper Collins.
Horne, A. (1989), *Macmillan 1957-1986*, London: Macmillan.
Howard, A. (1987), *RAB: The Life of R.A. Butler*, London: Cape.
Howe, G. (1994), *Conflict of Loyalty*, London: Macmillan.
Hurd, D. (1979), *An End to Promises: Sketch of a Government, 1970-1974*,
    London: Collins.
Hutchinson, G. (1970), *Edward Heath*, London: Longman.
Johnson, C. (1991), *The Economy under Mrs Thatcher*, Harmondsworth: Penguin.
Jones, B. (2010), 'Climbing the Greasy Pole: Promotions in British Politics', *Political
    Quarterly*, 81 (4): 616–26.
Joseph, K. (1976), *Stranded on the Middle Ground*, London: Centre for Policy Studies.
Kavanagh, D. (1987a), *Thatcherism and British Politics: The End of Consensus?*,
    Oxford: Oxford University Press.
—(1987b), 'The Heath Government 1970-74', in P. Hennessy and A. Seldon (eds),
    Ruling Performance: British Governments from Attlee to Thatcher, Oxford:
    Basil Blackwell.
—(1996a), '1970-1974', in A. Seldon (ed.), *How Tory Governments Fall: The Tory
    Party in Power since 1783*, London: Longman.
—(1996b), 'The Fatal Choice: The Calling of the February 1974 Election', in
    S. Ball and A. Seldon (eds), *The Heath Government 1970-1974: A Reappraisal*,
    Harlow: Longman.
—(2005), 'The Making of Thatcherism: 1974-1979', in S. Ball and A. Seldon (eds),
    Recovering Power: The Conservatives in Opposition Since 1867, Basingstoke:
    Palgrave.
Kavanagh, D. and Butler, D. (2005), *The British General Election of 2005*,
    Basingstoke: Palgrave.
Kavanagh, D. and Cowley, P. (2010), *The British General Election of 2010*,
    Basingstoke: Palgrave.
Kelly, R. (1994), 'The Party Conferences', in A. Seldon and S. Ball (eds), *Conservative
    Century: The Conservative Party Since 1900*, Oxford: Oxford University Press.
—(1999), 'Power in the Conservative Party: The Hague Effect', *Politics Review*,
    8 (3): 28–30.
—(2001a), 'Farewell Conference, Hello Forum: The Making of Labour and Tory
    Policy', *Political Quarterly*, 72 (3): 329–34.
—(2001b), 'Conservatism under Hague: The Fatal Dilemma', *Political Quarterly*,
    72 (2): 197–203.
—(2004), 'The Extra Parliamentary Tory Party: McKenzie Revisited', *Political
    Quarterly*, 75 (4): 398–404.

Kelso, A. (2009), 'Parliament on its Knees: MPs expenses and the Crisis of Transparency at Westminster', *Political Quarterly*, 80 (3): 329–38.

Kerr, P. (1999), 'The Postwar Consensus: A Woozle That Wasn't', in D. Marsh et al. (eds), *Postwar British Politics in Perspective*, Cambridge: Polity Press.

—(2007), 'Cameron Chameleon and the Current State of Britain's Consensus', *Parliamentary Affairs*, 60 (1): 46–65.

Kerr, P. and Marsh, D. (1999), 'Explaining Thatcherism: Towards a Multi-Dimensional Approach', in D. Marsh et al. (eds), *Post War British Politics in Perspective*, Cambridge: Polity Press.

Kerr, P., Byrne, C. and Foster, E. (2011), 'Theorising Cameronism', *Political Studies Review*, 9 (2): 193–207.

Kettell, S. (2008), 'Does Depolitisation Work? Evidence from Britain's Membership of the Exchange Rate Mechanism 1990-1992', *British Journal of Politics and International Relations*, 10 (4): 630–48.

Kilmuir, E. (1964), *Political Adventure*, London: Weidenfeld and Nicolson.

King, A. (1985), 'Margaret Thatcher: The Style of a Prime Minister', in A. King (ed.), *The British Prime Minister*, London: Macmillan.

King, A. (1992), 'The Implications of One-Party Government', in A. King et al. (eds), *Britain at the Polls*, London: Chatham House.

King, C. (1975), *The Cecil King Diary 1970-74*, London: Jonathan Cape.

Kirby, S. (2013), 'Prospects for the UK Economy', *National Institute Economic Review*, 223 (1): 43–62.

Knightly, P. and Kennedy, C. (1987), *An Affair of State: The Profumo Case and the Framing of Stephen Ward*, London: Jonathan Cape.

Kruger, D. (2007), *On Fraternity: Politics beyond Liberty and Equality*, London: Civitas.

Kyle, K. (2011), *Suez: Britain's End of Empire in the Middle East*, London: I. B. Tauris.

Lamont, N. (2000), *In Office*, London: Warner.

Laws, D. (2010), *22 Days in May: The Birth of the Lib Dem-Conservative Coalition*, London: Biteback.

Lawson, N. (1992), *The View from Number Eleven*, London: Corgi Books.

Lee, S. (2008), 'The British model of political economy', in M. Beech and S. Lee (eds), *Ten Years of New Labour*, Basingstoke: Palgrave.

—(2009a), 'David Cameron and the Renewal of Policy', in M. Beech and S. Lee (eds), *Built to Last? The Conservatives under David Cameron*, Basingstoke: Palgrave.

—(2009b), 'Convergence, Critique and Divergence: The Development of Economic Policy under David Cameron', in M. Beech and S. Lee (eds), *Built to Last? The Conservatives under David Cameron*, Basingstoke: Palgrave.

—(2011a), 'No Plan B: The Coalition Agenda for Cutting the Deficit and Rebalancing the Economy', in S. Lee and M. Beech (eds), *The Cameron-Clegg Coalition: Coalition Politics in the Age of Austerity*, Basingstoke: Palgrave.

—(2011b), 'We Are All in This Together: The Coalition Agenda for British Modernisation', in S. Lee and M. Beech (eds), *The Cameron-Clegg Coalition: Coalition Politics in the Age of Austerity*, Basingstoke: Palgrave.

Lees, C. (2011), 'How unusual is the United Kingdom Coalition (and what are the chances of it happening again)?', *Political Quarterly*, 82 (2): 279–92.

Lees-Marshment, J. and Quayle, S. (2001), 'Empowering the Members or Marketing the Party? The Conservative Reforms of 1998', *Political Quarterly*, 72 (2): 204–12.

Letwin, O. (2003), *The Neighbourly Society: Collected Speeches 2001–2003*, London: Centre for Policy Studies.

—(2009), 'From economic revolution to social revolution', in J. Cruddas and J. Rutherford (eds), *Is the Future Conservative?*, London: Lawrence and Wishart.

Lindsay, T. J. and Harrington, M. (1974), *The Conservative Party 1918-1970*, London: Macmillan.

Lord, C. (1994), *British Entry to the European Community under the Heath Government of 1970-74*, Aldershot: Dartmouth.

Lowe, R. (1989), 'Resignations at the Treasury: The Social Services Committee and the Failure to Reform the Welfare State 1955-57', *Journal of Social Policy*, 18 (4): 505–26.

Ludlam, S. (1996), 'The Sceptre Haunting Conservatism: Europe and Backbench Rebellion', in S. Ludlam and M. Smith (eds), *Contemporary British Conservatism*, London: Macmillan.

Lynch, P. (2012), 'European Policy', in T. Heppell and D. Seawright (eds), *Cameron and the Conservatives: The Transition to Coalition Government*, Basingstoke: Palgrave.

Lynch, P. and Garnett, M. (2003), 'Conclusions: The Conservatives in Crisis', in M. Garnett and P. Lynch (eds), *The Conservatives in Crisis*, Manchester: Manchester University Press.

Lynch, P. and Whitaker, R. (2013a), 'Where there is discord, can they bring harmony? Managing intra-party dissent on European integration in the Conservative Party', *British Journal of Politics and International Relations*, 15 (3): 733–57.

—(2013b), 'Rivalry of the Right: The Conservatives, The UK Independence Party (UKIP) and the EU Issue', *British Politics*, 8 (3): 285–312.

Macmillan, H. (1938), *The Middle Way*, London: Macmillan.

—(1969), *Tides of Fortune 1945-1955*, London: Macmillan.

—(1972), *Pointing the Way*, London: Macmillan.

—(1973), *At the End of the Day*, London: Macmillan.

Major, J. (1999), *John Major: The Autobiography*, London: Harper Collins.

Mandelson, P. (2010), *The Third Man: Life at the Heart of New Labour*, London: Harper Press.

Marsh, D. (1992), *The New Politics of British Trade Unionism: Union Power and the Thatcher Legacy*, London: Macmillan.

—(1995), Explaining 'Thatcherite' Policies: Beyond Uni-dimensional Explanation, *Political Studies*, 43 (4): 595–613.

Matthews, F. (2011), 'Constitutional Stretching? The Elasticity of the Westminster Model in the Era of Coalition', *Commonwealth and Comparative Politics*, 39 (4): 486–509.

Maudling, R. (1978), *Memoirs*, London: Sidgwick and Jackson.

Mayer, F. (1992), *The Opposition Years: Winston S. Churchill and the Conservative Party 1945-1951*, New York: Peter Lang.

McAlister, I. and Studlar, D. (1989), 'Popular versus elite views of Privatization: The case of Britain', *Journal of Public Policy*, 9 (2): 157–78.

McAnulla, S. (1999), 'The Post-Thatcher Era', in D. Marsh et al. (eds), *Postwar British Politics in Perspective*, Cambridge: Polity Press.

—(2006), *British Politics: A Critical Introduction*, London: Continuum.

—(2010), 'Heirs to Blair's Third Way: David Cameron's Triangulating Conservatism', *British Politics*, 5 (3): 286–314.

—(2012), 'Liberal Conservatism: Ideological Coherence?', in T. Heppell and
    D. Seawright (eds), *Cameron and the Conservatives: The Transition to Coalition
    Government*, Basingstoke: Palgrave.
McLean, I. (2001), *Rational Choice in British Politics: An Analysis of Rhetoric and
    Manipulation from Peel to Blair*, Oxford: Oxford University Press.
Meredith, S. (2008), *Labours Old and New: The Parliamentary Right of the British
    Labour Party 1970-79 and the Roots of New Labour*, Manchester: Manchester
    University Press.
Miller, R. (1993), *A View from the Wings*, London: Weidenfeld and Nicolson.
Mitchell, A. (2000), 'Reinterpreting Labour's History of Failure', in B. Brivati
    and R. Heffernan (eds), *The Labour Party: A Centenary History*, London:
    Macmillan.
Moon, J. (1995), 'Innovative Leadership and Policy Change', *Governance: An
    International Journal of Policy and Administration*, 8 (1): 1–25.
Morgan, K. (1992), *Labour People: Leaders and Lieutenants*, Oxford: Oxford
    University Press.
Mycock, A. and Tonge, J. (2011), 'A Big Idea for the Big Society: The Advent of a
    National Citizen Service', *Political Quarterly*, 82 (1): 56–66.
Nadler, J. (2000), *William Hague: In his Own Right*, London: Politicos.
Negrine, R. (1995), 'The Gravest Political Crisis since Suez: The Press, the
    Government and the Pit Closure Announcements of 1992', *Parliamentary
    Affairs*, 48 (1): 45–61.
Newton, K. (1992), 'The Long, Long Campaign', in A. King et al. (eds), *Britain at
    the Polls 1992*, London: Chatham House.
Norris, P. and Lovenduski, J. (2004), 'Why parties fail to learn: Electoral defeat,
    selection perception and British party politics', *Party Politics*, 10 (1): 85–104.
Norton, P. (1978), *Conservative Dissidents: Dissent within the Parliamentary
    Conservative Party 1970-74*, London: Temple Smith.
—(1990), 'The Lady's not for turning, but what about the rest? Margaret Thatcher
    and the Conservative Party 1979 to 1989', *Parliamentary Affairs*, 43 (1): 41–58.
—(1996), 'The History of the Party II', in P. Norton (ed.), *The Conservative Party*,
    London: Prentice Hall.
—(1998), 'The Conservative Party: In Office but not in Power', in A. King et al.
    (eds), *New Labour Triumphs: Britain at the Polls*, London: Chatham House.
—(2001), 'The Conservative Party: Is there anyone out there?', in A. King (ed.),
    Britain at the Polls 2001, London: Chatham House.
—(2005), 'The Conservative Party: The Politics of Panic', in J. Bartle and A. King
    (eds), *Britain at the Polls 2005*, Washington: CQ Press.
—(2009), 'David Cameron and Tory Success: Architect or By-stander?', in S. Lee
    and M. Beech (eds), *The Conservatives Under David Cameron: Built to Last?*,
    Basingstoke: Palgrave.
—(2011a), 'The Politics of Coalition', in N. Allen and J. Bartle (eds), *Britain at the
    Polls 2010*, London: Sage.
—(2011b), 'The New Politics and Constitutional Reform', in S. Lee and M. Beech
    (eds), *The Cameron-Clegg Coalition: Coalition Politics in the Age of Austerity*,
    Basingstoke: Palgrave.
—(2012), 'Margaret Thatcher', in T. Heppell (ed.), *Leaders of the Opposition:
    From Churchill to Cameron*, Basingstoke: Palgrave.
Nutting, A. (1967), *No End of a Lesson: The Story of Suez*, London: Constable.

Owen, D. (2008), *In Sickness and In Power: Illness in Heads of Government during the last 100 years*, London: Meuthen.

Parkinson, C. (1992), *Right at the Centre*, London: Weidenfeld and Nicolson.

Patten, C. (1980), 'Policy Making in Opposition', in Z. Layton-Henry (ed.), *Conservative Party Politics*, London: Macmillan.

Pattie, C. and Johnston, R. (1996), 'The Conservative Party and the Electorate', in S. Ludlam and M. Smith (eds), *Contemporary British Conservatism*, London: Macmillan.

—(2011), 'How Big is the Big Society?', *Parliamentary Affairs*, 64 (3): 403–24.

Peele, G. (1998), 'Towards "New" Conservatives? Organisational Reform and the Conservative Party', *Political Quarterly*, 69 (2): 141–7.

Pemberton, H. (2001), 'A Taxing Task: Combating Britain's Relative Economic Decline in the 1960s', *Twentieth Century British History*, 12 (3): 354–75.

—(2004), 'Affluence, Relative Decline and the Treasury', in L. Black and H. Pemberton (eds), *An Affluent Society? Britain's Post War Golden Age Revisited*, London: Ashgate.

Pierson, C. (1996), 'Social Policy under Thatcher and Major', in S. Ludlam and M. Smith (eds), *Contemporary British Conservatism*, London: Macmillan.

Pinto-Dushinsky, M. (1987), 'From Macmillan to Home 1959-1964', in P. Hennessy and A. Seldon (eds), *Ruling Performance: British Governments from Attlee to Thatcher*, Oxford: Blackwell.

Pinto-Duschinsky, M., McLean, I. and Lodge, G. (2011), 'The Alternative Vote', *Political Insight*, 2 (1): 16–17.

Pirie, I. (2012), 'Representations of Economic Crisis in Contemporary Britain', *British Politics*, 7 (4): 341–64.

Powell, E. (1968), *Conference on Economic Policy for the 1970s*, London: The Monday Club.

Prior, J. (1986), *A Balance of Power*, London: Hamish Hamilton.

Pugh, M. (2010), *Speak for Britain: A New History of the Labour Party*, London: Bodley Head.

Punnett, R. (1992), *Selecting the Party Leader: Britain in Comparative Perspective*, London: Harvester Wheatsheaf.

Pym, F. (1985), *The Politics of Consent*, London: Hamish Hamilton.

Quinn, T. (2008), 'The Conservative Party and the Centre Ground of British Politics', *Journal of Elections, Public Opinion and Parties*, 18 (2): 179–99.

—(2012), *Electing and Ejecting Party Leaders in Britain*, Basingstoke: Palgrave.

Quinn, T., Bara, J. and Bartle, J. (2011), 'The UK Coalition Agreement: Who Won?', *Journal of Elections, Public Opinion and Parties*, 21 (2): 295–312.

Qvortrup, M. (2012), 'Voting on Electoral Reform: A Comparative Perspective on the Alternative Vote Referendum in the United Kingdom', *Political Quarterly*, 83 (1): 108–16.

Ramsden, J. (1977), 'From Churchill to Heath', in Lord Butler (ed.), *The Conservatives: A History from their origins to 1965*, London: Allen and Unwin.

—(1980), *The Making of Conservative Party Policy*, London: Longman.

—(1995), *The Age of Churchill and Eden 1940-1957*, London: Longman.

—(1996), *The Winds of Change: Macmillan and Heath 1957-1975*, London: Longman.

—(1999), *An Appetite for Power: The History of the Conservative Party*, London: Harper Collins.

Rawlinson, P. (1989), *A Price Too High*, London: Weidenfeld and Nicolson.

Rawnsley, A. (2010), *The End of the Party: The Rise and Fall of New Labour*, London: Penguin.

Redmayne, M. (1963), *The Listener*, 19 December.

Redwood, J. (2004), *Singing the Blues: The Once and Future Conservatives*, London: Politicos.

Reynolds, D. (2000), *Britannia Overruled: British Policy and World Powers in the 20th Century*, London: Longman.

Rhodes-James, R. (ed.) (1967), *Chips: The Diaries of Sir Henry Channon*, London: Weidenfeld and Nicolson.

—(1972), *Ambitions and Realities: British Politics 1964-1970*, London: Weidenfeld and Nicolson.

—(1986), *Anthony Eden*, London: Weidenfeld and Nicolson.

Ridley, N. (1991), *My Style of Government*, London: Hutchison.

Rosamond, B. (1996), 'Whatever Happened to the Enemy Within? Contemporary Conservatism and Trade Unionism', in S. Ludlam and M. Smith (eds), *Contemporary British Conservatism*, London: Macmillan.

Rose, R. (1964), 'Parties, Tendencies and Factions', *Political Studies*, 12 (1): 33–46.

Roth, A. (1972), *Heath and the Heathmen*, London: Routledge and Kegan Paul.

Routledge, P. (1994), *Scargill: The Unauthorized Biography*, London: Harper Collins.

Rowland, C. (1960), 'Labour Publicity', *Political Quarterly*, 31 (3): 348–60.

Russell, A. (2010), 'Inclusion, Exclusion or Obscurity? The 2010 General Election and the Implications of the Con-Lib Coalition for third-party politics in Britain', *British Politics*, 5 (4): 506–24.

Russell, T. (1978), *The Tory Party*, Harmondsworth: Penguin.

Sanders, D. (1992), 'Why the Conservatives Won Again', in A. King et al. (eds), *Britain at the Polls 1992*, London: Chatham House.

Sanders, D., Clarke, H., Stewart, M. and Whiteley, P. (2001), 'The Economy and Voting', *Parliamentary Affairs*, 54 (4): 789–802.

—(2011), 'Simulating the Effects of the Alternative Vote on the 2010 UK general election', *Parliamentary Affairs*, 64 (1): 5–23.

Sanders, D., Ward, H., Marsh, D. and Fletcher, T. (1987), 'Government Popularity and the Falklands War: A Reassessment', *British Journal of Political Science*, 17 (3): 281–313.

Searing, D. (1994), *Westminster's World: Understanding Political Roles*, Cambridge: Harvard University Press.

Seawright, D. (2004), 'Geoffrey Howe', in K. Theakston (ed.), *British Foreign Secretaries since 1974*, London: Routledge.

—(2010), *The British Conservative Party and One Nation Politics*, London: Continuum.

—(2012), 'The Conservative Election Campaign', in T. Heppell and D. Seawright (eds), *Cameron and the Conservatives: The Transition to Coalition Government*, Basingstoke: Palgrave.

See, H. (2013), 'Guardians of the Public Sphere? Political Scandal and the Press 1979-97', *Twentieth Century British History*, 24 (1): 110–37.

Seldon, A. (1981), *Churchill's Indian Summer: The Conservative Government 1951-55*, London: Hodder and Stoughton.

—(1996), 'The Heath Government in history', in S. Ball and A. Seldon (eds), *The Heath Government 1970-1974: A Reappraisal*, Harlow: Longman.

—(1997), *Major: A Political Life*, London: Weidenfeld and Nicolson.

Seldon, A. and Sanklecha, P. (2004), 'United Kingdom: A Comparative case study of Conservative Prime Ministers Heath, Thatcher and Major', *Journal of Legislative Studies*, 10 (2–3): 53–65.

Seldon, A. and Snowdon, P. (2001), *A New Conservative Century?*, London: Centre for Policy Studies.

—(2005a), 'The Barren Years 1997-2005', in S. Ball and A. Seldon (eds), *Recovering Power: The Conservatives in Opposition Since 1867*, Basingstoke: Palgrave.

—(2005b), The Conservative Campaign', *Parliamentary Affairs*, 58 (4): 725–42.

Shepherd, R. (1991), *The Power Brokers: The Tory Party and Its Leaders*, London: Hutchinson.

—(1994), *Iain Macleod: A Biography*, London: Pimlico.

—(1996), *Enoch Powell: A Biography*, London: Pimlico.

Shore, P. (1993), *Leading the Left*, London: Weidenfeld and Nicolson.

Snowdon, P. (2010), *Back from the Brink: The Inside Story of the Tory Resurrection*, London: Harper Press.

Stark, L. (1996), *Choosing a Leader: Party Leadership Contest in Britain from Macmillan to Blair*, London: Macmillan.

Stennis, K. (1998), 'The European Challenge: Britain's EEC application in 1961', *Contemporary European History*, 7 (1): 61–90.

Stephens, P. (1996), *Politics and the Pound*, London: Papermac.

Stevens, C. (2002), 'Thatcherism, Majorism and the Collapse of Tory Statecraft', *Contemporary British History*, 16 (1): 119–50.

Stokes, D. (1992), 'Valence politics', in D. Kavanagh (ed.), *Electoral Politics*, Oxford: Clarendon Press.

Streeter, G. (ed.) (2002), *There is Such a Thing as Society: Twelve Principles of Compassionate Conservatism*, London: Politicos.

Stuart, M. (2011), 'The Formation of the Coalition', in S. Lee and M. Beech (eds), *The Cameron-Clegg Coalition: Coalition Politics in the Age of Austerity*, Basingstoke: Palgrave.

Taylor, A. (1994), 'The Conservative Party and the Trade Unions since 1900', in A. Seldon and S. Ball (eds), *Conservative Century: The Conservative Party since 1900*, Oxford: Oxford University Press.

—(2001), 'The Stepping Stones Programme: Conservative Party Thinking of Trade Unions 1975-79', *Historical Studies in Industrial Relations*, 11 (1): 109–33.

—(2005a), 'Economic Statecraft', in K. Hickson (ed.), *The Political Thought of the Conservative Party since 1945*, Basingstoke: Palgrave.

—(2005b), *The NUM and British Politics, Volume 2, 1969-1995*, Aldershot: Ashgate.

—(2010), 'British Conservatives, David Cameron and the Politics of Adaptation', *Representation*, 46 (4): 489–96.

Taylor, R. (1996), 'The Heath government, industrial policy and the new capitalism', in S. Ball and A. Seldon (eds), *The Heath Government 1970-1974: A Reappraisal*, Harlow: Longman.

Thaler, R. and Sunstein, C. (2008), *Nudge: Improving Decisions about Health, Wealth, and Happiness*, New Haven: Yale University Press.

Thatcher, M. (1979), 'Press Conference after the Dublin European Council', 30 November, http://www.margaretthatcher.org/speeches/displaydocument. asp?docid=104180.

—(1984), 'The Enemy within', Speech to the 1922 Committee, 20 July, http://www. margaretthatcher.org/document/105563.

—(1992), 'No Such Thing as Majorism', 27 April, http://www.margaretthatcher. org/document/111359.

—(1993), *The Downing Street Years*, London: Harper Collins.

—(1995), *The Path to Power*, London: Harper Collins.

Theakston, K. (2010), *After Number 10: Former Prime Ministers in British Politics*, Basingstoke: Palgrave.

—(2012), 'Winston Churchill', in T. Heppell (ed.), *Leaders of the Opposition: From Churchill to Cameron*, Basingstoke: Palgrave.

Thomas, H. (1967), *The Suez Affair*, London: Weidenfeld and Nicolson.

Thomas-Symonds, N. (2010), *Attlee: A Life in Politics*, London: I. B. Tauris.

Thompson, H. (1996), 'Economic Policy under Thatcher and Major', in S. Ludlam and M. Smith (eds), *Contemporary British Conservatism*, London: Macmillan.

Thompson, N. (2006), 'The Fabian Political Economy of Harold Wilson', in P. Dorey (ed.), *The Labour Governments, 1964-1970*, London: Routledge.

Thorpe, D. R. (1989), *Selwyn Lloyd*, London: Jonathan Cape.

—(1996), *Alec Douglas-Home*, London: Sinclair Stevenson.

—(2011), *Supermac: The Life of Harold Macmillan*, London: Pimlico.

Thorpe, J. (1999), *In My Own Time: Reminiscences of a Liberal Leader*, London: Politicos.

Tomlinson, J. (2007), 'Mrs Thatcher's Macroeconomic Adventurism, 1979–1981, and its Political Consequences', *British Politics*, 2 (1): 3–19.

Turner, J. (1996), '1951-1964', in A. Seldon (ed.), *How Tory Governments Fall*, London: Fontana.

—(2000), *The Tories and Europe*, Manchester: Manchester University Press.

Tyler, R. (2006), 'Victims of our History? Barbara Castle and *In Place of Strife*', *Contemporary British History*, 20 (3): 461–76.

Walker, P. (1991), *Staying Power*, London: Bloomsbury.

Walsh, K. (1992), 'Local Government', in P. Catterall (ed.), *Contemporary Britain: An Annual Review*, Oxford: Blackwell.

Walters, S. (2001), *Tory Wars: Conservatives in Crisis*, London: Politicos.

Watkins, A. (1991), *A Conservative Coup: The Fall of Margaret Thatcher*, London: Duckworth.

Watt, N. (2013), 'Gay marriage: MPs vote in favour leaves Cameron adrift from Tories', *The Guardian*, 6 February.

Watt, N. and Wintour, P. (2012), 'Gay Marriage Row: UKIP Plans to Derail David Cameron', *The Guardian*, 12 December.

Webster, C. (1991), 'The Health Service', in D. Kavanagh and A. Seldon (eds), *The Thatcher Effect*, Oxford: Oxford University Press.

Wheatcroft, G. (2005), *The Strange Death of Tory England*, London: Allen Lane.

Whitelaw, W. (1989), *The Whitelaw Memoirs*, London: Headline.

Whiteley, P. (1997), 'The Conservative Campaign', *Parliamentary Affairs*, 50 (4): 542–54.

Whiteley, P., Stewart, M., Sanders, D. and Clarke, H. (2012), 'Britain Says NO: Voting in the AV Referendum Ballot Referendum', *Parliamentary Affairs*, 65 (2): 301–22.

Wickham-Jones, M. (1997), 'Right Turn: A Revisionist Account of the 1975 Conservative Party Leadership Election', *Twentieth Century British History*, 8 (1): 74–89.

Willetts, D. (1992), *Modern Conservatism*, Harmondsworth: Penguin.

—(1994), *Civic Conservatism*, London: Social Market Foundation.

—(2005), 'The New Conservatism 1945–1951', in S. Ball and A. Seldon (eds), *Recovering Power: The Conservatives in Opposition Since 1867*, Basingstoke: Palgrave.

Williams, H. (1998), *Guilty Men: Conservative Decline and Fall 1992-1997*, London: Aurum Press.

Williams, P. (1978), *Hugh Gaitskell: A Political Biography*, London: Jonathan Cape.

Wilson, R. (2010), *Five Days to Power*, London: Biteback.

Wolfe, J. (1991), 'State power and ideology in Britain: Mrs Thatcher's privatization programme', *Political Studies*, 39 (2): 237–52.

Woolton, Lord (1959), *Memoirs of the Rt Hon The Earl of Woolton*, London: Cassell.

Wright, E. (1970), 'The Future of Conservatism', *Political Quarterly*, 41 (4): 387–98.

Worcester, R. and Mortimer, R. (1999), *Explaining Labour's Landslide*, London: Politicos.

Wring, D. and Deacon, D. (2010), 'Patterns of Press Partisanship in the 2010 General Election', *British Politics*, 5 (4): 436–54.

Young, H. (1989), *The Iron Lady*, New York: Farrar, Straus and Giroux.

—(1990), *One of Us*, London: Pan Books.

—(1998), *This Blessed Plot: Britain in Europe from Churchill to Blair*, London: Papermac.

Ziegler, P. (2010), *Edward Heath*, London: Harper Collins.

INDEX